A Final Encore

A Final Encore

The Life, Music and Tragedy of

Alexei Sultanov

J. W. WILSON

Fort Worth, Texas

Copyright © 2025 by J. W. Wilson
Library of Congress Cataloging-in-Publication Data

Names: Wilson, J. W., 1976- author.
Title: A final encore : the life, music, and tragedy of Alexei Sultanov /
   J.W. Wilson.
Description: Fort Worth, Texas : TCU Press, [2025] | Includes
   bibliographical references.
Identifiers: LCCN 2025002046 (print) | LCCN 2025002047 (ebook) | ISBN
   9780875658711 (paperback) | ISBN 9780875658797 (ebook)
Subjects: LCSH: Sultanov, Alexei. | Pianists--Russia
   (Federation)--Biography. | LCGFT: Biographies.
Classification: LCC ML417.S944 W55 2025 (print) | LCC ML417.S944 (ebook)
   | DDC 786.2092 [B]--dc23/eng/20250117
LC record available at https://lccn.loc.gov/2025002046
LC ebook record available at https://lccn.loc.gov/2025002047

Design by Adrienne Martinez

TCU Box 298300
Fort Worth, Texas 76129
www.tcupress.com

DEDICATION

For you, a spectacular gem of a human being, thank you for giving me my life, my purpose, my ability to see the good in all things. You taught me how life should be lived and why kindness and love matter. You treated each day like it was special, and you made those who knew you feel important. The world needs more of you.

You worked for the Cliburn organization as a volunteer and knew Alexei Sultanov, the subject of this book, personally. I was too young to know or understand much about this world then. You knew he was special. You were his chauffeur for much of the Cliburn Piano Competition in 1989 and after. I remember you telling me stories about this young Soviet pianist that you drove around. Incredible to think that thirty-five years later, he would be the subject of my book.

You gave me more than I could ever repay, but my desire to pay it forward initiated with you. Thank you, sweet lady, for loving me, Kristi, Andrea, Ryder, Reese, Hudson, and, of course, Wayne. We all are improved individuals because of you. Our lives richer and fuller with you beside us. It was March 6, 2023, that we lost you. An immeasurable loss to our family, our lives, and our hearts. Your legacy will live in us every day until our turn comes. Thank you for your life, your glow, your devotion, your smile, and your happiness.

Thank you for being my mom, Nancy Krstich Westphale.
(July 8th, 1950- March 6th, 2023)
"Do What's Right, Do Your Best, Do Unto Others"

"The individual has always had to struggle to keep from being overwhelmed by the tribe. If you try it, you will be lonely often, and sometimes frightened. But no price is too high to pay for the privilege of owning yourself."

— Friedrich Nietzsche (Alexei's favorite thinker)

Time! What is Time?
Time is infinity, it is near, and it is far. Time runs, time stays still. Time creates happiness, sadness, time searches, time finds. Time stabilizes and secures; time also ruins and destroys. Time gives answers to many questions; time leaves us in perplexity, incomprehension. Time heals, time retains, time preserves man's achievements, time also destroys it.

—Janis Abele
Translation of Latvian poem

CONTENTS

Acknowledgments   ix

1. A Star is Born   3
2. Making Mozart   5
3. Never A Snowflake is Repeated   11
4. Young Love   24
5. Horowitz   28
6. Tchaikovsky International Piano Competition   37
7. Back To School   41
8. Communism   48
9. Together   52
10. Van   54
11. Making the Cliburn   62
12. The Wilcoxes   69
13. Coming to America   71
14. Richard   82
15. The Draw   85
16. Opening Round   89
17. Semifinal Round   97
18. Final Round   102
19. The Cliburn Kid   110
20. Victory Lap   115
21. Meeting God   119
22. Together at Last   126
23. The Plan   133
24. Boo Si Ness   136
25. Mr. Cliburn   143
26. Carnegie Hall   147
27. Pupil, Pedagogue, Legend   150

28. The Sultanovs	153
29. 1993 Van Cliburn Competition	161
30. The Help	165
31. The Chopin	169
32. Pinprick	177
33. Light the Fuse	179
34. Appassionata Explained	183
35. Doctor Onboard	185
36. The 1997 Van Cliburn Competition	188
37. Riga	192
38. Tchaikovsky	194
39. Bump in the Night	203
40. Papulnik	208
41. Beverly	211
42. 2003	216
43. Rebirth	219
44. Never Give Up	226
45. The Grind	228
46. Beautiful Mind	232
47. Come On, Aileen	234
48. What So Proudly	238
49. James L. West	242
50. Overslept	244
51. Picking Up the Pieces	248
52. Mt. Fuji 2009	258
53. Final Curtain	262
54. Sitting on the Terrace	265
The Curse of the Cliburn	270
Where They Are Now (2024)	272
Appendix A	278
Appendix B	279
Notes	283
Bibliography	289

ACKNOWLEDGMENTS

I am indebted to Dace Sultanov for allowing me to write her story and sharing the most intimate details of her life with me. She is a perpetual ray of sunshine amidst a world increasingly full of confusion and struggles. Not once, during our lengthy time together creating this book, did I ever witness her mood or attitude anything less than supremely upbeat. I believe her to be a true treasure unto this world. Those who know Dace would likely agree. The common theme I encounter from those I interviewed was uniformly constant. She is the light wherever she goes. A woman born and raised in Latvia under Soviet oppression and musically trained behind the Iron Curtain at the Moscow Conservatory, where she found the love of her life. Dace's journey took her to the other side of the world to Fort Worth, Texas, where she experienced life's highs and lows only to emerge possessing the perfect gift of empathy and love. There is no one like her. I am lucky to now call Dace my friend.

    Also needing thanks are Jon and Susan Wilcox, the surrogate parents of the Sultanovs for many years. Their invaluable insight into the life of the young Sultanovs added color to this book. Jon's plethora of wonderful stories and introduction to Cusquena Peruvian beers are much appreciated. Aileen Hummel, the musical healer, exudes a gift for healing for those whom medicine has forgotten. Howard Reich's three-part story on Alexei in the *Chicago Tribune* was immensely useful. Beverly Archibald, thank you for your generosity and kindness. Denise Mullins, thank you for sharing your rare free time. Dr. Tamas Ungar, I have known you since I was a child, but I never realized how incredible you really are until recently. Thank you for all you do for music, pianists, and your gift of teaching. Your life is a gift to the world of music. Maris Abele, what an incredible caring brother you truly are. John Giordano, Maestro, thank you for your passion for music and the effort you gave to share it. Donna Witten, what an amazing addition to the Sultanov story. Your unwavering passion to help people shines brightly. Sasha Korsantia, thank you for your lifetime dedicated to the piano as well as your friendship with Alexei, which opened the story up with some wonderful memories. I am amazed by your professional life of performing and subsequent travel. Vika, your continued friendship with Dace since the conservatory days came with many humorous and interesting stories. Thanks to June Naylor Harris for connecting me with the people who wrote about the Van Cliburn International Piano Competition and for marrying such an interesting guy. Mary Rogers, your long and illustrious career telling stories makes you an instant favorite of mine. Janis and Benita Abele, I loved you from the moment I met you. Please forgive my butchering of the beautiful Latvian language. What truly amazing people you two are. Sasha Shtarkman, the consummate professional and supreme talent, thank you for digging into your memory bank for insight into your early years in the Soviet Union and sharing the details of your life. Your knowledge of the tremendous challenges pianists face, even the gifted sort, helped tremendously. Danny Saliba, I thank you for the crash course on the most incredible piano company, Steinway & Sons. Bryan Elmore, you gave my family the most memorable experience with the tour of the Steinway & Sons factory in New York. I am indebted to you for your generous time under the Steinway hood. My family are now Steinway fans for life. Alann Sampson, your patronage to the arts has made you a guiding light in the classical music arena. You have been there and done that, which helped me tremendously. Richard Gipson, thank you for your professionalism and introduction to the musical world here in Fort Worth. Your career in music, mainly percussion, has brought so much to so many at TCU. The university is lucky to have a man like you in its sphere. James Williams, from oilman to piano man, you have to be one of the most interesting people I met and not anything like I expected. Thank you to the most passionate Alexei Sultanov fan there is, Yusuke Murakami. Yusuke, no one unrelated appreciates the magic of Alexei like you. Thank you to Eugene and Larissa Cherkasov for your valuable insight into the world of classical music and years of patience teaching children the beauty of the piano. Ryder and Reese have grown as humans under your tutelage.

    Piano teachers everywhere face a generation of children hard pressed to spend quality time learning to play. The outside influences make the work piano teachers put forth such an invaluable commodity in our precious world. Thank you to the multitude of piano and musical competitions worldwide. In this increasingly competitive world, competitions receive ongoing negative pushback. Musical competitions have the unique ability to make or break theirs competitors. Lack of proper preparation for a competition can destroy a young pianist's confidence and quite possibly their careers. Piano competitions inherently breed a gladiator style event where one champion is crowned, which appeals to the masses and thus strengthens their popularity. Thanks, in recent times, to the advent of the Internet and streaming capabilities, competitors are no longer subjugated to the winner-take-all mentality. Conductors and promoters across the world can and will discover talent appropriate to their cause—often in the early rounds and from those not necessarily suited to the jurors' tastes. The Internet has opened the doors of opportunity to those capable of knocking. On the flip side, the magnitude of preparation for a piano competition cannot help but further a pianist's talent by the sheer hard work involved. Practice makes perfect, after all. Whatever the issues at hand, musical competitions bring wonderful music and real artists to the masses, and for that, we should embrace them. For those who play the piano at any level, I salute you. My comprehension of this king of instruments has grown a hundredfold while writing this book. I feel as if I have acquired a master's degree in classical music appreciation by working on this book. Dace, a remarkable cellist and person, made me realize the true power of music. Music has the ability to touch our souls and brains in a way nothing else can. Musicians feed the soul of the world with what it really needs more of—beauty.

I never had the opportunity to meet Alexei Sultanov, but I now know his life's story intimately, and for that I am a richer person. He was a diamond in the rough and most worthy of having his story told. His influence on the world was far reaching and amazing. Dace very easily might never have left Latvia or the Soviet Union, but by her sheer determination to survive and live fully, she has created a life of purpose. The world is a much better place because of the Sultanovs, and I hope you enjoy this amazing story as much as I enjoyed researching and writing it.

A million thank-yous to my exceptional wife, Andrea. This book took time from us that is increasingly rare. I hold in my heart a debt of gratitude for your constant support. You are the rock in our marriage.

1
A Star is Born

Upon birth, the human experience is circumscribed by the support systems of caregivers. A baby's future is undetermined, but the traits of a genius are typically discovered fairly early through the course of reasonable childhood activities. Traits such as insatiable curiosity, the ability to learn quickly, making sense of incoming complex information, and the heavy need for attention are recognized markers of potential genius. A child's magical grasp and understanding of a skill far advancing his or her age are often found by accident. The discovery of this trait typically results in a severe redirect in that child's life. A rare and recognized intellectual gift leads to parental dreams of fortune and fame, with significant resources leveraged on this child. The coupling of genius and opportunity might even change the world for the better. It can also take its beneficiary to the darkest depths of life. Alexei Sultanov wasn't like other children, and his gift couldn't stay hidden for long.

Alexei (pronounced "Alec-Say") was born August 7, 1969, to Natalia Pogorelova and Faizul Sultanov in the Soviet Central Asian Republic of Tashkent, Uzbekistan. Natalia, a Russian, made a life as a professional violinist. Faizul, a native Uzbek, provided as a concert cellist. A foundation in music brought the two together and sustained their relationship. The family struggled mightily to earn a living on the professional stage and thus lived a very lean existence. The pressure of raising a child only added to the load. The weight increased as Natalia gave birth to a second boy, Sergei, six years later, which completed the family. Alexei

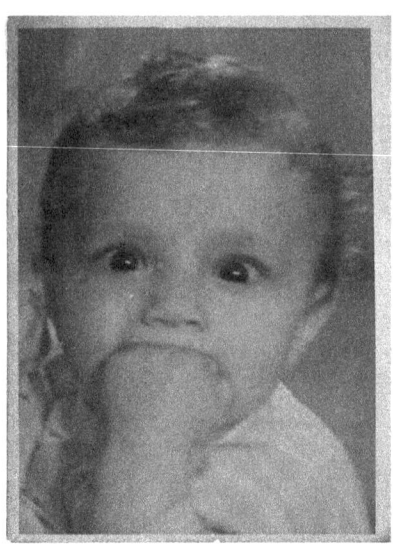

Baby Alexei Sultanov. *Dace Collection*.

spent much of his early childhood battling illnesses like chronic pneumonia and rheumatic fever, which limited him physically. Faizul and Natalia played professionally when they were called but taught music lessons for their livelihoods. They were forced to teach their students from home so that they might be close to their often-sick child. Alexei's close proximity to his parents' lessons allowed him to hear the constant background of their music. Along with cello and violin lessons, the piano was also taught at home. On occasion, a very young Alexei corrected the students' pitch when he noticed inconsistencies. He would cry out when a student missed a note or failed to play in tempo. His interest in music did not go unnoticed, and his parents stepped in.

Alexei's ear for music was countered by his tremendous tantrums when things didn't go his way. Natalia, realizing his potential opportunities, dreamt that her son would develop into the next famous Soviet violinist. She cobbled her money together and bought him a tiny violin. However, Alexei would have nothing of it and smashed the violin on the floor in protest, ending his mother's dreams of another violinist in the family. Faizul introduced him to his cello but had similar luck. It seemed the piano was all that soothed the young child. The boy's mood was often affected by music he heard from street musicians while out in public. A violinist on the street could send him into a meltdown if the song was too melancholy. Natalia was seen from time to time begging these musicians to play pieces with uplifting melodies or to stop playing altogether. A minor-keyed melody on the radio often sent him reeling.

The young family lived in a cramped one-bedroom apartment in Moscow. Alexei slept in the one bedroom beside the family piano, which he would begin to tap on as a six-month-old. Natalia and Faizul gave up

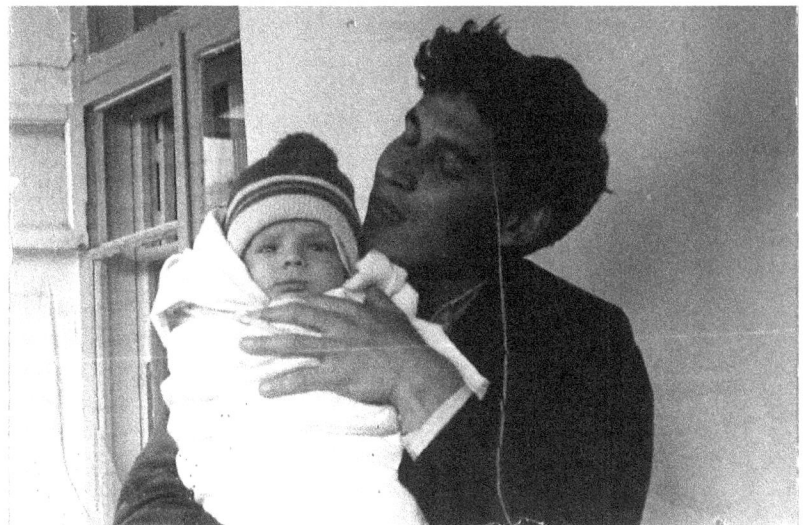

Alexei with his father, Faizul. *Dace Collection*.

their bedroom to their precious son and instead slept on a bare mattress on the floor of the apartment. Natalia warned Faizul early on that, "We are doomed and are destined to be slaves of this child for the rest of our lives." He displayed at age two that he was not like other children. While not quite able to talk, Alexei fingered short yet creative melodies by request on the family's Soviet Red October branded keyboard for friends and family. Natalia realized the potential magnitude of the situation when one day she sang Alexei one of her beloved songs, and Alexei hummed it back to her perfectly. He seemed to have an exceptional ear for tone and pitch, well ahead of the curve. His underdeveloped voice still carried the tune perfectly.

Born into a musical family, he began basic piano lessons at the age of three and, with guidance from Natalia, began to compose his own short musical pieces. He also discovered that he could transcribe the notes of Beethoven works onto score paper simply by listening. Often, Alexei heard Faizul playing the piano and became agitated as he missed notes that were unnoticeable to most. He would call out to him in Russian emphatically the correct note, "Play the 'A' Papulnik! Play the 'A' Papulnik!"![1]

Two-year-old Alexei Sultanov learning the piano. *Dace Collection*.

2
Making Mozart

Being mentioned in the same breath as Mozart is reserved for a special few within the confines of musical history. Only the most exceptional and creative prodigies ever garner such a designation. The singular name of Mozart carries with it implied terms such as genius, pioneer, and savant. Mozart, after all, carved his name into history in a noticeably short period of time, before his untimely death at thirty-five years old. The world celebrates with reverence January 27 as the birthday of Mozart. Increasingly, musical geniuses have become easier to recognize with the advent of the Internet. People love to ascribe the Mozart label to young prodigies, but confirmation requires much time and accomplishment to warrant a proven comparison. Most geniuses can be validated with testing, performance, and accomplishment, but very few reach the Mozart apex. While most children Alexei's age were playing games, exploring their surroundings, and learning life's basics, Alexei had been assigned a different path. Music would consume his life for the foreseeable future.

Natalia knew early that Alexei needed more guidance than what she could provide. If Alexei was to be the prodigy that she felt him to be, then he needed the best teachers available. Tamara Popovich, who was a revered music teacher in the capital city of Tashkent in Uzbekistan, had her pick of only the finest students that were offered to her. Popovich was a plain-looking, highly focused, highly skilled Soviet-styled master of piano education. She met young Alexei at age five and was floored by the vastness of his music talents. Tamara left the interview stunned.

She expressed to Natalia and Faizul that he possessed a unique ear for music and could sing in perfect pitch. She explained why she could be of use to him. A talent like his required a steady regimen designed to push him. Although money was very tight for the teaching family, Natalia and Faizul purchased a camera and a tape recorder to capture and document their young sensation. Popovich began teaching him and found him to be a very quick study. Alexei understood what the seasoned Popovich was saying. Two years later, at age seven, Popovich's youngest student wowed a curious crowd by playing Mozart's *Concert Rondo in D Major* with the local symphony orchestra. The crowd was joined by the orchestra in their complete amazement. The boy's age, along with his small size, bewildered those expecting far less. Alexei was no longer a secret. Natalia and Faizul's private recording of this moment caused critics to describe him as brilliant, phenomenal, and Mozartian.

The praise was high for Alexei, but with it came the certain catch. His genius was certainly established now, which created a cocoon around him that consisted of one thing: music. Alexei began his schooling as was required for his age but left little else for him except the piano. His small complex world was overwhelmed with music and its required practice. Practice was not measured in days of the week but more succinctly in hours per day. His meals were brought to him at the piano. Tamara convinced the Sultanovs that Alexei needed a strict regimen of practice and more practice to harness and control his gift. A childhood of playing with toys and other children was out of the question, as it would simply diminish his greatness. Alexei learned that his mother knew what was best for him, and a smack from the back of a shoe awaited him should he forget that. Discipline played a central role in the next few years for Alexei. It would be easy to say that Alexei suffered from severe over parenting and a childhood that never happened, but on the flip side, the results were astonishing according to all who bore witness to his incredible development. Howard Reich, famed *Chicago Tribune* music columnist, years later, likened Alexei's seven-year-old debut performance of Beethoven's massive *First Piano Concerto* to playing major league baseball as a teenager.[1] Over the next several years, Alexei's abilities blossomed as did his command over the music he practiced. He was without equal amongst the children in his school and thus felt the weight of his world squeezing in on him.

As Alexei's life plan took shape under heavy pressure from his parents, he developed a volatile defense mechanism. His behavior became erratic at times as he increasingly lashed out against those who controlled him. His class time at school unveiled the omnipotent and manipulative system into which he was born—communism. It was the constant pressure at home coupled with the pressure to conform to the Soviet model at school that eventually stoked a fire inside Alexei. Alexei loathed having to be told what to do all the time but lacked the ability to change any of it. He subsequently developed and cultivated the beginnings of a lifelong resistance to the communist model of sharing and doing what's best for his country rather than serving himself. His childhood hatred of sharing, which was implemented early on at school, morphed into a rabid rebelliousness not often seen behind the Iron Curtain. This trait would intensify as he aged.

He found an outlet for his anger that would come from outside his family. A family friend who emigrated from North Korea several years prior introduced Alexei to tae kwon do around the age of eleven. The discipline of this Korean martial art would help Alexei control himself when the pressures of practicing threatened to stall his progression. This combative art form, which appeared at the conclusion of World War II, promoted striking, kicking, and self-discipline that appealed to Alexei's towering need for an emotional outlet. When time would allow, Alexei threw himself into its culture and rudimentary training. The release it offered would benefit him throughout his life.

Upon turning eleven, Alexei also began regularly visiting the Russian capital of Moscow for private lessons with the conservatory's legendary professor, Lev Naumov. The costs of travel, even by train, were steep in those days but necessary to connect Alexei and this highly sought-after professor. Alexei had indeed been identified as a prodigy, but the state hadn't yet footed the bill for these trips to Moscow. The conservatory was Russia's highest educational insti-

Alexei showing off his martial arts skills. *Dace Collection.*

Alexei as a young man practicing. *Dace Collection.*

tution and reserved for the best and brightest talents the country had to offer. The communist model sought to protect its talent once identified, in all forms, by paying for training and development by the communist state in its revered conservatory. The Sultanovs, in the meantime, ran up a tremendous debt funding these trips to Moscow. They began asking friends and family to borrow money to keep Alexei on track with the bright future that everyone seemed to recognize.

When Alexei was thirteen, he applied to the International Radio Competition for Young Musicians Concertino Praga. This Czech Radio competition, formed in 1966, was held every three years for young performers. This competition sought to unite and promote the best young musicians who applied to the public contest. The competition's focus included stringed instruments, woodwinds, and chamber music. The first prize brought with it a celebratory concert in Prague, which was broadcast live on the radio. Often the winners played in front of radio microphones for the first time. The solo performers were joined by the Prague Radio Symphony Orchestra. The laureates were invited to perform at the South Bohemian festival Concertino Praga, which took place in the historic South Bohemian castles. Alexei impressed many but surprisingly did not garner any accolades there. Yet his appetite and understanding for musical competition was

Hall of Moscow Tchaikovsky Conservatory (view from scene) Est. 1866. *Photo by Pavel Losevsky*

ultimately born. He realized that the competitive piano world involved a tortuous practice schedule and little room for anything else. After all, what better way to evaluate Alexei's talent than to be judged by his peers? Music competitions, especially pianistic, sought out a winner, and Alexei knew he was of this ilk. Perhaps, if he could prove himself the best, then he might find some respite from his complicated existence. He had witnessed how significant accomplishment in music gave its performers seeming control over their lives; something he desperately craved. With Alexei's brutal practice schedule under Popovich's watchful eye, he developed a rebellious habit of injuring himself in an attempt to push back against the unrelenting pressures. Afterall, he could not be expected to play if he was injured. The local emergency room in Tashkent knew Alexei by name and often sent him home with bandages to his bruised and cut hands. This self-mutilation afforded him some reprieve from his tortuous practice schedule. It would also manifest itself into bulimia, which haunted him throughout his life.

From 1984 to 1986, Alexei spent his summers not playing outside like most kids his age but at his aunt Svetlana's apartment in Balashiha on the outskirts of Moscow in front of the piano, with Tamara Popovich at his side. His days consisted of endless cycles of practicing. As grueling as they were for Alexei, the results were magnificent. Alexei quickly became a performer

Alexei with his long time teacher, Popovich. *Dace Collection*.

Young Janis Abele wearing his Red Army issues uniform. *Dace Collection*.

of unspeakable range. His ability to hear a piece of music and unlock its stylistic mysteries became second nature to him. Tamara was constantly forced to find harder regimens for Alexei when he would make quick work of some of her difficult lesson plans. The cycle was endless but ultimately effective. When Popovich would leave his side to run errands, she would load Alexei with practice work. Alexei took advantage of the lack of supervision to create jazz tunes which helped him keep his sanity. Soviet talent scouts, who were composed mainly of pedigreed musical professors in positions of influence, had identified Alexei early, and thus his secret was out, much to the gratification of Popovich, Natalia, and Faizul. He was rewarded for his exceptional abilities at age fifteen with early acceptance into the Moscow Central Music School, where he would train for the Moscow Conservatory, where talents like Alexei ended up. Alexei then began spending much more time in Moscow honing his craft with Russia's most distinguished teachers. He discovered that his conservatory professor, Naumov, desired him to compete in one of the Soviet piano competitions. It was during this time that Alexei met fellow pianist, Georgian born Alexander Korsantia. Sasha, as Alexander was known, was four years older than Alexei, but a lasting friendship was formed. Alexei was indeed ready, but at fifteen he wasn't old enough to compete in the official Chopin competition in Poland. Korsantia was, though, and became one of the Soviet entries. Korsantia's talent was exceptional and would take him into working as a touring professional pianist, but his friendship with Alexei remained on solid footing.

3
Never a Snowflake is Repeated

Janis Abele adored his beloved Benita (or *Bebsitis* as he referred to her). As a young Latvian man, he feared serving in the Soviet Red Army. The fortunate few received assignments with the Red Army band or with the Soviet railroad, which offered a much safer path than the militaristic route. Janis (pronounced "Yan-is") enjoyed his childhood, including school and the time he spent learning to be an engineer. One afternoon, Janis would borrow from a young woman he knew a book entitled *Lazdu Laipa*, written by Latvian author Ilze Indrane. When he went to return the book, the woman's younger sister, Benita, answered the door. The two quickly became interested in one another. Janis would spend every minute of his free time with her, and the couple fell madly in love.

However, their time was interrupted when Janis turned eighteen and was conscripted to the Red Army. After indoctrination, Janis was turned over to the railroad for deployment. Along with his company, basic cold weather gear, and meager rations, he boarded his designated train for assignment. They knew only that they were headed north but not where. As the days passed, their excitement diminished. The train ride lasted five endless days spent sleeping and waiting. When the train finally slowed, the recruits jumped up and searched the horizon for anything civilian. Aside from a small military barracks, all they

Dace Abele as a infant. *Dace Collection.*

saw was a vast expanse of frozen wasteland. A dreaded place known throughout the world as Siberia. Here, they would spend the next three years in some of the harshest conditions on the planet.[1]

Siberian life was very difficult as he labored mightily for the railroad. He spent his free time writing letters and dreaming of the woman he would one day marry. Her return letters always took months to reach him, and he could always tell that the letters had been opened and censored multiple times before they reached him. At the conclusion of his conscription, Janis returned to civilian life and married Benita.

Life for Janis and Benita progressed steadily for the new couple. He reveled in being home in Riga with familiar scenery surrounding him. Life now would require an occupation, as the Red Army no longer supported him. Latvia's economy lacked a multitude of options for new civilians. The Soviet control of Latvia added to the constant struggle of the young couple. As tough as it was, the couple stayed close together and found happiness. In the older sections of Latvia, which was sandwiched between the countries of Estonia and Lithuania, just off the Baltic Sea, the country homes had names, and the Abeles' home was called *Skujinas* (Skoo-yee-nyass). Their country escape sat in the Daugmale region smack dab in the middle of Latvia, just off the Daugava River.

As the blissful time continued, the couple realized they were ready for a family of their own. Benita quickly became pregnant, and the two prayed for a healthy child. A gentle snow—exceptionally early for that time of year in Latvia—fell the morning of the birth. Dace Abele was born at two o'clock in the early morning hours on October 12, 1968, in Riga. This day would also mark the opening ceremonies of the XIX Olympic Games in Mexico City.[2] These summer Olympic Games found an audience in front of the Abeles' small black-and-white television. As tightly controlled as the media was in Latvia, via the Soviets, the Olympics were a nationally celebrated event. Every television could be found tuned into the games, which historically showcased the Soviet Union's dominance. The Soviets always felt highlighting their athletic stars on the world stage was a matter of national pride.

The fervor that resulted from these games nearly resulted in a baby girl named Olympia, but higher motherly powers prevailed, and Dace (pronounced "Dot-Say") had her start. Benita recalls the church bells ringing at the precise moment of her birth. Men in this part of the world weren't allowed in the delivery room, so the cold dark street below would have to do for Janis. He paced the streets below the hospital window as the snow fell to the ground. His nervous concentration was interrupted when a commotion arose from the delivery room window above, and Dace was held up at the window for Janis to see and admire. Janis tearfully stood there beaming at the distant sight of his baby girl. He hurriedly ran up the stairs to the room to meet her. Dace was everything a father could have hoped for. *Tetis*, the Latvian version of Daddy, as she would one day call him, became the proud father of Riga's newest baby. In Riga, life was simple and perfect for this child. The Soviet occupation of Latvia was seen and felt throughout, but nonetheless, Dace's upbringing was a peaceful one and not one marked by the many difficulties in this area of the world.

Dace's childhood was somewhat typical of those musically inclined families behind the Iron Curtain. The Abeles survived as a middle-class family who had the good fortune of living in a house built by Dace's grandfather, Reinhold Lukstins. This house would accommodate more and more kin as Benita and her two sisters married and had children. The ample house would shelter more than its intended design at various points. The family would eat its meals at a large circular table on the first floor. The tableside discussions were part of family lore as nary a meal was served when there wasn't a debate or argument over matters that only close families know. Mornings, though, always saw any hostilities restored to decency, with the smell of coffee permeating the entire house. Family stood as a pillar in Latvian culture, which couldn't be easily broken by the constraints of Soviet oppression.

The Republic of Latvia was founded on the eastern shores of the Baltic Sea in 1918, with the declaration of their independence from German control after the conclusion of World War I. The country desired its independence from all its powerful neighbors. The country labored hard to rebuild what the Great War had destroyed or robbed from it. Peace never lasted long as the neighboring Russia utilized its size and power to keep Latvia under its thumb. Latvia never enjoyed full freedom, but Russia's strategic interests and lack of resources kept the country under occupation. Russia lacked enough financial resources to fully manage this Republic amongst its many interests. Latvia's limited freedom was short lived, for the Nazis invaded in 1941.

Janis grew up undersized and under stimulated in his country home on the outskirts of Riga. Riga is the largest city in Latvia and its capital; it is home to one-third of the country's population. This ancient port city lies on the banks of the Daugava River and reigned as the European Capital of Culture in 2014. Richard Wagner, Mikhail Baryshnikov, and the World Chess Champion Mikhail Tal, called the Wizard of Riga, all call Riga home. It's generally recognized as having the finest and largest collection of Art Nouveau buildings in the world.[3] Latvian and Russian languages both originate from the Baltic-Slavic language group, and they share a synthetic design. Regardless, Janis and his countrymen still resisted learning the language of their oppressors.

The Abele family was no stranger to the horrors of war. Both brothers of Dace's grandmother would be lost to the Nazi regime. After the Nazis acquired Latvia during their European expansion, its culture and treasures were once again exploited. The Nazi war machine brought along with it an incessant thirst for resources. The Nazis incorporated Latvia on July 10, 1941, as Reichskommissariat Ostland or General Province of Latvia. The Latvian town of Salaspils sat eleven miles to the southeast of Riga and was one of the oldest settlements in Latvia. The Nazi invasion found new purpose for the once peaceful town. The Nazi SS erected a concentration camp on the outskirts of Salaspils, hidden in the middle of the forest. This concentration camp was originally designed to destroy the incoming trainloads of Jews but was reimagined as a police prison and work education camp. Its true purpose left no confusion. It would undoubtedly enter history as one of the largest civilian concentration camps in the Baltics during the war. The concentration camp saw around twenty-three thousand prisoners enter its gates with nearly two thousand deaths—due to illness, executions, and exhaustion.[4] Most of the dead were children who suffered from primarily typhoid fever, measles, and brutal treatment. Latvia's wartime population of nearly two million people saw over three hundred thousand of its civilians murdered during that period.[5] It was a time of chaos.

Some Latvians initially welcomed the Nazis, as they represented the long-awaited end of their Soviet occupation, only to discover the magnified horrors that awaited them under the new occupation. Many of the Latvians were forced to pick between fighting for the Soviets against the invading Nazis or joining the incoming Germans, knowing fully that joining either side might result in their deaths. As the Nazis took possession of Latvia, the country was pillaged of its important resources, including its people. The war years crushed almost everything of perceived value that existed in Latvia. As the Axis powers lost momentum and the Nazis were on the verge of defeat, Latvia again dreamt of their independence. This was not to be. The Soviets reoccupied Latvia in 1944 after driving the Nazis out and forming the Latvian Soviet Socialist Republic, which held firmly in place for the next fifty years. Independence would not come for these historically oppressed people until 1991, when it was restored by a Declaration of Independence of the Republic of Latvia after many years of peaceful protests. Latvia to this day remains an independent democracy, with its capital of Riga housing one third of its citizens. Its official language is Latvian, but a strong Lithuanian influence took a foothold here due to the lengthy Soviet occupation. Latvia contains many ethnic Russians amongst its citizens.

However, Dace's watchful parents minimized the impact of the Soviet occupation during her early years. The first few years were joyful and happy. Benita had been an accomplished pianist and well known throughout Riga for her musical talent. Benita loved to take Dace to the opera house in Riga, Dace's first childhood memory. Dace memorized and fell in love early with the Italian opera *Tosca* by Puccini. The unique opera house smelled of wood, upholstery, and paint remained a constant so many years later. Benita worked as the piano accompanist for the Riga Boys Choir, which gave her and Dace regular access. Her skill in performance accompaniment, or providing the background music for the main performance, was popular and garnered her some acclaim. Benita worked in this capacity with the Riga Opera House, which then changed its named to the Riga Doma Music School. Her talent made her a sought-after piano teacher. Benita's music career, though, was put on hold once Dace's brother, Maris, was born in 1974, and the demands at home became too great to continue.

In need of money, she discovered she could teach students at her home, so she could be close to Maris and Dace. Benita possessed the extraordinary patience and thick skin to teach piano even to the most difficult students. She had the distinct pleasure of teaching piano to the conductor of the Riga Opera when all others would not, since he was known to be especially cruel to his subordinates. Benita spent much time with young Dace teaching her basic music, piano, and singing, which uncovered within her daughter a special music talent. It seemed Dace was destined for a career in music. Her mother had high hopes that her talent would impress enough people to attend the famous conservatory in Moscow.

Since she was the firstborn child, Dace received the lion's share of the attention. She quickly learned how to interact with people and developed a bubbly and outgoing personality. She spent much time with her baby brother Maris, born six years after her. She helped to tend to his needs while she followed Benita's musical education. When Dace met her newborn brother, she reported that he gave off the intoxicating odor of a baby elephant. Of course, Dace had never smelled a baby elephant. She loved to dress up baby "Maritis," as he was affectionately nicknamed. Dace, when alone, loved to play next to the window with her mother's extravagant button collection, which she had accumulated over the years from sewing.

She began her formal schooling when she was seven years old. She sat at the same desk as her younger cousin Anta, who lived with the family and kept careful watch out for her. The two became very close, but music would begin to define Dace. In Latvian schools, music was often combined with general education. That same year, Benita brought Dace to Emila Darzina Music School to have her tested for music talent. In this part of the world, to have music ability was normal, but to excel put one on the fast track to a better life. Most seven-year-olds with basic musical prowess were expected to carry a tune and stay on key. Dace Abele found singing in key and carrying a tune for the examiners quite intimidating. She was asked to stop amid a Latvian children's tune she was nervously singing. The teachers informed Benita that Dace wouldn't last long with her musical career. She didn't have what they considered basic talent. They advised her to consider other forms of work.

For a young child, this wasn't crippling news, but for her mother it was troubling. The daughter of musician parents certainly expected their offspring to excel at some level. As Dace grew up, she believed her answer was playing the drums. This didn't sit well with Benita. She gently encouraged her to try something softer, and the cello made its appearance. Benita lobbied Dace's school to allow her to take cello

Baby Dace with mother, Benita.
Dace Collection.

Country home of the Abeles, a favorite spot.
Dace Collection.

lessons. The school acquiesced and gave her a shot due to her mother's fame. They felt Dace wouldn't make it once the workload piled up.

The school day began at 8:30 a.m. with general education, which consisted of math, literature, writing, and science. Under the Russian model, classes on communism and Marxism found their way into the Latvia educational experience. Capitalism was systematically taught as evil and bad. Under communism, she learned, the government took care of its citizens and provided them with free education and medical care. Students were taught that a better life was the reward if one subscribed to the teachings of communism. Dace's teachers reinforced that the state owned all property as well as the means of production, and everyone was equal and without wealth divisions. Essentially, she was taught to keep her head down, follow instructions, and make no trouble. Trouble never interested Dace. She was far too busy. Music classes commenced in the afternoon with piano, chamber music, cello classes, and orchestra, and didn't finish till 5:30 p.m. This was Dace's schedule Monday through Friday from age seven to sixteen.

The idea of playing the cello wasn't a complete surprise, based on Benita's internal feeling for Dace's gift. Janis Abele may have also had a hand in its origination. Although he never played an instrument, he loved listening to music and cellist compositions were often heard on the family's radio. Janis also was the registered owner of a small country house the family named *Skujinas*, which he considered his sanctuary. He would often escape from the pressures of city life here. He relished the open land and forests that covered the area. Janis could go to *Skujinas*—a Latvian word for pine needles—with its quiet, peaceful location and listen to music uninterrupted and paint, which was his hobby. Dace also developed her intense love of the outdoors here. What began with her playing her cello outside in *Skujinas*, for all nature to hear, matured into a lifelong passion of playing in remote and incredible settings in nature.

Aside from school, daily chores, and now cello lessons, Dace did not have time for much else. Her parents kept her busy at *Skujinas* by helping the family in the fields and tending to their small herd of livestock. Dace often was up at five in the morning to shepherd the cattle as part of her responsibility. When back in the city, Dace kept her nose out of trouble and avoided any type of conflict. The Riga school system allowed its students the summer off, which Dace enjoyed immensely. Outdoor dances called *Zionball*, or *zalumballe* in Latvian, were all the rage for a budding teenager in Riga. However, Dace's summers were not spent idly. The cello always found ample time and a place to be practiced. There was always room for improvement according to her instructors.

Growing up in Latvia was typical of most Soviet-controlled countries. After the Second World War eradicated Hitler from the earth and dissolved the German empire, Latvians held out hope again for their independence. When the power grab commenced, Latvia was quickly gobbled back up by the Soviet Union. Latvia lacked a force capable of defending herself and the war-torn country and government were far from recovering. Under Soviet control, the Latvian culture, irreparably damaged by the Nazi occupation, underwent a rewriting that had a very pro-Soviet angle. The Soviet perspective, which began at the elementary school level, taught that the Soviet dictator Joseph Stalin, was a national hero. People learned the socialist way of life where people took what they needed and nothing more. Basic public services were free, and people worked for the betterment of their fellow man, not themselves. The United States was a faraway land full of loose women and lazy men, and thus a threat contrary to the Soviet way of life. The United States was always referred to as the enemy of the Soviets. Most modernized Latvian schoolbooks utilized dark colors whenever a map depicted the United States.

The Soviet message was promoted and spread though fear and intimidation, not unlike the Nazis had done before the war. Fear played a prominent role in both cases. Soviet propaganda, a method utilized to control their citizens, was also far reaching throughout the world in areas such as technology, sports, art, and music. Soviet musicians were exported throughout the world to showcase their dominance. Ninety miles off the coast of Florida sat one of the Soviet strongholds. Soviet musicians were routinely sent to Cuba to perform as part of the Communist Party outreach program.[6] Soviets, did in fact, lead the world in many cultural facets, but none more so than music, given the sheer number and level of talent of their classical musicians. The Soviet promotion of its musicians to the world did carry a risk. On a regular basis, musicians turned up missing when time to return to the motherland. These defectors discovered the outside world was not as terrible as they had been taught. Their potential and new opportunities outside the Soviet Union opened up a world of possibilities. The freedoms enjoyed by Americans became the stuff of fantasy to the Soviets, which a very select few had an opportunity to experience. The documented stories of defectors became legendary to those permanently living behind the Iron Curtain. The Soviets had little interest in revealing to the world its subversive inner workings. The defectors, who risked their lives for a chance at a better one, often left everything and everyone behind.

Young Dace with pigtails.
Dace Collection

In Soviet Latvia, Christmas was strictly prohibited as a religious holiday, not accepted under Communist Party mandates. Those willing to celebrate the birth of Christ did so under careful lock and key.[7] Dace's aunt often snubbed her oppressors and adorned a large Christmas tree at her house but kept it carefully out of sight behind a large curtain. Dace's parents instilled in her caution enough to not talk to anyone about the family celebrating Christmas. Rumors of the Soviet security agency, the *Komitet Gosudarstvennoy Bezopasnosti* (KGB), arresting celebrating Christians often surfaced around this holiday. The KGB system utilized fear to keep Christians in constant hiding.

The Abeles sheltered their children as best they could from the undesirable influences inside of Latvia. Dace's increasingly rare time with her brother Maris often found them fishing at *Skujinas* or playing ice hockey in the homemade backyard rink. Maris discovered a love for books and was often found reading anything he could get his hands on. Dace was always very protective over her baby brother and the two formed a lasting bond. Maris had early aspirations to play the clarinet professionally, until years later at the Latvian Conservatory when he was involved in a serious auto accident that left him concussed and no longer able to play the clarinet. The two shared a love of music though that was fostered throughout their adolescence. At age fifteen, Benita decided to expand Dace's cello training, so she sought out the best cello teacher she knew.

    Arvids Tareila was hired and became Dace's first paid cello teacher. She disliked him from the start. Arvids was rather strict and pushed her hard all the time. He had a habit of locking her in the classroom alone while she practiced so she could focus on nothing else. These practices typically lasted two to three hours, leaving Dace exhausted. On occasion, when she happened to be in classroom #33, she would climb down a tree that grew outside the third story window and visit the local coffee shops for a bulcinas, a delicious small Latvian pastry roll filled with fruit. This was a wonderful respite from the monotony of practice, and Arvids was none the wiser.

    When she was sixteen, music professors from the conservatory in Moscow visited Dace's school to teach the students a master's class. The famed cello professor, Alexander Fedorchenko, made the sixteen-hour train trip and was among the visiting professors. His appearance to Dace was strikingly similar to Winnie the Pooh and he was nearly as kind and thoughtful. Fedorchenko's stated goal of teaching a master class in cello performance came with a secondary purpose. He was tasked with finding a worthy student to bring to the conservatory in Moscow to demonstrate his teaching skills exhibited through his student playing. The other professors visiting from the conservatory completed their teachings and quickly initiated their evaluations of the respective talent pool that existed in this musically rich region. Those lucky enough to be identified were sent to Moscow for further education, which was indeed a huge honor. The selection process took place in the school's auditorium with the professors judging the students' recitals in their respective instruments—piano, violin, or cello. Fedorchenko straightened up in his chair whenever the cellists took the stage. When Dace's turn came, emotions welled up inside her as she performed Haydn's *Cello Concerto no. 1 in C major*, a piece that she knew very well from years of practice. Dace was mere minutes into the first movement, when professor Fedorchenko raised his hand to interrupt her. He wasn't disappointed but rather satisfied and even offered some constructive criticism on how she could get more out of her cello. After the day's audition was completed for all the students, Professor Fedorchenko approached Benita. His first pick had taken ill and thus had to decline. His second pick was Dace Abele.

In the Soviet culture, speaking honestly to someone is the norm regardless of feelings or political correctness. These conservatory professors were especially blunt. If they didn't like someone's style of playing and felt they were better suited to a life of menial labor, then they would suggest it. Fedorchenko had some very useful comments for Dace, but she exhibited talent enough that Fedorchenko wanted her to continue her musical education in Moscow. This honor is akin to a collegiate athlete getting drafted by a professional team. Benita was obviously thrilled but knew this substantial opportunity would require her daughter to leave home. The decision, albeit sad to imagine, was easy to make. Dace would be studying under the best music professors the Soviet Union had to offer. Most of the greatest Soviet musicians in history had studied at the Moscow State Tchaikovsky Conservatory, named appropriately for Russia's most famous musician, Pytor Tchaikovsky. If a student could make it at the conservatory, their lives and subsequent careers would be valued differently and likely better by their country. The road would not be easy, but if students applied themselves and worked hard, they could advance out of whatever challenging situation in which they found themselves. Life was very difficult for many people in Latvia and there were few ways to climb the socioeconomic ladder, but having musical talent was one of those ways. Financial security and, more importantly, safety were not assured for anyone in Latvia. The conservatory offered its students certain protections by the Soviet government as well as the best teachers available. These students were a source of national pride and much effort was taken to develop them fully.

The life Benita knew was coming to an abrupt halt. She couldn't keep her protective bubble over Dace once she left. What opportunity awaited Dace in Moscow? What unknown perils awaited her daughter? As in most life decisions of this magnitude, the opportunity ultimately outweighed the risk. It was months later when Dace graduated Emila Darzina Music School and traveled to Moscow to begin anew. She never had time for a boyfriend until she reached the conservatory, but that was about to change, as was the course of her life.[8]

Dace arrived in Moscow after the longest train ride of her life to enroll in the Moscow Central Music School. Her excitement got the better of her, as she bounded into her new dorm room anxious to meet her roommates. She discovered two women, both surprised by her arrival and both perplexed by the nonsensical Russian-like words emanating from her mouth. Dace's limited Russian took some getting used to as it lacked the fundamentals of the mainstream Soviet students. The Latvia language made her sound funny to her new roommates. It would not take long under her Russian immersion before she quickly improved her mastery of the language.

Dace laughed out loud at the peculiar sight of the two women before her. One of them, a young conservative woman wearing a ponytail and "Shastakovichian" glasses, which were thick-rimmed spectacles, sat on the corner of the bed. Victoria, or Vika as she was known, quickly took interest in the free-spirited and younger Dace. As the two settled their differences, their new world opened up to them.

They quickly realized the tremendous collection of unique cultures and people that existed here. Their arrival at the prestigious school designated them as the newest generation of prominent musicians, expected by their country and, more so, their parents to excel. Most students there were gifted in one way or another, but not everyone was happy to be there. Dace met many who were attending at their parent's behest. For Dace, it was exciting and unknown, and she relished it. It was widely known that the teachings of the Central Music School and then, if they were lucky, the Moscow Conservatory, offered a better life to those who seized the opportunity. The student mixture consisted of children of prominent parents, diplomats, high-ranking military officers, factory workers, common laborers, or musicians from Latvia and every region of the Soviet Union and its territories. They were all different, but ultimately, they knew why they had been selected. The pressure exerted by parents here was substantial. This opportunity offered a potential big break should they choose to accept it. Failure could bring shame upon the family. It was considered a great sin amongst Soviet culture to not develop a gift awarded to these children from "above," as was the common euphemism for God in communist culture. The mandatory entrance exams for the Moscow Central Music School were incredibly difficult and each student labored to get through it.

4
Young Love

Alexei Sultanov, in 1986, was quickly accepted as a sixteen-year-old to continue his musical education at the Moscow Central Music School. For him, leaving home was a welcomed event. Alexei relished the thought of the end to his brutal training regimen. Fortunately, Lev Naumov, a remarkable man who would become his professor, identified Alexei at an early age. Naumov was widely considered the godfather of the Russian piano school and had been awarded the People's Artist of Russia award, the highest Soviet civilian musical honor. This honor signifies outstanding achievement in the field of music within the Soviet Union. Lev Naumov was a classically trained pianist, composer, and legendary educator. He had himself studied under the legendary conservatory pianist and teacher, Heinrich Neuhaus. Naumov's strictly business and technical approach to teaching made him one of the premier professors at the conservatory. He simply was not interested in the world's outside influences. He was there to teach in the Soviet manner and that is what he did. Alexei had tremendous respect for Naumov, as he would greatly expand his talent and work ethic that his long-standing teacher, Tamara Popovich, had instilled into him. Alexei would remain under Naumov's tutelage throughout his time at the conservatory. Naumov was credited with producing many of the most famous Soviet pianists ever to live. He felt Alexei would be the next.

Alexei also benefitted from the additional tutelage of another legendary Soviet pianist and professor, Sergei Dorensky, at the conservatory. Unlike Naumov, Dorensky had some English language skills, and he possessed a much higher opinion of himself than he did of Naumov. Dorensky and his membership in the Communist Party caused Alexei to suspect he was also KGB. Dorensky, and his well-known birthmark on his right cheek, would join Naumov as legends in their fields and each were responsible for a large contingent of Soviet pianist exports over their careers. Each also pulled many strings to keep Alexei in school when administrators attempted to expel him for his perpetual bad behavior issues. His talent was deemed worthy of saving even though administrators felt differently.

Alexei had arrived on the scene in Moscow several months after Dace walked from her train into this new overwhelming place. Alexei was held in great esteem amongst his fellow students even before his arrival. He was not regarded as a regular amongst the new class. His talent was widely known and respected among those at the Central Music School. His schedule was also uniquely a hot topic. Alexei spent half his time at the conservatory with Naumov and Dorensky and then would disappear and spend the other half his time in his hometown of Tashkent, Uzbekistan, with his nemesis, Popovich.

Vika, Dace's newest friend, met Alexei by accident one day during a break in class. Vika had been hiding in the corner of a small room situated behind the school's own concert hall ditching biology class, as was customary for her. Her hiding spot afforded her some free time to read, which she greatly loved. Vika's mother had rented a small apartment near the conservatory by the hour for her daughter to practice piano and compose, but the bad weather wouldn't allow travel there on this day. The peculiar woman who ran the apartment house gave her the creeps as she always kept a very close eye on her and the other tenants, as did the caretakers of the Central Music School and conservatory. Someone always appeared to be watching them or at least trying to. It was customary to sign out when leaving the building for any purpose. The school seemed to have great interest in keeping account of its students.

As Vika pored over the book, two boys suddenly opened the door and entered. She recognized one of the boys from Dace's class, but the other one was a short stranger with a mop of hair and vivid dark eyes. They nodded politely to each other, and Vika buried herself back into her book. The two boys sat and became engaged in a game of chess. The hushed room was interrupted when the new short boy howled with laughter at an apparent mistake his friend had made. A few minutes later, the peace was once again ruined by the sound of the class bell announcing the end of the biology class that Vika was skipping. The trio split from the room, but Vika left with questions. She would later learn that the new boy was none other than the prodigy everyone had been talking about named Alexei.

Dace and Vika spent as much time together as their schedules would allow. The first time Dace was introduced to Alexei at a casual gathering by their dormitory, she initially was not interested. Alexei was several inches shorter than her and seemed overly confident. He possessed a charming yet devious smile that suggested he was someone who liked to cause trouble. Dace had heard many people talking about him. He was known as the star student, and the girls all knew his name. Dace had seen him walking around on occasion at school and wasn't overly impressed by his looks. She tended to avoid giggling with the girls about someone she knew little about. Then came a concert in which Alexei was performing with the Moscow State Orchestra. The public and students alike filled the auditorium to hear Alexei, along with the orchestra, perform the beloved *Tchaikovsky's Piano Concerto no. 1*. The crowd immediately became transfixed by this young man as he played. Dace's interest in Alexei changed in the space of one rendition of the world's most famous piano concerto. She became instantly entranced with him and the powerful and creative way in which he played. Most of the girls studying at the conservatory became enamored with him. The boys in turn likely experienced a tinge of jealousy. His command of the music captured everyone's attention. The professors, who hadn't already, took notice as well with several penciling his name in their notebooks as a potential for their class. This was no ordinary talent even in a land known for its talent. Alexei was talked about around every corner at the conservatory. Dace left the performance with a newfound curiosity about this strange guy. His talent and ability to capture the audience created an attraction she had never felt before.

The second encounter between Dace and Alexei happened several months later when the Choir of Spain visited the conservatory for an engagement. The tickets sold out quickly as the popularity of the choir was vast. Those that were lucky enough to procure tickets made their way easily to their seats. Those not so lucky, utilized the tried-and-true method of rushing the door all at once, which seemed to be a regular occurrence at the conservatory. Oddly, people often found seats by being especially crafty. Dace was one of these lucky students to gain entry through this non-traditional method. On this particular evening, Dace and a small contingent of coeds gained entry into the hall and managed to elude the understaffed and overwhelmed ushers. Those who made it in without tickets would scramble for an empty seat or to the balcony to hide. Once in a seat, some were often safe from expulsion due to the size of auditorium and reluctance of the limited security to chase them down. Alexei, who had also finagled his way inside without a ticket, using nothing more than his wits, found several seats close to the stage. Several smitten girls immediately joined him before Dace found herself scrambling for a seat in Alexei's row. Noticing her standing alone without a seat, Alexei made a generous offer to Dace. He offered her a seat on his lap. The shy Dace, under duress from potential expulsion, accepted his offer and spent the next several hours in this precarious position. The next two hours were so nerve-racking for Dace that she doesn't recall a single note sung that night by the choir. Alexei helped by adding some playful flirting to the mix. The night ended with the group walking back to the dorm together, and the stage had seemingly been set.

Alexei's legend around the conservatory grew with each passing performance he gave. He wasn't naive to this fact and began to embrace his growing celebrity and equally to rebel against those that wished to control him. He would find ways to push the professor's limits. His exceptional talent was recognized, which granted him a very long leash. When the conservatory announced the field for the upcoming Tchaikovsky International Piano Competition, the students' excitement surged when Alexei's name was announced. His schooling and practice load hadn't lessened as he had imagined it would after leaving his hometown teacher, Popovich. In fact, it remained so severe that Alexei often lashed out at those he deemed responsible. His chronic mischief often found him reprimanded, which by design allowed him a break from practice. His professors all recognized Alexei's talent and as such piled onto him enormous amounts of work, much to his dismay.

As summer arrived, after the completion of the first year, Dace returned to the quiet of Riga. There she worked with her family, practiced her cello at Skujinas, and daydreamed about this interesting boy named Alexei. There was no contact between the two during the summer. Dace was eager to return to school as the summer waned. When she returned to the conservatory for the fall semester, the school was hit with startling news. The conservatory would be visited by a true legend for a very special performance.[1]

As the legend goes, when Vladimir Horowitz arrived at the gates of heaven, the angel presiding over the music shouted to the harp-playing angels, "Put your harps away and roll out the Steinway: Horowitz is coming!"

5
Horowitz

Vladimir Horowitz, a Soviet-born American citizen, is widely considered one of the greatest pianists of all time. As a child, Horowitz's father changed his birthdate to make him younger than he actually was, to keep his son's special talent safe from the rigors of the Red Army. Horowitz showed exceptional talent early in life and enrolled early at the Kiev Conservatory, where his fame grew as he toured the country. As popular as he had become, the economic and political hardships within the Soviet Union kept him struggling to provide for himself. In December 1925, a twenty-two-year-old Horowitz crossed the border into Germany with the pretense that he would be studying with pedagogue Artur Schnabel in Berlin. Secretly, he vowed to never return to his homeland and the sure economic and political dangers that awaited him. In 1927, his secret desires were exposed when he was selected by Soviet authorities to represent Ukraine at the inaugural 1927 International Chopin Piano Competition in Warsaw, Poland. He declined his selection by the Soviets to play, thus revealing his true intention, to defect. He would not be returning to the Soviet Union and measures would likely be implemented by the Soviet government to limit his advancement. Horowitz's defection opened his eyes to the opportunities available within his newly found freedom. It was an empowering sensation that he quickly realized. While he was no longer willing or able to play in the Soviet Union, he found a much broader audience and rapid fame.

Horowitz's "emigration" to Germany gave him solace, for the time being. Several successful concerts in and around Europe drew remarkable praise for his pianistic skill. His reputation and talent quickly garnered international interest, especially in the United States, where the allure of the young Soviet prodigy intrigued most concert halls. He gave his United States debut performance at Carnegie Hall in 1928, playing Tchaikovsky's *Piano Concerto no.1*. The reception for his brand of playing was magnanimous. Everyone now wanted a piece of this superstar as his fame grew exponentially from that first performance. In 1929, he would immigrate to New York City and find a true home. He would later become a United States citizen in 1944. His body of work earned him celebrity through the world, and he won twenty-seven Grammys.

The entire ordeal was an embarrassment to the Soviet Union and poked holes in the Iron Curtain. Sixty-one years after crossing the Soviet border to Germany, Horowitz announced to the world that in 1986 he would return to the Soviet Union to play recitals in Moscow and Leningrad. These recitals were viewed as groundbreaking events politically and musically between the US and Soviet Union.[1] This came at the end of the Cold War and aided the repair of relations between these two volatile world powers. This trip was in part due to his desire to return and play at his home as much as it was to initiate his return to playing the piano, from which he had been on a long hiatus. His refusal to return home for so long was spurred by his mistrust of the powerful Russian elite and as a protest against the oppressive communist model. The cooling fires between the two nations coupled with Horowitz's waning years prompted him to return to his birthplace and remaining family. He was indeed a living legend to the students at the conservatory and the people of the Soviet Union.

Horowitz's trip would last three weeks, and he would be bringing along his famed Steinway & Sons Model D Concert Grand Piano CD 503. The Steinway & Sons family gave this exquisite piano, built in the 1940s, to Horowitz as a wedding present. His legendary tuner Franz Mohr painstakingly maintained it. The piano notably had a very responsive action, which required a very light touch to play. The piano keys responding uplift was extraordinarily strong as they quickly returned to their resting position. Horowitz was widely known for his attention to detail, mostly in regard to his piano's maintenance. This particular piano went everywhere Horowitz went as well as did Mohr, who would become close friends to Horowitz.

Franz Mohr was designated as the head concert technician for Steinway & Sons. He would work with Horowitz for twenty-five years and was present at every concert and recording. He even turned pages for Horowitz while he played on specific occasions where that was needed.

The trip back to the Soviet Union for Horowitz became front-page news across the world. His arrival became the most anticipated event ever for many Soviets. Days prior to the performance at the conservatory, Horowitz was invited to a dinner party at the beautifully adorned American ambassador's home, named the Spaso House. Mohr, who attended as well, ran into his old Soviet pianist friend, Vladimir Viardo. Viardo had become a household name after he had won the gold medal at the 1973 Van Cliburn International Piano Competition held in Fort Worth, Texas. Shortly after Viardo's gold medal win, the two became friends while he was in New York for his Carnegie Hall recital under contract with Cliburn. This reunion in Moscow was special since it had been thirteen years since the two had seen each other. Soviet artists had been banned from the United States after the onset of the Soviet-Afghan War in 1980.

The tickets to Horowitz's return at the Moscow Conservatory were wildly coveted and unavailable to nearly everyone not part of the Soviet hierarchy. Horowitz recognized the difficulty in acquiring a ticket for the conservatory students and thus opened his Saturday rehearsal for just the students. The student line for this rehearsal was long and formed early. However, the Sunday Horowitz recital was still the most sought-after ticket in conservatory history. The absence of tickets to purchase caused panic among those determined to see the recital. This resulted in a number of conservatory students, among others, rushing the entrance in a last-ditch attempt to gain entry, which was overheard by microphones recording the internationally televised event. The recital was telecast live in the United States and the whole of western Europe. *Horowitz in Moscow*, an album on compact disc featuring this conservatory concert, was released by Deutsche Grammophon in 1986 and topped the Billboard classical charts for over a year.

Horowitz's return to his birth country had been orchestrated by heavy political maneuvering from both Cold War rivals. The international press clamored for information. From the moment his plane touched down in Moscow, a constant stream of media and video cameras followed Horowitz's every move. He was greeted at the airport by a host of Soviet officials. He was driven to see his remaining family members in the days before his performance, which brought forth feelings unusual for the aged icon. Horowitz was introduced to Marina, the daughter of his most beloved composer, Alexander Scriabin, and was filmed playing for her the composer's *Etude Op. 2 no.1* on her personal Bechtel piano. Horowitz was scurried around on several sightseeing tours along with producer Peter Gelb to witness what had become of his former land. Despite being continuously hounded by the media, he offered his time and even reminisced about his early life in the Soviet Union for them. Horowitz made a special personal visit to Tchaikovsky's house fifty-two miles north of Moscow in Klin. The house[2], now a museum, was where Tchaikovsky wrote his iconic Sixth Symphony and finished proofreading the scores for *The Nutcracker and Iolanta*, as well as eighteen other pieces. Tchaikovsky would breathe his last breaths in this home. The visit overall tested the strength of Horowitz, as he rested very little.

On the rainy Sunday afternoon of April 20, 1986, Horowitz made a grand return to the conservatory. Horowitz always scheduled his Saturday rehearsals and Sunday performances meticulously. These two days were sacred for him when performing. He detested practicing and thus rarely did. Despite appearing unprepared, he consistently gave amazing performances—which only added to his legend.

In the afternoon of the performance, Dace found herself amidst a group of young students, all vying for a place to gaze upon this transcendent performer. After many initial groups rushed the entrance and caused the commotion heard on the television broadcast, the authorities, who were well staffed that day, managed to remove most non-ticketed persons. Those most sly managed to avoid detection. Dace found herself in another group next to Tchaikovsky's monument in front of the Grand Hall searching for leadership with a plan to gain entry. Her eyes and focus met Alexei's. Alexei Sultanov, with his natural gusto and obsessive quest for adventure outside of piano practice, took the reins and convinced the group he had a plan. The sixteen-year-old Alexei was continually in and out of the Moscow Central Music School as a portion of his education continued with Popovich in Tashkent, musically speaking. He bounced back and forth between Tamara Popovich in Tashkent and the best musical professors the country had to offer in Moscow. He was still technically too young to enroll at the conservatory but was assuredly being fast tracked. Alexei's star power afforded him many privileges within the conservatory and its adjacent structures where his schooling often took him. He knew the floor plans of the buildings from his constant visits.

Alexei, with his plan in mind, led the small group including seventeen-year-old Dace to the six-story building next door to the conservatory that was closed that day. This particular building was composed of a multitude of classrooms, but it was primarily used to teach English to Soviet students. The heavy security at the conservatory was nonexistent at this spot. However, the doors were locked, and no entry seemed possible. Alexei decided the group could and should force open the locked double doors. Their makeshift human battering ram delivered enough pressure that the door's lock broke and their entry was secured. The group hustled up the six flights of stairs, which were built in such a way that you could see the first floor from the top of the six-floor stair. Once on the top floor, they encountered a large, spindled gate that blocked their access to the roof. This new obstacle with its spike deterrents refused most guests but their mission would not be given up on. If one were brave enough, they could climb onto the stairway wall and squeeze through a small opening and bypass the large gate. Any errors on the stairway wall could find its aggressor falling the six floors to a sure death. Not settling for failure, the team carefully climbed the stairway one by one and squeezed past the dangerous gate avoiding any of its immediate problems.

The sixth floor behind the gate turned out to be the attic, which had a small opening to the outside nearest to the conservatory. The rarely visited attic contained much of the school's unused tables, chairs, and equipment. The opening to the outside became the new target. As they crossed through the dusty space, a large flock of nesting doves burst forth from behind a table, frightening each person. The doves had been seeking respite from the rain until invaders rushed their hideout. The doves made the most amazing racket as they took flight all around. Surely, they felt the doves would alert the security with the amount of noise they made. As the doves made their exit and the groups' nerves were calmed, they followed the birds through the rooftop opening. This small and amazing vantage point of the conservatory was nearly as high and unveiled their next move. The rain was drizzling as Alexei planned the inevitable. The conservatory roof had a small platform roughly four feet across and several feet below their position. The jump would require a leap off their current balcony to the small, slippery, and wet conservatory platform. The group fed each other encouragement for the unforgiving four-foot jump to the platform below. Then they would follow that leap with an additional and more challenging four-foot jump to a pitched roof of the conservatory. Their desire to see the great Horowitz and the added peer pressure easily squashed their fears. The falling rain only added to the experience.

Alexei jumped first and made it across both gaps with little trouble. Alexei, now safely across, became the de facto jump director as he stood on the roof of Moscow's most celebrated musical hall in the rain and gave detailed instructions to each oncoming jumper. The pitched roof didn't come with solid footing due to the steady rain, but this didn't deter anyone. Dace found herself at the back of the line to jump and felt empowered when everyone before her made it successfully. She made the initial jump to the platform with relative ease. On the second leg of the jump, Dace had the distance and landed on the pitched roof but immediately felt her feet begin to slide backward. She placed herself on all fours but couldn't stop her backwards momentum. A fall from the conservatory roof held only one outcome—certain death. Dace, now faced with sheer panic at what awaited her, looked around for anything to grab onto. Nothing. As the eyes of the group ahead all watched horrified, Dace quickly slid to the roof's edge, when suddenly a hand appeared out of nowhere and extended out toward her. She quickly snatched it, squeezing with all her might. The hand didn't seem familiar, but the face did. Alexei had grabbed a nearby radio antenna and lowered himself close enough to grab her hand as she teetered on the edge. He reeled her up to the safety of the group and gave her a smile that bonded them instantly. Alexei would tell the story later in short form to all within earshot, "I see a girl falling, I grab her hand. I look at this girl, I think not bad, so I save this girl."

With Dace now safe, the new hero wasted little time and led the group toward the center of the roof where they found small window-shaped doors, which begrudgingly opened after some jostling. These doors opened into rooms that housed the anchor points for the Grand Hall's chandeliers. From this high perch, they could peer through a small opening and see the crowd below. The group then spread out in search of their own opening to observe from. Alexei and Dace, now inseparable, partnered up and shared a spot that held the massive chandelier directly over the stage. Dace and Alexei smiled at one another both understanding how special and remarkable this moment really was.

Their attention to each other was interrupted several minutes later when the eighty-three-year-old Vladimir Horowitz walked slowly onto the stage where he gently patted the lid of his old and cherished Steinway. The rumble of the applause was felt in the rafters. The significance of this moment was recognized even from their high position. Horowitz's presence drew audible gasps from the audience. The crowd's applause was tremendous and full as they welcomed back their long-lost hero after his sixty-one-year absence. Everyone here had only heard and read about this man. This spectacle allowed the Soviet people in attendance to finally see their hero in person. Patrons could hardly hold back their tears just seeing Horowitz in the flesh. As the ticketed crowd of 1,793 and estimated two hundred gate crashers finally hushed, those lucky few gripped their seats, wiped their eyes, and stared in disbelief. Security had initially caught six illegal entrants before they gave up finding them altogether.

As he began, the audience held their breath as Horowitz performed in splendid fashion, reminding the Soviet people what an extraordinary musical icon he was. They watched in awe with stunned looks on their faces at what they were witnessing. The Soviet people felt a tremendous sense of pride build inside them. Many of those lucky enough to attend would describe this experience as one of the greatest of their lifetimes. Alexei and Dace were spellbound in the rafters of the conservatory as the intimacy and power of the moment united the pair in a way only these circumstances could. As they looked at one another in awe, they discovered the powerful forces of attraction at work. This moment would remain one of their most cherished memories. Horowitz gave the audience everything his aged body could give.

His two-hour performance entailed three sonatas by Scarlatti, the Mozart Sonata in C Major, two preludes by Rachmaninoff, and two etudes by Scriabin before an intermission. After his needed break, he returned with pieces from Schubert, Liszt, and Chopin. Every note fell onto welcoming ears. He then rose to an instant standing ovation and slowly walked off the stage with stiff legs, knowing full well he would be right back. For his encore, he played for his adoring crowd three short pieces by Schumann, Moszkowski, and Rachmaninoff. Horowitz stood to receive his audience, waving back, bowing, clapping back towards them, and waving a handker-

Picture of Russian Pianist Vladimir Horowitz inside of Conservatory Hall. *Photo by Jean Pimentel/Kipa/Sygma via Getty Images*

chief. The Soviets showered him with love and appreciation, and bouquet after bouquet of flowers piled up on stage for an unprecedented eight-minute standing ovation. The Horowitz in Moscow performance would make music history and still remains a very popular recording[3] throughout the world. He would perform a second recital a week later in Leningrad, before flying back home to New York to recover.

While Alexei and Dace wanted to soak it all in, they only survived till intermission. As Horowitz left stage for his intermission to euohoric applause, voices alerted the rooftop intruders that authorities had discovered them and were approaching. The group simultaneously realized the moment had passed and it was time to flee. In the confusion, the two got separated when Alexei discovered an opening into the ceiling of the men's bathroom, and Dace, unwilling to take that route, fled the scene only to find a nearby firemen's ladder that allowed her access to the attic below. Several members of the renegade group were caught but received only minimal reprimands from the school. Dace and Alexei both avoided capture, and after descending many flights of stairs, they arrived safely out of the building. While they were separated in the escape, the two would become inseparable from that day forward. Their improbable story circulated across the campus the following day, only adding to the mystique of the young Alexei.[4]

The upcoming Tchaikovsky Competition and its worldly allure immediately became the priority for Alexei's circle of influence. As the pressures on

Alexei increasingly mounted, his parents decided to temporarily move him back to Tashkent in preparation for the 1986 Tchaikovsky Piano Competition that was coming up in the summer. The distractions back home were minimal compared to the assumed freedoms Alexei had access to in Moscow. Popovich was in Tashkent, which added a kink to Alexei's freedoms. Popovich took control of Alexei's practice regimen and cut out anything that didn't benefit his lessons. Dace unfortunately fell into this category. Alexei would attend a local class in the morning, then practice from two to seven in the evening. The efforts Popovich took to ensure Alexei remained disciplined were grueling and extreme, but the results were impressive. Alexei's reputation had spread throughout the Soviet Union, making him a notable entry in this edition of the Tchaikovsky International Competition. He was not able to see Dace in preparation for the competition, which added to the complications. Phone calls were not commonplace in this part of the world, and the distance between them made it difficult to communicate.

Before Alexei departed for Tashkent, he shared an emotional goodbye with his new love. It was clear that they belonged together. They both expressed mutual feelings for the other. Their relationship was considered exclusive. While Dace worked diligently in the Central Music School's classrooms, Alexei was consumed by his preparation some seventeen hundred miles away to the southeast in Tashkent. The sixty-six-hour train ride was brutal for Alexei though it did offer him time to think about Dace and even relax a bit. While each progressed in their respective worlds, their blossoming passion for one another remained in the forefront of their minds. No amount of distance or practice could block out their feelings. As Dace played her cello, her thoughts would often drift to her Alexei. Alexei would steal bits and pieces of time from his practice and Popovich to think of his Dace, who eagerly awaited his return.

Alexei believed his extraordinary talent at the piano would be his avenue out of this unrelenting existence. He had begun to develop a deep-seated animosity against the pressures that were levied on him. He knew he could not change it now but perhaps he could harness this talent achieve what people like Vladimir Horowitz had been brave enough to accomplish. Freedom. Freedom from the things he wanted to change. Freedom to live according to his wishes. Freedom to practice when he wanted to practice. The piano was his escape, and he would somehow take Dace with him.

6
Tchaikovsky International Piano Competition

The Tchaikovsky International Piano Competition, named after Russian immortal Pyotr Llyich Tchaikovsky, remains one of the grand musical competitions in the world. This quadrennial competition resides in Moscow, Russia, for disciplines of piano, violin, cello, singing, and most recently added violin making. The Soviet community holds competitors in the highest regard and requires them to be between the ages of sixteen and thirty. American Van Cliburn first gained international fame by shockingly winning the inaugural Tchaikovsky competition in 1958 under the careful watch of Communist Secretary Nikita Khrushchev. The competition's underlying purpose was more than just a world-class music competition. The Soviets used it as a marketing event designed to highlight their cultural superiority over the rest of the world. This seemingly backfired when Cliburn was handed the first prize, but fate stepped in. Van Cliburn's win created an avenue in which the two world powers could coexist without further aggression. Essentially, it opened the door for discussions of peace, thus helping to bring about the end to the Cold War.[1]

Alexei's preparation for the Eighth Tchaikovsky Competition in 1986 was all consuming but on par with the training regimen for most prodigies of this magnitude. The five-foot, two-inch musical sixteen-year-old giant was pushed ferociously and nearly to the point of exhaustion. June's competition finally arrived, and Alexei found himself under tremendous pressure. Additionally, Dace, his one true escape, remained back home in Riga during the summer of the competition. The family television was tuned in to broadcast the competition into their dining room, which was the norm for nearly all Soviets and many of their European counterparts. The media storm over the young Uzbekistani created pandemonium in his hometown and around Moscow, where his legend was growing daily. Alexei and his entourage made the return to Moscow for the competition with exceedingly high hopes. On the day of the drawing for playing position, Alexei found himself in a practice room inside the conservatory going over last-minute details for his performance. Alexei understood what was at stake for him, his family, and his country.

The pressures, which most sixteen-year-olds should never feel, were tearing him up inside. A moment of exhaustion came when he sat staring at the practice piano all alone as the adults had left the small room for a period of time. The passion and anger seemed to boil over. Alexei wanted control of his life again and felt no way out. He rose from the piano bench and screamed out at the top of his lungs. He curled his highly dexterous hands into fists and slammed his right hand into the wall next to the piano. The concrete wall gave little ground. The result was severe pain and several bleeding knuckles and what soon would be diagnosed as a cracked bone on the pinky finger. For someone on the doorstep of the world's largest piano competition, this was not an encouraging start. As Popovich returned to the scene, she was horrified to learn that Alexei had damaged his right hand when, as Alexei explained, the piano lid had inadvertently dropped onto it. The hand swelled over the crack and caused Alexei extreme discomfort. The story leaked to the press quickly about the local favorite who had injured his hand yet planned to continue in the competition. This storyline only helped bolster his reputation further with a story of inspiration and true determination.

The competition jury held an emergency meeting to decide what to do, as Alexei's turn to perform was approaching. The jurors made a ruling that would allow Alexei to postpone his appearance as long as he was willing and, more importantly, able. A sports doctor was located and began a series of massages on the afflicted area along with oral medicines, which offered no relief. Alexei was administered an injection of Lidocaine into his broken hand just prior to his first performance. The numbing agent allowed Alexei to play but failed to cover him for the duration of the forty-five-minute recital.

As he took the stage, he was met with roaring approval from the audience. Alexei's confidence was shaken though as he lacked any sensation in his pinky. He experienced growing agony toward the end of his performance. His pinky began to quiver from his violent brand of pounding upon the keys, which increasingly sent shooting pain across his hand. His intensely passionate and forceful finger technique on the piano showcased his incredible mastery of the instrument. A delicate yet tornadic movement of his hands danced around the keyboard. His power was much greater than his small stature suggested. Alexei utilized some of his training in the martial arts to help him find strength to play Chopin's demanding Polish dance titled *Scherzo no. 2 in B Minor, Op. 31*. The mental focus required to perform at this level is well documented, but what makes it truly remarkable is the extent to which he had to endure severe pain. Alexei was allowed to receive a subsequent injection into his pinky finger just minutes prior to each of his performances. The pain would return before he completed the piece. After completing his first-round performance to a packed audience, he received a standing ovation. However, Alexei was suffering intolerably.

Alexei easily made it to the second round of the Tchaikovsky Piano Competition out of the 109 piano entrants from across the globe that were selected to compete. Round two, days later, found the injured virtuoso among twenty of the best young contemporaries in the world. With the lidocaine injection administered, he again took the stage to an enormous crowd of his countrymen. Making the finals was never a question to anyone close to Alexei. He performed flawlessly even as every right fifth-digit key made him visibly wince. The audience, who had been clued into his injured hand, watched him suffer on stage, but few felt his performance diminished as a result. He lost himself in his Beethoven *Appassionata*, which would become a staple piece for Alexei. The crowd's reaction at the end supported the idea that Alexei ought to be a finalist and the clear favorite to win. Alexei was usually highly critical of his performance, but this time the pain kept him subdued.

After an extended jury deliberation, a shocking decision was reached that included a stellar field of twelve finalists including two Americans, four Soviets, a Frenchman, a Briton, a Bulgarian, a Chinese, a Cuban, and a Czech. The twenty-two-member jury contained fourteen from Soviet bloc countries. Critics found it concerning and odd that several Soviet jurors were the current teachers or coaches of some of the entrants. The twelve talented finalists earned their way into the gold medal showdown with one exception, Alexei Sultanov was not one of them. The jury chairman took the stage to announce the finalists. As the last name was read and it was not Alexei, shouts from the crowd were heard protesting their disappointment. Although he had played beautifully and flawlessly in rounds one and two, the jurors had collectively decided that the prospect of Alexei further damaging his hand was too great to allow him to continue in the Tchaikovsky Competition. The press knew instantly that politics had been at play. This wasn't simply the jury protecting its competitors, as there was no protocol for this type of situation. The jury members had their own favorites, and Alexei apparently wasn't among them.

The next morning a local newspaper article told of how the jury members used his injured hand as their scapegoat to oust him. Certain members of the jury saw this as a way to ensure their students had better odds at victory by removing the crowd favorite, Alexei, from contention. This would not be the last time politics played into Alexei's career. Deserving or not, Alexei was out of the competition. The decision devastated Alexei. Dace, who had been glued to her television back in Riga, broke down in tears upon hearing the news. Counter to the ongoing claims of Soviet nepotism, the gold medal was awarded to another crowd favorite, Barry Douglas of Northern Ireland. Douglas, the first non-Russian to win since Van Cliburn's legendary triumph in 1958, had won the bronze medal the year prior at the Van Cliburn International Piano Competition in Fort Worth, Texas. The Soviets did finish strong at the Tchaikovsky, winning second and third prize. After the conclusion of the Tchaikovsky, one of the American jurors, Daniel Pollock, referred to sixteen-year-old Alexei Sultanov as one of the greatest piano talents he had ever heard as he exhibited an "unbelievable depth of emotion."[2]

7
Back to School

It was during this period in Alexei's life that his parents downgraded their living conditions in their small Tashkent home to a tiny apartment in Ramenskoe, on the outskirts of Moscow, to be closer to the conservatory. Alexei had remained under careful parental control, bouncing between his mother and Popovich in Tashkent and his teachers in Moscow. Alexei and Dace were both accepted into the Moscow Conservatory, as their progress warranted it. Alexei's parents had been bringing him to the conservatory for weeks at a time to work with conservatory professors.

His professors quickly grew tired of his constant departures to go home and finally gave the Sultanovs an ultimatum: Alexei must remain at the conservatory indefinitely for his studies, or else. The Sultanovs relented. Tamara Popovich convinced the family to move where she could keep her watchful eyes on her prodigal pupil while he studied at the conservatory.

Faizul and Natasha both quit their jobs in Tashkent and their routine three day train ride to Moscow, for the sake of Alexei's career. In a sense, Alexei's training became their primary occupation. Faizul would continue to work teaching music lessons to support the family and pay for Alexei's lessons with Popovich. Alexei's lessons often took priority over other family needs and desires. Dace wouldn't see Alexei again until she returned to Moscow in September 1986. Her days back in Riga were spent worrying and waiting after watching the debacle at the Tchaikovsky Competition.

Dace's studies, cello lessons, and practice regimen had earned her exemplary marks from her professors, and she even managed to garner some high praise from Professor Fedorchenko. He was always very straightforward and kind to her, even when she erred. He rarely showed much emotion, but he began to take more of a fatherly interest in Dace. She would become one of his favorite and cherished students. He would even go on, years later, to name his daughter Dasha after Dace. Dace became the original babysitter for young Dasha. One of the peculiar hobbies of Fedorchenko was searching through old, abandoned buildings and junkyards for potential lost treasures. This unique habit would lead him to discover the discarded pieces of a cello that he would one day piece together. He took these pieces to his friend, a luthier, who painstakingly found more pieces to repair it and patch it up. When crafted together, it became a beautiful and seasoned makeshift cello. Fedorchenko would present this makeshift cello to Dace when she graduated. It was very rare at that time for professors to give students their instruments. The original stamp from the year the cello was made, 1888, was still present on one of its patchwork pieces. This cello became Dace's instrumental soulmate, and she appropriately named him Mr. Cello. She plays this same cello today.

Although she was not a prodigy, the talent she was born with coupled with hard work had developed her into a virtuoso. Her passion for the music was apparent to those who saw her play. Her style of play carried audiences on a journey through her soul, which she displayed often by shedding tears while she played. Dace treasured playing Mr. Cello and the solace it gave her awaiting Alexei's return to school. The time off that Alexei's professors granted him—to let his hand heal—allowed him to recover from the disappointment at the Tchaikovsky competition. This was all made easier by having his beloved Dace back into his life as classes resumed. Because of his growing fame, Alexei would often take himself out of public scenarios, as he did not care for the attention, especially the way the girls would fawn over him. He now loved Dace and leaned on her for an escape from the growing pandemonium.

While prodigies in any discipline greatly excel with their gifts, they can often suffer in some other fundamental areas of life. Albert Einstein was arguably the greatest scientist the world has ever known, but what most find hard to realize is that he was a human and thus had flaws. Einstein was a chronic absentee father of three and had several bouts with infidelity resulting in several failed marriages. Einstein's brain was exceptional on many levels, but he did suffer intolerably in the sphere of everyday life.[1] The musical genius of Mozart and Beethoven also largely overshadows the fact that these icons were largely despised by the ones who knew them best. The point being the words genius and prodigy designate a person who embodies significant creativity or achievement, but the people behind these talents suffer much like the general population. Alexei Sultanov's career trajectory followed a pattern of one-sidedness. His gift was strengthened at every turn at the expense of the other necessary qualities of human life. Alexei's incurable immaturity demanded constant attention. Luckily, he found Dace, who was his enabler and the love of his life.

Dating life at the conservatory wasn't simple, but as teenagers are apt to do, sheer determination led to bold and exciting schemes to pay each other an unsanctioned visit. The dormitories, where the majority of the conservatory students resided, were a few blocks from the school. The main dormitory building was a large six-floor mansion ruled by Soviet governesses called *Vospidatil,* who ruled on high with an iron fist. These governesses were ladies of middle-to-upper ages that kept eyes on everyone. They sat out in the hallways during the nights, conducted nightly bed checks, and patrolled freely throughout the building in an effort to curb any behavior deemed inappropriate, especially the comingling of the boys and girls. Dace lived on the third floor, which housed only girls. When at the conservatory, Alexei lived with the young men on the second floor. Coed visits, which were forbidden, required risk and creativity, which Alexei seemed to be writing the book on. The infrequent bathroom breaks by the governesses typically created opportunities for the determined youngsters. These windows of opportunity usually required a steadfast watch through cracked doors for long periods of time. Dace and Alexei often garnered personal time together utilizing the bathroom breaks of these women. Dace also learned to feign sickness, which would typically afford her a visit to the infirmary that was under a strict locked-door policy. Alexei realized that this was an opportunity for extended time together, so he tested and mastered the scalability of the water pipes that climbed the building and offered exceptional access to restricted parts of the building, including the sick bay.

During evenings, the governesses added additional checks of the rooms. On occasion, Alexei fooled the governesses with carefully placed pillows beneath his sheets that convinced the bed checkers that he was asleep and accounted for. Alexei's insatiable curiosity for adventure allowed him to learn how to pick the simple locks of the dormitory doors with a small knife, which granted him further access to Dace. The governesses, during the overnight hours, would sit vigilantly in hallways to monitor and keep the sexes apart. The couple's romance blossomed during this time. Dace and Alexei found reasons to visit the conservatory to practice in the confines of its many piano practice rooms, which often led to time together. The simple application of a chair braced against the back door kept out unwanted entrants. When the teachers would knock to need of the room for the next lesson, Dace and Alexei would carefully make their escape without detection.

Alexei's time at the conservatory was preceded by his reputation. His talent was undeniable, but he developed another reputation for trouble. He systematically became one of the most notorious uncooperative students in the history of the school, a fact that would come back to bite him later on. His propensity for trouble stemmed from his severe dislike of the communist structure. He fancied himself a free thinker and not willing to simply fall in line as expected. Alexei pushed back against authority whenever he could, when away from his parents. His Soviet professors, all staunch and disciplined communists, struggled mightily to tame the wild Alexei. Alexei quietly referred to communists along with music critics as "talent killers." His repeated actions so inflamed the conservatory officials that he was kicked out of school twice. One of those times was for playing jazz on the classroom piano during a lull in a course on communist history. Jazz music and its American roots did not meet the strict conservatory guidelines. Professor Lev Naumov, Alexei's primary professor, used his tremendous influence to get Alexei back into school on both occasions.

Nevertheless, Alexei's relative freedom in Moscow helped him develop his other interests. The Arthur Conan Doyle stories of Sherlock Holmes were especially interesting to Alexei and kept his curiosity engaged during his formative years. As he matured, he found great understanding with the literature and controversial philosophy of Friedrich Nietzsche. His books and beliefs made sense to Alexei and help shape his approach to critical thinking. Alexei also found continuing solace in the self-discipline of Tae Kwon Do, where he achieved a third-degree black belt and immersed himself in its culture. He considered himself a warrior who needed to keep his body and mind finely tuned, much akin to a ninja. He could control his environment with knowledge coupled with the gifts he possessed. He felt supremely confident in his abilities to perform on the highest level.

Nothing, he believed, could inhibit his ascent. He felt nearly indestructible. There were only two things that Alexei feared and posed the most challenge for him: wasps and Tamara Popovich.

One particular weekday, Alexei feeling unmotivated to participate in the act of learning, hatched a simple plan to avoid going to class. He feigned illness and thus confessed to the governess that he wasn't feeling well. She fetched a thermometer to check his temperature. When she left the room for a brief minute, he violently rubbed the thermometer on his pants to heat up the mercury. When the governess returned and discovered his temperature greatly elevated, she followed protocol and immediately ordered Alexei to the hospital. At that time in Moscow, there had been an outbreak of hepatitis, marked by feverish symptoms and a yellowish tint to the skin, so the governess had cause to worry. Alexei, a native of Uzbekistan, also seemed to the governess to have this yellowish tint to his skin color, an unfortunate stereotype of the times, which made him look different and furthered her suspicion. An ambulance was summoned to take Alexei away. His plan to play hooky from school quickly progressed out of his control. After he was admitted, Alexei was immediately put into the isolation ward alongside other confirmed hepatitis cases. Alexei underwent a series of tests and was released several hours later once he was determined to be of sound health. Alexei returned to the dormitory safely free from any school activity for the day. Two days later, he awoke to a legitimate fever and was back in the hospital, diagnosed with actual hepatitis. He contracted the virus during his previous visit. Alexei was confined to his hospital room amongst other hepatitis cases, where his treatment began. Faizul and Dace would coordinate efforts to smuggle in improved rations to his hospital window on the fifth floor. Alexei somehow loosened his window and lowered a bucket on a rope where he could retrieve their offerings, along with passionate love notes penned by Dace that the couple shared back and forth for the ten days Alexei spent in confinement.

The normally reserved and shy Dace grew to love Alexei's passion for life, his spontaneity, and his insatiable thirst for fun and adventure. It wasn't long until the relationship matured from young love to a much deeper form. The two musicians knew that their lives would now be centered around each other. Alexei's zest for life also came with bouts of extreme jealousy. Alexei couldn't stomach the sight of other males talking to Dace. Often the mere act of talking to her would send Alexei over the brink. When confronted with another man who was clearly flirting with Dace, he routinely would fly into a rage, confronting the perpetrator and his imagined attempt to steal away his girl. These episodes would land Alexei in trouble with school administrators for behavior detrimental to the school's code. This also led to a passionate love affair often played out throughout the bowels of the conservatory. The unnecessary risks Alexei would often take were fueled by the passion they shared for each other.

Whenever possible, they would skip classes to be together. Alexei loved to tease Dace about her accent, which was unique to that part of the world. The basic educational portion of school, while required but not emphasized, came easy for the both of them, as they were quick studies of the general courses. All conservatory students were required to learn piano, regardless of whether this was their instrument of choice. Dace did not like to practice piano and was often at the mercy of Alexei's criticisms. One piece Dace had been tasked to learn was Beethoven's famous *Pathetique*, with which she had great difficulty. Alexei, with his patience worn thin, slapped at her hands when she missed a note and even cursed her for not playing it the right way. He was perhaps covertly lashing out against those who pushed him so hard, making Dace the unfortunate victim. His gift of music had not matured yet into the patient ability to teach another. The pair shared a passion for music that at times found them playing chamber music together.

As talented as she was, Dace could not match step for step with his talent. Dace did though exhibit certain gifts for music. She had an exceptional ear for music and all its nuances. Her ability to hear a song and replicate it on her cello was substantially above par. Professor Fedorchenko taught her that when learning a piece of music, repetition, repetition, and more repetition had no limit, but one must be able to suddenly wake up at four in the morning and play the piece in question to know if it has been memorized. Dace took great joy in testing her memory. She often used champagne as a self-imposed test to see if she could play a certain piece. She would begin with a few glasses and play. Then a few more with a repeat performance. If she could consume the entire bottle, which was well past her threshold, she knew the piece satisfactorily. This gave her the confidence to perform on command. She found little music to fear, but contemporary compositions gave her fits. While Dace's recitals remained inside the walls of the conservatory, Alexei had begun to play concerts outside the conservatory. The national Soviet music management company, GosKoncert, often arranged paying recitals for the worthy conservatory students.

While the demand for his talent earned him money, the majority of this income would ultimately end up in the conservatory's coffers. He received requests on an increasing basis to play at different concert halls across Europe. Alexei financially was still on shaky ground, much like the majority of the conservatory students. More importantly, Alexei was learning the business side of performing. Dace and Alexei remained inseparable while at the conservatory. The couple loved to take long walks together— often going miles upon miles around the Moscow campus. Dace also continued to perform well as a student in the music department. Her cello repertoire quickly improved, as did her technical mastery of her instrument. Alexei though, who had never touched a cello, but certainly understood its dynamic, was often critical of Dace's abilities on the cello. These criticisms were perhaps his misguided attempts at motivation. Basic piano was a required course for each student at the conservatory. Alexei tried to help Dace learn the piano as best as a savant could relate to someone with little interest in learning the piano. Alexei's unorthodox and sometimes cruel methods helped Dace pass her introductory piano class. He continually was very tough on her playing. Often, he modified her professor's instructions and taught her his way, which entailed untested methods. The conservatory loved to orchestrate performing tours by their students to give them public experience. The pair were partnered up by their teachers at times to perform in and around Moscow along with their classmates. Their first performance together included Antonin Dvorak's *Piano Quintet no.2*, *Beethoven's Cello Piano Sonata in A Major*, and Prokofiev's *Cello Piano Sonata. Op. 119, C Major*. In 1988, during one of their regular meetings, Professor Naumov asked Alexei about his willingness to travel to the United States to compete in a piano competition named after Van Cliburn, the beloved American pianist. The thought of traveling to faraway America fascinated Alexei, so he pushed Naumov to get him an application. Naumov knew well of this competition, its namesake, and its level of competition. Alexei wasted no time filling it out and sent it back with a recorded sample of his talent. The wheels had been put in motion, and Alexei began daydreaming. Once the application had been sent, Professor Naumov sat Alexei down with the assurance that he could not win this competition, due to his lack of experience. He just wasn't ready. Naumov had much experience in these sorts of competitions. Perhaps it was just a motivational ploy.[2]

8
Communism

The communist experience loomed large for anyone born inside the Soviet empire. Its ideology, simply put, sought a society without socioeconomic classes. Common ownership of their capital goods required collective efforts of the masses. In essence, everyone is equal and shares in the common good. Communism is in sharp contrast to capitalism, which is a two-class system—the working class and the capitalist class. Communists consider the bourgeoisie, or the capitalists, the root of all problems. Communism calls for a revolution of the working class to overthrow the capitalist class, establishing common ownership of all capital goods. Iron Curtain was term originally coined in 1920 by Soviet travel author E. Snowden, but it meant very little to the Soviet people. Communism, by design, cuts its citizenry off from the world by keeping everything Soviet in and all else out. The Soviet leadership thus inhibits any opportunity for worldly growth by limiting outside information and knowledge.

Their world of music, sports, and academia had drastic differences from the capitalist model as well. The management of talent inside the Soviet Union reveals just why the Soviets promote such a vast number of prodigies. If you were identified at an early age to be talented in such areas as athletics, music, or academics, the state would assume responsibilities of your management. The opportunities to further your talents within the Soviet model would be unlimited and without cost to the parents. The parents wouldn't have to pay for tutors, coaches, or professors, as they were provided for by the state. Alexei was a prime example of this model. When he was identified early on as a child piano prodigy, the Soviet state made sure his gift was tended to and nurtured once he reached the Moscow Central Music School. Alexei's parents never had much money, but never needed any at least as Alexei's extraordinary education and training was concerned.

Growing up in the Soviet Union is markedly different from the American experience. The Soviet people feel the influence of communism at every step but are unaware or unable to do much about it. In addition, upon turning the age of eighteen, regardless of ability or talent, every Soviet man received in the mail a draft notice into the Red Army. Many male citizens endured basic training, which included being taught to use a rifle. Those with social or economic privilege utilize avenues of influence to avoid the grueling assignments thrust upon so many from the poorer classes—mainly assignment to dangerous locales such as Siberia. It is no secret how the Soviets coddled their athletes. Watching Olympic games in the eighties, the Soviet Union emphasized and showcased athletics as a show of national strength. Athletes in Russia typically had access to the best coaching, training, and sometimes performance-enhancing drugs. If in the Soviet Union there stood a higher calling than sports, it was assuredly music. Music in the Soviet Union was the powerful cultural gold standard in worldly exports. Those fortunate to possess the gift of music early on follow a completely difficult set of rules from the general public.

In Alexei's case, his basic education, although required, was never a priority, as his path was laid out in stone. His music took precedence in every aspect of his life. He was identified early on and thus his life no longer belonged solely to him. Musically inclined students were given an exceptionally preferential opportunity. They would often be sent to special classes, not available to the commoner, with exceptional tutelage. These gifted students though enrolled in basic education courses to earn the required credits in areas such as reading, writing, and arithmetic. In every case, courses related to communism were taught as part of each student's core curriculum. Alexei, as did many Soviet musicians, viewed these classes with a bit of irony. The liberal perspective often associated with artists found little purpose for big government in their lives. The communist model wasn't always in conjunction with creative-thinking

Soviet musicians. The strict Soviet doctrine of common ownership controlled by powerful politicians rubbed Alexei wrong and therefore could not be considered at full value. The associated rebelliousness of the enlightened Soviet youth was spurred on by the philosophies and writings of Tolstoy or Dostoevsky. Aside from getting through course requirements, the conservatory promoted a superior product with an enriching educational experience afforded only to the few lucky ones.

This comprehensive training method was responsible for rewarding the world with an abundance of exceptional masters. It was expected and programmed into the curriculum that Soviet musicians played not only for themselves, but also for love of their country. Failure to do so was to disrespect the homeland. When a Soviet musician reached the age of eighteen, musical talent, or a lack thereof, could dictate your quality of life.

Musicians, although not excused from the Red Army draft, could greatly improve their deployment. Drummers and violinists could find themselves in the Red Army band. But what do you do if you're a pianist? Alexei wasn't looking for a cushy deployment, as his status would have certainly allowed him. He was looking for an all-out exemption from his service in the Red Army. Alexei's exceptional talent at the piano though did not save him from being drafted. His talent at bending the rules did though. In a stroke of Sultanov luck, perhaps due to his noted talent, Alexei simply ignored his draft notice. This was a clear violation of Soviet law under regular circumstances. The risk was severe. Each time he left and entered the country and passed through customs, he risked his very freedom. An investigation from a customs official could easily discover that Alexei was long overdue to report for duty. His recitals outside the Soviet Union always concluded with a visit through the customs line. The Soviet customs process then wasn't highly technical, nor was it efficient. The system was also rife with corruption. If one could afford a bribe, then things could be done. Alexei had no real money but instead had his wits. The sheer number of people entering and exiting the Soviet Union made it common for a citizen to show a passport without a lengthy examination. Alexei always hoped the customs officials found him uninteresting enough to not check his records.

His luck was solid but ultimately would come to an end two years later when he was stopped by customs in Moscow at the end of

September after returning from a recital. A young immigration officer ascertained his identity and subsequent absence from military duties, which made Alexei's immediate situation sticky. The agent following protocol informed Alexei that a call would be made to the Red Army office to let them know Alexei was now in their custody and would be delivered to them. Alexei had prepared for this potential problem as best he could. As Alexei's freedom hung in the balance, he produced from his suitcase a carton of his personal favorite Marlboro cigarettes. This American brand of smokes was banned in the Soviet Union and thus highly coveted. Alexei dangled the bait in front of the agent and calmly suggested that he was never there. As they say, every man has his price and, for this Soviet official, the cigarettes were enough. The agent quietly turned off his computer, slid the gift into his desk, and Alexei was given the nod to proceed ahead. The then eighteen-year-old ran this tremendous risk whenever he traveled. GosKoncert had its students to protect from possible draft duty, and did not share information. The Red Army also kept its data close to the vest. The lack of collusion between GosKoncert and the Red Army resulted in cracks in the law that allowed for Alexei to evade the draft. Male students at the conservatory occasionally disappeared from school upon turning eighteen. Any student with familial wealth or connections always found ways out of draft, but those with backgrounds similar to Alexei's required added vigilance and luck.[1]

9
Together

Life together for the inseparable young couple at the conservatory was blissful even as Alexei continued to flirt with danger. With the application in the mail for the Van Cliburn International Piano Competition, Alexei continued along his path. Alexei's spontaneity always kept the atmosphere charged with excitement. Dace felt especially alive when she was around him. Alexei felt early on that Dace was the one he would spend his life with. Dace needed much less time to come that same conclusion. Every time she was around him, she felt the nervous butterflies. Dace's unwavering love for Alexei always enabled him to dominate the relationship. He loved to be in control, and Dace blindly followed along. She felt loved in his presence and thus had few qualms about the direction he chose.

When the occasional argument ensued, Alexei always wanted to hasten the solution when the patient-headed Dace took time to cool off first. On rare occasions, when the solution couldn't wait, Alexei would throw a few dishes out of frustration. However, the reconciliation was never far behind. This period for the two often combined their love of each other with drinking, the popular Soviet pastime. Most Soviet teenagers then were seasoned drinkers and even smokers before they reached adulthood. The preferred *Papirosa* type of cigarette was popular to Soviets for its low price and high strength due to its lack of a filter. Vodka remained dominant in the Soviet culture and is constantly portrayed in the media as such. Champagne, though, was a favorite of the young couple. The Soviet Union had grown to be one of the highest consumers of alcohol in the world, much to the detriment of its citizen's health. Soviet leader Mikhail Gorbachev would implement controls in 1985 to slow this problem. His very unpopular partial prohibition succeeded in reducing the country's consumption, but the countrywide pushback was far more than he was willing to endure. The program would ultimately fail. In the more liberal circles around the conservatory, these anti-alcoholism measures only increased the student's indulgence.

Alexei was outwardly immature but profoundly deep in his thoughts and prophetic warnings. His career as a pianist was all but assured, but his longevity was much less certain. As the couple enjoyed a leisurely stroll one afternoon around the conservatory grounds, Alexei shared with Dace that he felt most certainly that his life would not be a long one. It was his full belief that he would only live to be thirty-five years old. He didn't know how or why, but some unknown force compelled this belief within him. As Dace heard this, she couldn't fathom life beyond their current situation. As concerning as this should have been, her love for Alexei trumped his belief that one day he would perish prematurely. Dace loved him with all her heart, and that was enough for her. As teenagers, the age of thirty-five seemed as far away as the United States. They had each other, and the future was theirs to chart.

When Dace's friend and former roommate, Vika, was moved to another school building outside the central tube of Moscow, due to a large building remodeling project, the two began to see much less of one another. The distance between them simply wouldn't allow it. One day, Vika's room phone rang. On the other end was Alexei. He got quickly to the point. Alexei and his male cellist friend were in a situation and desperately need to borrow some money from Vika. Not wanting to disappoint her friend Dace, Vika agreed to meet Alexei and his friend later that day at the train station. As Vika arrived at the station, the two beggars were waiting. After she endured a continuous barrage of pleas from the two, reeking of alcohol and in need of a shower, she reluctantly opened her wallet and gave them the requested fifteen rubles, or the equivalent of a few dollars. Alexei asked Vika to keep this a secret and promised to repay her for her generosity one day. The two then promptly disappeared into the crowd at her next train stop. Vika doubted whether she would ever see those rubles again.

10
Van

Harvey Lavan Cliburn Jr., or Van as he was known, became the embodiment of the American success story. Van Cliburn was born in Shreveport, Louisiana, on July 12, 1934, and later moved to Kilgore, Texas. His father, Harvey Lavan Cliburn Sr., was an executive with Magnolia Petroleum (now ExxonMobil). At the age of three, Harvey Lavan Jr. began piano studies with his mother, Rildia Bee O'Bryan Cliburn, a talented former student of Arthur Friedheim, who had been a pupil of Franz Liszt. Van began to learn to play by watching his mother's students play the family's Steinway piano. Van made his public debut at the tender age of four with a Bach Prelude and Fugue, a remarkable feat for that age. Van was twelve when he played with the Houston Symphony Orchestra, earning him significant acclaim from critics. At the age of sixteen, he had amassed more than ten thousand hours of practice time—turning his exceptional aptitude into magical artistry. After he graduated from Kilgore High School in 1951, his mother sent him to study with Madame Rosina Lhevinne at the famed Juilliard School in New York City, where he trained in the tradition of the Great Russian Romantics. Juilliard was long considered one of the most prestigious schools for music in the world. The acceptance rate at the Upper West Side school hovered between 5 and 8 percent, making those admitted exceptional. Van felt comfortable there and grew in stature and as an artist. In 1954, Van Cliburn entered and won the Leventritt Piano Competition in New York City. The competition implemented higher standards than just popularity amongst the jurors. With a focus on finding the most remarkable musicians, the first prize was sparingly awarded. Cliburn's win was the competition's first since 1949. The prestigious Leventritt Competition award offered important appearances with such major orchestras as the Cleveland, Denver, Indianapolis, and Pittsburgh, as well as a coveted New York Philharmonic debut with the great Dimitri Mitropoulos, which took place in Carnegie Hall on November 14, 1954. Mitropoulos garnered international fame as a Greek composer and conductor and was a rumored lover of composer Leonard Bernstein. From lessons at the age of three to eventually playing personally for every US president from Truman to Obama, Van was as big in the piano world as he stood in his own world. At a towering six-foot four-inch and rangy frame, he was as unique as he was masterful. Van was a consummate gentleman who preferred the reclusive life to the public variety.

It was 1958 when the popular Juilliard prodigy was convinced by his professors and mother to compete in the inaugural International Tchaikovsky Competition in Moscow of the Soviet Union. This period in world history was dubbed the Cold War due to an ongoing conflict between the Soviet Union and the United States. The term Cold War was appropriate as it encompassed every aspect typical of war except actual fighting. The ideological differences between the two world powers were severe and threatening to one another's place on the world stage. Notably, the Soviets had recently and successfully launched into orbit a 184-pound metallic sphere named Sputnik. This historical first launch was a successful effort to demonstrate Soviet technological superiority over the rest of the world. The United States nervously deemed this event an extreme threat to national security, and thus the space race was born. Americans perceived the Soviet Union as bloodthirsty for world domination. Nuclear arms testing between the two powers kept each on edge, coupled with ongoing posturing on both sides for control over Berlin. The first International Tchaikovsky Competition was another well-coordinated Soviet attempt to prove to the world that Soviet culture also stood alone on the world's stage. In January 1958, efforts came forth from the two world powers to warm the Cold War deadlock. The two countries signed the Lacy-Zaroubin Agreement, named after its chief negotiators, allowing the exchange of cultural, educational, and technical ideals between the two. This agreement opened the door for America's participation in the inaugural Tchaikovsky Competition. This initial competition included two disciplines—piano and violin—for its sixty-seven competitors hailing from twenty-one countries. It was later decided that the competition would take place every four years.

   A certain American competitor arrived with nervous elegance and wonderment into a place that most people only read about. Van Cliburn's natural, beautiful tone and captivating style quickly made him a hot ticket. Curious Soviets clamored to see this tall, skinny, and unusual foreigner play. The contest called for each competing pianist to play three times over the three-week span. The competition would prove to be another Soviet success, and Cliburn quickly became a fan favorite. When he earned his way into the finals from an initial pool of fifty competing pianists, Cliburn would seize a moment of historical and musical significance for the ages. His final performance left a difficult decision to the star-laden jury but not in the traditional sense. Van's performance in the finals was strategically played for the Soviet people with what would become a legendary performance of Tchaikovsky's *Piano Concerto no.1* on April 13, 1958.[1]

   The competition was indeed fierce, and its final competitors were all worthy of such an award. The women swooned with adulation for the towering American, and the showering of Cliburn with flowers upon the stage after his performance made the jury's job that much more difficult. He had outperformed the field. But how could the Soviet-heavy jury award an American the grand prize at the inaugural Tchaikovsky Competition, given all the political pressures being levied upon them? This was, after all, a showcase of the Soviet masters and their dominance on the pianistic world stage. When it was time to announce the winner, the jurors feared potential backlash should they reward the American with the gold. Jury president Emil Gilels approached the attending Communist Secretary, Nikita Khrushchev, to explain the situation. As Gilels nervously posed his dilemma to Khrushchev, he was asked sharply in response, "Is he the best?" Gilels pondered his reply and offered up an unmistakable nod. "Then give him the prize!" Khrushchev demanded. Afterwards, at the reception, Khrushchev was captured on camera giving Cliburn a Soviet-sized bear hug. Even in the absence of the Internet and its influence, the photo didn't take long to appear in every newspaper across the world. The effects of the Soviet leader happily cavorting with the lofty American sent ripples out that further softened the rift between the two nations. Cliburn's victory encore performance stole the show with his Rachmaninoff's Piano Concerto no. 3 and earned him a roaring standing ovation lasting eight minutes, which was also a first.

This was the victory heard around the world as the news media spread it like wildfire. The reception for Cliburn after his win found people clamoring to put eyes upon him and perhaps touch him. Women wiped away tears being in his presence. His performance of the Tchaikovsky no. 1 deeply moved many people. Cliburn had conquered the Iron Curtain with his Steinway and, in doing so, had ripped down a tremendous political barrier towards peace that the world so desperately needed. Cliburn's patriotic homecoming in New York found him as guest of honor in a ticker-tape parade, which remains to this day the only time the honor has been ever bestowed upon a musician. He was hailed and celebrated as a conquering hero. Time magazine awarded him the cover, proclaiming him "The Texan Who Conquered Russia." Van could not have known the immeasurable impact of his victory.

Shortly after his triumph, as he returned home, he was asked to appear on NBC's *The Steve Allen Show* in front of his huge national audience. His face would become associated with the piano as he made many appearances on television including *What's My Line?* and *Mister Roger's Neighborhood*. Cliburn's triumph in Moscow turned him overnight into the most famous classical musician in the world. As a known recluse, he now had little choice but to become a public figure.

Seven months after winning the Tchaikovsky Competition, back in Texas, the Fort Worth Piano Teacher's Forum hosted a dinner honoring Van's first and most important teacher, his mother, Rildia Bee O'Bryan Cliburn. The night belonged to Rildia Bee, but every eye was fixed on Van. Strategically seated between Van and his mother was Dr. Irl Allison, founder of the National Guild of Piano Teachers, who, en route to the banquet, brainstormed a crazy idea. He shared in a surprise announcement after dinner that the National Guild would provide a ten-thousand-dollar cash prize for a brand new international piano competition to be named in honor of Rildia Bee's son. When Irl

The Russian people celebrate their beloved Texan, Van Cliburn. *Everett Collection Historical / Alamy Stock Photo*

Allison opened the doors for the Van Cliburn Competition with some big promises and a tip of his hat, the deal was sealed. The location for the competition was yet to be determined, but surely a competition named in honor of a man of such prestige, talent, and international celebrity would be held in New York City, or so they thought.

In the audience that evening sat the notable Fort Worth piano teacher named Grace Ward Lankford, who was the cofounder of the Fort Worth Piano Teachers Forum in 1950. Lankford knew instantly in her heart and thus spent the remainder of her life demonstrating to the world that no city other than Fort Worth—with its community support, tradition of volunteerism, dedication to arts and culture, and gracious hospitality—could host such an international event. The city of Fort Worth itself contains a proud and rich history of hardworking people, but most international music competitions take place in cities of musical prominence. Fort Worth isn't typically a place those outside the United States can easily identify. Fort Worth, considered the gateway to the West, made its name in the cattle industry. The cattle business was booming in the early years, as was the labor required of the horse-riding cowboy. These cowboys worked hard and died harder but left an indelible impression on the legacy of Fort Worth. Its nickname, "Cowtown," leaves little doubt as to its roots. Fort Worth has thrived in the shadow of its giant neighbor, Dallas, but kept its small-town charm and limitless attractions to families. Fort Worth wasn't quite a place that those in the know distinguished as a locale for an international piano competition, except for one overwhelming reason. Van Cliburn called it home.

In contrast to the music capitals like New York and Los Angeles, Fort Worth was an unlikely host for such a competition, but an overly enthusiastic community of volunteers rallied around their new virtuosic hero to establish the Van Cliburn Foundation, and in 1962, it hosted the inaugural Van Cliburn International Quadrennial Piano Competition. Van Cliburn's name on the competition quickly elicited international draw power. The Soviets, due to Van's victory in Moscow, raced to get in line.

The Cliburn competition successfully capitalized on Cliburn's name to compete on the world music stage. The inaugural Van Cliburn International Piano Competition operated on a seventy-thousand-dollar budget, a partnership with Texas Christian University for use of their concert hall and practice rooms, and management for the winner from Van's own manager, Sol Hurok. The competition also boasted hundreds of hometown volunteers, and the climax, a ten-thousand-dollar grand prize from the National Guild of Piano Teachers, which collectively opened the doors for the fledgling competition. Fort Worth would play host to forty-six worldly contestants from sixteen countries in 1962.

The first three quadrennial competitions showed wonderfully on the world stage and steadily grew in popularity, but the real growth came in with the presence of formidable civically minded woman, Martha Hyder. Hyder appeared on the Cliburn scene in 1973 after her children's piano teacher, Grace Ward Lankford, original Cliburn competition advocate, asked her to join her Cliburn efforts. The scope of the Van Cliburn Competition found new aggressive international growth under Hyder, a local oil heiress and grand philanthropist. Hyder, an unstoppable supporting force for the arts, and consummate go-getter, who constantly spread the message of the Van Cliburn Competition around the world, added to her endless list of international contacts. Hyder remained on a first-name basis with a multitude of world leaders and never settled for anything but the best for her little town of Fort Worth. Her marriage to prosecutorial whiz Elton Hyder became the stuff of legend. In 1944 Elton, at the age of twenty-eight, became the youngest assistant attorney general in Texas history. He also was among the youngest ever to bring a case before the US Supreme Court. Known for his voracious work appetite, Elton supervised a much older legal staff that led to the conviction and hanging of World War II war criminal Japanese Prime Minister Hideki Tojo, in 1948. His attention to the legal profession waned at age forty-five as he concentrated on real estate and his investments.

Martha's influence in Fort Worth and the world helped place the city and its piano competition firmly on the international stage. Martha was elected chairman of the Van Cliburn Foundation in 1973, the same year she and Elton hosted Soviet Vladimir Viardo, who deservedly took home Cliburn gold. The competition she inherited had been successful but had developed a stigma of crowning winners whose careers never materialized. Martha intended to change this. She traveled the world seeking favor amongst the most important concert halls throughout the globe. Her hard work and determination fueled the creation of a two-year management contract for the winner. She secured national television exposure for the Cliburn competition. Martha also convinced enough concert hall promoters into giving Cliburn finalists and potentially all contestants a vast array of opportunities and bookings to help further their careers. Vladimir Viardo would become her pet project as she orchestrated a red carpet of opportunity to help blossom his extraordinary talent. The Cliburn competition soared to new heights under the stewardship of the unflappable Martha Hyder. Her time as chairman of the Cliburn competition would last just one competition cycle, but her influence never waned. Leadership would pass along several times, including to the local Cliburn proponent Alann Sampson and ultimately to Richard

Rodzinski in 1986, but Martha's fingerprints were seen at every level. Martha was close to Van Cliburn himself and often telephoned him or Sampson at ridiculously early hours in the morning with a new idea to improve the Cliburn competition.

11
Making the Cliburn

The 1989 Van Cliburn International Piano Competition's solid reputation around the world still needed a Soviet presence to keep its international reputation strong. Two competitions had passed without a Soviet entry. The rift between the United States and the Soviet Union grew deeper in part because of the revolving boycotts by each superpower aimed at undermining the other country during the lingering Cold War. The 1980 Olympics held in Moscow elicited an American boycott due to ongoing tensions. The Soviets would miss the brilliant victories of pianistically flawless American André-Michel Schub in 1981 and of Brazilian Jose Feghali in the seventh Van Cliburn Competition in 1985. Incredibly, Feghali's victory almost never happened. He would pull a muscle in his back during rehearsal for the finals that required a visit to the doctor. He was prescribed a muscle relaxant that caused dizziness and a violent rash so bad that he was not able to practice for the two days leading up to the finals. Feghali called the Cliburn director at that time, Andrew Raeburn, and told him that he was pulling out of the finals, as he was not able to perform. Fortunately, the director refused to let him out of the competition. Feghali would play on through his added suffering to win the audience and the gold. Feghali would enjoy a tremendous concert career as well and became a tremendous ambassador to the Cliburn competition for years to come.

Four years later in 1989, luckily for the preservation of the world and for music, the pressures cooled as *Perestroika*, the reforming of the political and economic system, had begun to crumble the old Soviet Union, ushering in a more liberal-thinking world power. The re-energized Soviet music machine felt it might be time to offer up their best piano talents to the competition. As the new Cliburn executive with worldly influence and persuasiveness, Richard Rodzinski was sent to Moscow to get the Soviets back in. Several reports circulated that Van Cliburn had made a quid pro quo deal with the Soviets involving their return to the Cliburn competition in exchange for his return to the Soviet Union for a recital tour. Rodzinski's meeting with the Soviet state-run artist agency, GosKoncert, finally sealed the comeback deal. The Soviets, though, wanted to send whom they deemed appropriate for the Cliburn competition, a direct conflict with the audition and selection rules. Rodzinski skillfully convinced GosKoncert that the Cliburn selection committee must audition and choose who they felt should participate in the Cliburn, thus preserving the integrity of the competition. To keep the Cliburn competition fair and by the book, the Cliburn could not allow it any other way.

The Eighth Cliburn Competition would mark the beginning of a new compromise between the two world powers. It was no secret that the Soviets produced some of the finest pianists the world had ever heard. The United States, much newer to the world music stage, still exhibited many remarkable players and beating the Soviets remained desirable whenever the two competed. Several of the talented American performers were, in fact, defectors or expatriates from the Soviet Union. The previous Soviet absence from the Cliburn had left an obvious gap in the remarkable talent pool. At the conclusion of each competition, the Van Cliburn Foundation wastes little time in initiating its worldwide talent search in its never-ending role of prepping for the next upcoming competition. This remains an unenviable task of epic proportions. The constant search for talent is the lifeblood of any legitimate piano competition.

In 1989, the Cliburn Foundation mailed out eight thousand application books to the major musical institutions, schools, orchestras, conservatories, presenters, festivals, managers, and musical publications, along with direct requests across the world to outline the opportunity open to them. Only the most advanced pianists, who possessed a broad enough repertoire, were eligible. In response, the Cliburn received nearly 250 vetted and qualified applicants from every part of the musical world. Each of those applicants were then scheduled to perform at the closest prearranged venue, a fifty-minute recorded recital in front of an invited public. These auditions required a tremendous amount of time and effort to put together. A team of engineers led by Tom Frost was sent to every locale to manage the recordings. Frost, a CBS executive, was the producer of the audio feed for the radio, television, and subsequent recordings for the 1989 competition. The selection jury would travel to world musical hubs such as Beijing, Tokyo, Warsaw, Leningrad, London, Venice, Budapest, Munich, Los Angeles, New York, Chicago, and Fort Worth, with the goal of locating the next class for this grand quadrennial competition. The applicants were given a stipend by the Cliburn Foundation to assist in getting them to these auditions. Each applicant would then select the best twenty-minute segment from their fifty-minute recording to submit. These recordings were then sent to Fort Worth and its screening jury.

The Cliburn selection committee consisted of known musical personalities John Giordano, Minoru Nojima, Ralph Votapek, Maxim Shostakovich, and Joaquin Soriano, who would hunker down in a video viewing room at a four-story office building at 2525 Ridgmar Boulevard, where they raked through the submitted videotape auditions. John Giordano despised this process, as the video recordings tended to be subjective. The contestants' submission would be at the mercy of their venues, recording quality, piano quality, and tape editing. Giordano, the chairman of the selection committee and the Cliburn competition jury, knew that the recordings created further issues because some contestants were just simply more photogenic than others and, like it or not, people made decisions from this. For this initial and expensive selection process, the selection committee utilized the state-of-the-art equipment from long-time local audio and video business Marvin Electronics to view and critique the tapes. The selection panel that year took eight days to pore over 193 approved videotapes, containing each applicant's twenty-minute showcase. It was from these tapes, which consisted primarily of Betamax video recordings and VHS camcorder recordings, that they pulled the final forty pianists they invited to the competition. Two quickly dropped out for personal reasons, creating the field of thirty-eight competitors for the Eighth Van Cliburn International Piano Competition. Each competitor had exhibited talent consistent enough to compete for the prize. The Cliburn first prize held its weight easily with other grand piano competition prizes. For the eighteen- to twenty-nine-year-old contestants, the Cliburn prize was among a handful of life-changing awards. The winner would be awarded two-year Van Cliburn competition contracts for management, thus launching their careers. The Cliburn winner experienced a form of instant stardom and access to the largest and most desirable venues throughout the world. Based on worldwide desirability, the top six finalists each received bookings for an accelerated performance calendar, with a combined schedule of over four hundred engagements worldwide in the two years after the competition. The Moscow Conservatory chronically receives regular visits from talent seekers from classical music competitions throughout the globe. The Cliburn selection committee descended upon Leningrad and Alexei Sultanov almost by accident. The young boy prodigy impressed crowds throughout his country, but there were older, more experienced, and more high-profile pianists at the conservatory that first caught the Cliburn selection committee's eye. The Soviet Union's Alexander Shtarkman, Elisso Bolkvadze, and Veronika Reznikovskaya had all auditioned in Leningrad and been pegged for the Cliburn competition now that the political gates had been loosely opened. Alexander Shtarkman held the enviable distinction of being the top Soviet prodigy and the most accomplished entry from the Soviet Union. Sasha, as he was known throughout the Soviet Union, was an incredible young talent and the son of celebrated Soviet pianist Naum Shtarkman, who was a disciple of Soviet great Konstantin Igumnov. Naum notably placed third behind grand prizewinner Van Cliburn at the inaugural 1958 Tchaikovsky competition.

Shortly after the competition, Naum's promising career quickly unraveled when he was arrested as he prepared for a performance in Kharkov, Ukraine. Article 21 of the Soviet Criminal Code RSFSR would place Naum in prison for eight years for the crime of homosexuality. His criminal record after his release severely limited his tremendous talent. Naum was relegated to playing tier-two venues across the Soviet Union. Ultimately, in 1987, he found a professorship at the Moscow Conservatory, where previously as a twelve-year-old, he performed a solo recital in the Great Hall and would later attend school. His prodigal son, Sasha, found his way on the piano like his father, and was held in high regard by his peers. His acute attention to detail and work ethic made him a favorite amongst the professors at the conservatory. His selection to the Cliburn competition was assured unanimously after a few minutes into his audition in Leningrad. He would arrive in Fort Worth as a favorite as far as the Cliburn staffers were concerned, and being the elder of the Soviet group, he felt the pressure to win. Sasha and Alexei had met originally back at the 1986 Tchaikovsky Competition, where neither of the teenagers made the finals. Now they existed as friendly rivals, sharpening their talent with every competition. Back in 1986, as Alexei and Dace were getting a bird's-eye view of Horowitz's legendary concert below, Shtarkman had made the miracle concert in a much different fashion. He had procured a ticket for a different artist performing days later and carefully changed the name and date on the ticket. The counterfeit ticket got him through security, and he witnessed this monumental moment from the safety of a stairwell. Shtarkman had even brought along a bouquet of carnations that he was able to lay on the stage at the conclusion of Horowitz's performance. These specific carnations laid upon on the edge of the stage, as well as his backside, can be seen on the existing black and white video recording of the performance's last moments.

Also, amongst the throngs of Soviets lucky enough to have procured a legitimate seat to Horowitz, was soon-to-be eleven-year-old Olga Kern. Kern sat mesmerized as she gazed upon the stage where Horowitz soon would be. As a piano prodigy herself since the age of five, she soaked in the excitement and energy that poured out from all around. She stared at the behemoth piano that occupied the center stage. Kern's grandfather, an accomplished pianist himself, had gifted his prized granddaughter the one ticket he was able to purchase. He sensed that this monumental event would best inspire her and further her young talent. The emotional performance hit its mark with Kern. It's an experience Kern still considers one of her life's most memorable. Her pianist future did indeed soar and hit its pinnacle years later in 2001 when—at the age of thirty—she won the gold medal at the Eleventh Van Cliburn Piano Competition, making her an international star.

Alexei's audition for the Cliburn selection committee in Leningrad initially brought skepticism due to his young age, but it was not long after he began playing that the committee members were looking at one another in amazement. He played with great fire and passion, much more akin to an older, more experienced pianist. His selection was unanimous, and so the Soviet ticket now stood at four competitors. The Cliburn selection committee knew these four were each capable of winning the gold. The committee left the Soviet Union satisfied with their choices. These artists had something to say with their playing styles, and Fort Worth would be ready.

For the Eighth Van Cliburn International Piano Competition, the four Soviets were to be matched up with thirty-four other carefully selected competitors from countries such as Japan, China,[1] Australia, Germany, Italy, Ireland, South Korea, Yugoslavia, Hungary, Indonesia, France, Portugal, Brazil, Bulgaria, Netherlands, Italy, and Canada. The Cliburn committee also selected eight Americans to fill out the card. The preparation for the Van Cliburn competition began for the Soviets in 1988, as it did for all, once they learned of their acceptance. Alexei Sultanov was sent to St. Petersburg by train during a fierce winter for his preparation leading up to the May departure to the United States. The separation from Dace kept Alexei frustrated yet focused on performing flawlessly for a chance at greatness.

Vika, now a budding young composer, received another visit from a wishful Alexei once he returned to Moscow and several weeks before leaving for Texas. Dace had shared with Vika and several others Alexei's upcoming trip to the United States, but very few people at the conservatory knew about his participation. Perhaps it was the superstitious nature of the Russian people that kept this information private until something significant was worthy of mentioning. Dace and Vika had luckily been spending more time together those days. On their most recent visit, they shopped at a new clothing store near the student dormitory. They both fell in love with and purchased identical pairs of blue velvet trousers. The gorgeous trousers were covered in small black dots which reminded them of the staccato musical sign. Pietro Locatelli was an Italian composer whose Baroque style works were very popular with cellists. These small dots when written above or below a musical note signify to the musician to play a shorter duration of the note. This trousers pattern and their mutual love of Locatelli resulted in the girls giving them a nickname—the Locatelli trousers. Days later, Vika joined the couple at the movies and became amused when Alexei wore the other pair of Locatelli trousers, not Dace. He apparently loved them so much that he began wearing them, much to Dace's chagrin. Before he departed for the United States, Alexei had visited Vika. He had taken great interest in the moccasins she wore to the movies. He pleaded and begged to borrow them and talked the moccasins right off of her feet. Vika knew those moccasins might never be returned to her.

Months later, as the Soviet team congregated back in Moscow for the upcoming departure to someplace called Fort Worth, expectations were high. Shtarkman, Bolkvadze, Reznikovskaya, and Sultanov were handed their visas and marching orders. Excitement was everywhere as this trip to America was everyone's first.

Alexei told Dace on departure day—perhaps half in self-motivation and half in a lover's goodbye—that he would bring her home a gold medal. The goodbye was tearful, as both understood the distance between them wouldn't allow for any easy form of communication. Alexei departed for the Van Cliburn International Piano Competition on the other side of the world, wearing Dace's Locatelli trousers and Vika's moccasins, ready to make his mark on the world.

Dace would remain at the conservatory to finish out the remaining school year before the summer break as Alexei crossed the world to compete. Dace's summer back in Riga with her family awaited her. In lieu of any familial support for the competitors, the Soviet government sent two KGB agents, also publicly referred to as translators, to keep tabs on their talented exports and, more importantly, handle any and all business related to the Soviet musicians. The hospitality that awaited the incoming class of Cliburn competitors stood at the ready. Visiting competitors at the Cliburn competition would be assigned to a host family to live with during their stay. This highlighted the volunteer aspect and hometown charm of this event. The host family would be carefully matched up for convenience's sake when possible and become the de facto handler for the competitor. This removed the empty and cold environment of a hotel room and created a positive and warm environment from which to showcase themselves to the world. It was not required that the hosts speak their competitors' native languages, but efforts were made to accommodate when options were available. The requirements to be a host were simple, but the host committee labored hard to find the closest match. The host families operated under three strict Cliburn rules: They were to have their competitor at their respective events on time. They must allow for an atmosphere conducive to practice, and they must maintain a flexible schedule to allow for scheduling changes. These volunteer chauffeurs benefitted not just by all access to the Cliburn events, but more importantly each home would hold a world-class private concert as their competitor practiced. For lovers of classical music, it was a jackpot.

12
The Wilcoxes

In 1989, the US Department of Defense budget was a whopping $427 billion, which supported vast international interests, among them the dwindling Cold War efforts, and gave smart people like Jon Wilcox jobs. The threat of communism still loomed large for Americans, although their fears were in sharp decline. Fort Worth's Bell Helicopter hovered in the upper echelon of defense contractors—creating helicopter war machines with monikers like the Yankee, Zulu, and V-22 Osprey. Working there amidst the human resources department was local mainstay Jon Wilcox. Wilcox, a Texas Christian University grad, had been at Bell since 1981 after leaving a five-year stint at aerospace and defense pioneer Northup. His humble beginnings as a math teacher at Fort Worth Country Day School were cut short when he received an unsolicited phone call from Northup offering him double his salary to leave. The decision was easy and ended what may have well been a long and illustrious teaching career after just one year. His prior college experience at TCU though had been productive. When faced with the course requirement of taking a language, he selected Russian along with twenty-two others, and due to the lack of interest in the course, he made it to his third year as the only student left in the class. The one-on-one instruction with his professor, Dr. John Loud, gave Jon an accelerated Russian education in that short period of time. On the other hand, his would-be wife, Susan, also had a background in language. She had spent two years studying abroad in Krakow, Poland. It was in a later class while attending San Diego State that the Wisconsin-born Susan was showing some friends some postcards of Krakow that caught Jon's eye. Those postcards opened the door to a conversation, and the two quickly fell in love and married in short order.

Years later, a Van Cliburn competition volunteer named Lynn Searcy worked regularly at the local branch of the YMCA alongside then Chief Financial Officer Susan Wilcox. Searcy learned through her Cliburn duties that two of the four Soviets entering the upcoming Van Cliburn competition did not speak any English. Lynn, who held the Cliburn title of director of development, also knew Jon Wilcox spoke Russian and thus the question was posed: Would the Wilcoxes consider hosting the nineteen-year-old Soviet prodigy named Alexei Sultanov? Alexei, it was shared, was quite a talent indeed but spoke no English. The young couple thought the idea sounded fun and consented. The Wilcoxes could never have foreseen how this innocent decision would change the rest of their lives. A few weeks later, Alexei Sultanov and the Soviets arrived.[1]

13

Coming to America

Alexei stepped off the plane at Dallas Fort Worth International Airport, much to the delight of Susan and John Wilcox. A weather delay in the area had forced him to spend the previous night in New York City. Alexei nervously carried with him a small duffel bag that the conservatory had issued him, which included a few basic items of clothing and necessary toiletries. This duffel would constitute everything that he owned on this planet. Alexei deplaned to a world immeasurably different for him, thus making Jon so pivotal from the start. Alexei walked into the airport terminal accompanied by his three Soviet co-competitors. Trailing slightly behind and inconspicuous by all measures were two older Soviets dressed in business attire. The woman introduced herself as Marina Mitareva in accented English to the lot of American hosts. Her accompanying male counterpart, Vladimir Soukhanov, said nothing. Their stated roles were translators, which held some level of truth. These Soviet chaperones' cover fooled very few people. The reputation of the KGB preceded their arrival and naturally put everyone on slight edge, albeit much subdued due to the safety of the United States. These KGB agents were not here for pleasure but rather to look after their Soviet investments. They were charged with keeping their Soviet prodigies from losing their way in this land of overindulgence and corruption. These KGB agents would shadow the five-foot, two-inch Alexei, along with the other competitors, for the duration of the Cliburn competition in Fort Worth.

After the initial and unique pleasantries, Alexei was led to the car where he took the back seat of the Wilcoxes' brand-new Acura Legend. The KGB had prior arrangements for transportation, but they were aware of each competitor's lodging and schedule. The short thirty-minute drive home was riddled with awkward silences and Jon's attempts to break the ice. Alexei gazed wide-eyed out the window at the unfolding scenery. The Wilcoxes realized quickly that Alexei came here on business and not just a free vacation. The serious demeanor he exhibited portrayed a focused young man, or perhaps it was also his uncertainty about this new situation. His short answers suggested that he was a very confident young man. He was very respectful to his new hosts, but all signs pointed to an underlying sense of duty instilled in him. That focus lifted as the garage door opened at the Wilcoxes' house, which revealed Susan's car parked inside. In the Soviet Union most people were very lucky if they could afford one car, but it was unheard of to own two.

Alexei quizzed Jon as to who else lived in the house, assuming the car belonged to another family. This caused some much-needed chuckling. When Jon asked Alexei what he wanted to do first, Alexei responded in Russian that he wanted to have a douche. This caused Susan and Jon to pause, glance at each other, and nervously ponder their next move. It would take them a few additional seconds to realize that the poor boy merely wanted the Russian version of a shower. Alexei settled into his appointed room and got the lay of the land. Everything was bigger here, and what Alexei considered opulence was abundant. This would be his home for the next three weeks, if he survived that long. Then something caught his eye that brought a smile to his face.

There, sitting in the Wilcoxes' living room, glistening in the daylight, was a brand-new Steinway & Sons Model B piano, awaiting someone worthy of its beauty. Alexei could not have imagined the incredible series of events that led to this piano being available to him. The early years of the Van Cliburn competition found the pianists playing whatever piano the host family or host's friends could muster. In many cases, the pianos were worn out or aged relics not representative of what they would be playing at the competition. Those host homes with larger piano budgets seemingly gave their competitor a slight advantage in their preparation. Danny Saliba, the Steinway & Sons representative for the Southwest region of the US, over several years had convinced the Cliburn executives not only to make Steinway a bigger part of the competition, but also to place Steinways in the homes of competitors when their hosts didn't own a piano. The Wilcoxes, fortunately for Alexei, did not own a piano, so they received one of the three brand-new Steinways delivered to host homes that year.

Each subsequent Cliburn competition, Saliba added more Steinway pianos to the host homes. Ultimately, he would place one in each host home, thirty-five total pianos for the 1997 Van Cliburn competition, to ensure there was no equipment advantage for the practicing pianists. This wonderful perk of the Cliburn competition would continue in perpetuity for all future Cliburn competitions. After the competitions ended, the Cliburn Steinways would end up at the Fort Worth Steinway & Sons showroom owned by local dealer Luke Wickman. Van Cliburn, a notable night owl, would visit that showroom after each competition in the early morning hours to play and autograph each Cliburn competitor-used Steinway. These pianos soared in marketability, quickly launching the Steinway Model B Cliburn Signature Series. Van would autograph more than 140 over the years before his death. The partnership shared between Saliba and the Cliburn competition blossomed for both, making Steinway & Sons the brand of choice in the DFW metroplex and the competition.

Over the years, Danny Saliba developed a remarkable relationship with the competition as well as with Van Cliburn himself. Saliba even taught Van a useful trick to help alleviate having to shake hundreds of hands after each performance, with his right hand already tired from the performance. Saliba suggested that if Van would place a towel over his right hand after he left the stage, then people would assume his hand was not open for shaking and simply converse with him in lieu of offering their hands. The trick worked brilliantly, and Van utilized it often after difficult performances. Saliba's foray into pianos began at the age of sixteen selling the synthesizer, a relative of the organ. Saliba learned the business well and found success selling the instruments. While in Chicago on a work trip early in his career, Saliba was introduced to John Steinway—the great-great-grandson of Steinway & Sons founder, German piano builder Heinrich Engelhard Steinweg.[1] Heinrich would build, in 1836, his first instrument in the kitchen of his Seesen, Germany, home, thus creating the "Kitchen" piano. Henry E. Steinway, as he later anglicized his name to, immigrated to the United

States due to the limited opportunities and dangerous political environment that existed in Germany. After leaving his fledgling company to one of his sons, he moved with his wife and the remainder of their eight children and founded, in 1853, the original Steinway & Sons factory in Manhattan, New York, in a small loft on 85 Varick Street.[2]

In the 1860s, Steinway & Sons moved to Queens as the handmade quality craftsmanship of Steinway jumped in popularity, and the New York side of the family business set out to supply the Americas. Henry Steinway's original family piano-making business, which began in the 1820s, was then being run by his sons. The family company had also grown, and in 1880 they would build a new factory in Hamburg, Germany, that would handle the rest of the globe. Steinway & Sons became synonymous with exceptional quality throughout the world by pianists, patrons, and concert halls alike. The craftsmanship and attention to detail made Steinway & Sons the most sought-after piano in the world.

The onset of World War II created a unique situation for Steinway & Sons. In America, the company was forbidden from making pianos for three years, as their materials were better served to fight the Axis powers. In 1939, Nazi officials nationalized the Steinway & Sons factory in Hamburg and the retail store in Berlin, believing erroneously through false rumors that it was a Jewish-owned company. The more accurate reason was that it was now an American company operating in Germany. Sadly, the New York Steinway & Sons competition in America circulated a rumor that the Steinway family were Nazi sympathizers. The American Steinway factory did in fact contribute to the American war effort with a contract for the CG-4A troop carrying gliders and, eventually, upright pianos for the entertainment of the troops. The contract Steinway struck with the US War Department saved the company from closing its doors, as the market for the luxury items had all but dried up. The government contract also opened the door to employ hundreds of women in the factory, a significant step for Steinway. The Nazis killed the manufacture of pianos in Hamburg, instead opting for construction of fake gliders, wooden swastikas, gunstocks, coffins, and bunk beds for the German Army. The few pianos in inventory were sent to Nazi strongholds for their entertainment. Steinway & Sons pianos held little cultural value to the Nazis since the Bechstein piano had been declared the official piano of the Nazis as its ownership came from within. Its founder's son, Edwin Bechstein, was well connected in Berlin society and on close terms with Hitler. Bechstein's wife let it be known that they wished Hitler to marry their daughter. Once the war came to an end, rebuilding all that was lost took monumental efforts from all. The Hamburg Steinway & Sons factory barely survived the war and did not reopen fully until seven years later. The majority of the workers kept their jobs to continue building the Hamburg Steinway. The Bechstein company had been obliterated by Allied bombing raids and took much longer to reopen.

The fifties and sixties saw slow improvement for the restarted Steinway. The worldwide demand for custom-made pianos also grew, and things began to look up. In the early seventies, the Steinway & Sons factory in Queens, New York, had been cited by the Environmental Protection Agency for its use of a certain lacquer, which was sprayed on the pianos after construction. This lacquer posed a significant health hazard to the residents of Queens, and thus the citation. The EPA ordered the growing piano maker to install specialized walls utilizing a special oil inside the lacquer rooms to capture the harmful chemicals released by the lacquer. The prospect of building this newly required room proved so expensive that its implementation would force Steinway & Sons out of business. The hundreds of shareholders and Steinway family members met and ultimately decided that their only option was to sell the company or close. The answer came in the form of an old Steinway family friend, entrepreneur Bill Paley.[3] Paley rented space in the basement of the Steinway factory in 1928. There he ran a fledgling company created when he purchased a collection of sixteen struggling radio stations called United Independent Broadcasters Incorporated. Columbia Phonographic Company, as it was renamed, took flight and enjoyed limited success. Paley desired originally to use the broadcasts to advertise his family's cigar business. He quickly realized the potential of radio and altered the name again to Columbia Broadcasting System (CBS). Under Paley's leadership, the iconic American company quickly surged to prominence.

As Steinway & Sons faced insolvency, CBS, now a giant broadcasting conglomerate, stepped in to keep them afloat. Paley and Steinway negotiated a twenty-million-dollar stock swap, which saved the company from extinction.

CBS at that time also happened to own the organ manufacturer that Saliba worked for. A chance meeting in 1980 with John Steinway endeared Saliba to the famed piano maker, and a friendship was born as Saliba began working for John Steinway and Steinway & Sons. It was in John Steinway's Manhattan apartment that a young Van Cliburn would often stay during his Juilliard years.[4] The two developed a close bond, as did Cliburn with the instrument when he became a Steinway artist.[5]

It was John Steinway's friendship with Van Cliburn that resulted in Steinway sending Saliba to Texas and the Southwest to represent the company. An early roadie for the Silver Bullet Band in Detroit before Bob Seager became its full-time front man, Saliba experienced an overnight transition from his beloved rock and roll to classical music. John Steinway taught Saliba how to properly listen to the piano—a skill which he would develop into a highly acute sense of hearing. In fact, he could determine a piano's brand while listening through the radio. Saliba's talent for selling and promoting the instrument would significantly further the New York Steinway brand. The American Steinway, as it is known, is carefully built for filling the larger performance halls typically found in the United States and specially designed to handle the power of Chopin's compositions. The Texas connection, coupled with a friendship with Fort Worth's Van Cliburn, created a substantial opportunity for Saliba. He sold the Steinway ideals to the Cliburn competition and launched his ingenious marketing plan to make Steinway & Sons its most prominent instrument. It was 1992 when John Steinway suggested Saliba buy the Whittle Music business in Dallas, Texas, which he promptly turned into Steinway Hall–Dallas, giving him a permanent presence in the Dallas–Fort Worth metroplex.

As Steinway & Sons continued to make giant strides revolutionizing their high-quality pianos, trouble loomed around every corner. Through its history it had taken many remarkable triumphs over seemingly insurmountable obstacles for Steinway to innovate and improve its product. During the 1970s, Steinway & Sons received an important visit from the officials at LaGuardia Airport. The new-age airport sat on the former Gala Amusement Park land, which was owned by Steinway & Sons to lure employees from the city. Steinway sold the land to the city of North Beach in 1929. The airport had just installed a new radar system in their modern air traffic control tower that was experiencing mysterious trouble in the southern part of its coverage. An investigation was performed to determine its cause. The Steinway & Sons factory was the main source of the investigation, as it stood in the heart of the problematic echo or return. In the wood-forming room, the piano rims made of hard rock maple and other high-quality woods needed a heating element to help dry the glue inside the wood layers. Thin copper sheets were wrapped around the wood and electrified to heat and help dry the glue. It was the substantial use of electricity combined with the copper sheets that was identified as the cause of the partial radar blackout at LaGuardia. Once the problem was ascertained, Steinway was ordered to cease use of this process. The solution led to a redesign of the wood forming process and a multitude of further innovations. Steinway's methods to solve complex issues led to 139 granted patents that continually push the frontiers of their craftsmanship.

Alexei was amazed by the standard of living the Wilcoxes presented. He was not accustomed to such luxuries, or any, for that matter. Alexei imagined that Jon and Susan were quite wealthy when, in fact, they were navigating through middle-class struggles during those days. When Jon introduced Alexei to his Atari game system, the trap was sprung. The nineteen-year-old prodigy had never imagined such entertainment existed. It took but a few days for Alexei to quickly surpass Jon's skill level at his favorite martial arts game *Ninja Gaiden*. Sensory overload ensued as Alexei explored his surroundings, but it would never interfere with his mission. The boy wonder that hated to practice back home had no reservations about time well spent in the Wilcoxes' living room at the piano. The Wilcoxes' three-bedroom, two-bathroom house was perfectly complemented by the living room Steinway piano. Whenever Alexei sat before the Steinway, the house erupted into what the Wilcoxes described as their very own private, world-class concert. They knew within seconds of his first practice run that this was no ordinary kid. His complete and utter mastery of that Steinway kept the Wilcoxes spellbound every single time he practiced. It became increasingly more difficult for Jon and Susan to leave for work knowing what was transpiring back home in their living room. The Wilcoxes found ample time to give Alexei a tour of Fort Worth to introduce him to its culture. The differences were enormous and extremely exciting to him.

Alexei's small duffel bag of possessions held nothing close to a tuxedo or appropriate dress in which to perform. He was keenly aware he needed clothes appropriate for the competition. Part of the host family's responsibilities were to assist their contestant's preparation, which included proper attire. Each performer was given a stipend for clothing, which they could use to work with several prearranged Fort Worth clothiers. Jon took Alexei to the Tom James Company, where he was outfitted in the course of two business days in his very first tuxedo for the competition. Alexei had to learn to wear this new tuxedo on the go. He implemented some changes to the traditional look with a white turtleneck in lieu of the formal dress shirt. His new tailored tuxedo, or tails as it was, fit Alexei like a glove. Susan, in turn, took him to Neiman Marcus, which handles the highest end apparel known to the city. It was the Neiman Marcus brand underwear that grabbed his interest the most. He spent his stipend on a year's supply and promptly made them his go-to undergarments.

The Wilcoxes' home had another extraordinary luxury for Alexei in the backyard pool. This was the first swimming pool Alexei had ever seen, and he was mesmerized by it. After practicing on those hot Fort Worth afternoons, he would race to jump in, not bothering to change into a swimsuit. In fact, Alexei had never owned one and knew little of its usefulness. Alexei found time enough for the pool in between monumental practice sessions.

Alexei was introduced to the concept of an American restaurant with seemingly endless options. Ordering from a menu of unknown words and dishes proved to be a difficult endeavor. For Alexei and Dace, dining out in Moscow wasn't unheard of, but they rarely had enough money. When Alexei returned from a performance with the few rubles he earned, the couple loved to dine at a traditional Georgian restaurant, where they enjoyed their favorite meat dumplings called *pelmeni* or *shashlik*—a Russian version of the Americanized shish kebob. These outings were especially rare, as they generally would eat their meals at the conservatory dormitory, which allowed them access to free food that they would cook themselves. The process of sitting down in a Fort Worth restaurant and studying a menu containing more options than one could handle left Alexei wide-eyed. The new stimulus seemed to overwhelm their new guest, but the Wilcoxes sensed Alexei's drive and mission and thus tried to keep his home life quiet and comfortable. He always found ample practice time and never skimped on putting in his work.

As his competition performance time drew close, he would stay at the piano morning, noon, and night—ensuring he would perform well. An occasional dip in the pool, a cartoon, a video game, or visit to a restaurant found its way into his schedule. Alexei was not able to communicate with Dace or family back home, as phone calls were very costly and difficult to string together. Internet service providers were just beginning to take off at this time, but being in its infancy kept adversarial countries like the Soviet Union well behind the curve. Dace and her family were left in the dark on the competition updates, as news wasn't easy to come by behind the Iron Curtain. The family began their impatient wait for news from across the world. The Van Cliburn piano competition required sixteen days to complete if a competitor made it to the end, so hypothetically, the longer they waited, the better the news.

The Wilcoxes' television captured Alexei's attention when practice wasn't on the menu. His childlike personality found respite in the cartoons he discovered. Alexei's demeanor was extremely shy and reserved in this new country, but his English and confidence improved rapidly with his new immersion in American cartoons. He quickly picked up some of the vernacular of modern America. In fact, Alexei learned a few basic English phrases from these cartoons. He engrossed himself in these cartoons each morning and oft repeated their respective catch phrases for the Wilcoxes' amusement. Almost as impressive to the Wilcoxes was how effortlessly Alexei remembered the background music from these cartoons and then played it back for them on the Steinway—often adding complexity to the music. The Wilcoxes felt that Alexei had a solid chance to place in this competition. There was just something about him that reeked of stardom. In Fort Worth, Alexei moved about freely, without any of the usual pressures from home. Alexei's perceptive nature taught him the value of this misunderstood thing called freedom. The KGB escorts did not visit the Soviet competitors at their host homes but rather could be found at all the Cliburn events, attempting to blend in.

Back home in Tashkent, the common everyday experience was exceptionally different. When the family needed food, the options were quite simple and left much to be desired. Farmer's markets were a common sight for produce and dairy. When the family needed meat, they stood in line at a butcher's window until their turn to choose between the few options. Everything one might need typically required standing in line to request it. If Natalia Sultanov needed bread for the family, she would visit the *Khlebnaya*, a small neighborhood bakery, to order light, rye, or dark bread. The decision depended on what she could afford. If demand was high, she might return home with whatever was left to buy. The *Ovoshnaja* handled the vegetables, beets, carrots, onions, and, of course, cabbage. This experience for those living in the Soviet Union made first visits to the US eye-opening experiences. When the Wilcoxes took Alexei to his first grocery store, he went into sensory overload. He had never seen or heard of such a place in his life. Rows and rows of colorful and unimaginable food in every conceivable form. More food than he had seen in his lifetime. America, to him, was indeed the land of plenty. Alexei smirked as he recalled from his schooling that he was not supposed to have these types of feelings toward a sworn adversary of the Soviets. Danger and deceit should be lurking around every corner. Alexei intuitively reasoned that perhaps all was not as bad as he was led to believe. He quickly fell in love with this place.

Once all the contestants had finally arrived in Fort Worth and got settled in, the schedule of activities kicked off. Competitors were required to attend the meet and greets, host parties, patron parties, and promotional appearances. Although Alexei's piano performances suggested he had a demonstratively outspoken personality, he reverted to shyness when he was around large groups of people. He preferred the company of a few at home. The Wilcoxes struggled mightily to ensure that Alexei was where he was supposed to be. The contestants' schedules were carefully planned, and their execution took incredible efforts by all involved. The schedule was set in motion weeks prior to their arrival. The two accompanying KGB agents had been copied with this schedule and thus always appeared at group functions and performances. When the Soviet competitors were not on the move, the agents were holed up in their hotel room, coordinating their efforts. Wherever the four Soviet competitors performed, there was always at least one of the KGB agents in close proximity. The agents were not hard to identify, but they were never actively engaged in the goings-on. Susan Wilcox fondly remembered how friendly they were when she spoke to them. English came easily to the KGB agents, as their assignments likely depended on it. It was obvious to her that they were focused on doing their job. Business aside, the KGB agents were decent enough to hold a conversation with anyone interested when engaged. These were hardly the monsters the media had portrayed them to be. Cliburn Executive Director Richard Rodzinski had snuffed out a potential issue early on when the KGB agents were pushing the Cliburn Foundation to keep them apprised of any schedule changes or new incoming information. Richard flexed his muscles and told them to do their jobs but not interfere with his competition. The message was received loudly, as there were no further interferences. The Cliburn had plenty of international affairs to manage, and the KGB would not be one of these moving forward.

14
Richard

Richard Rodzinski had been the president and executive director of the Van Cliburn Foundation since 1986. His musical roots were most assuredly passed down from his Polish father, Artur Rodzinski, the famed conductor for the New York Philharmonic and Cleveland Orchestras in the 1930s and 1940s. In honor of Richard's birth, his distinguished family was presented with two compositions written by the legendary Samuel Barber and Igor Stravinsky. Richard would go on to make a name for himself in the classical music world. His leadership of the Van Cliburn Foundation for twenty-three years encompassed six competitions. The Cliburn saw tremendous growth under Rodzinski's direction. He felt the Cliburn competition was an audition for significant careers in music for its competitors. Rodzinski quipped, "All must recognize that, unlike the Olympics where winning a medal is the end, winning the Cliburn is merely a beginning." To Rodzinski, classical music was much more than wonderous entertainment; it was essential in cultivating a more complete human being. Rodzinski had a certain knack for managing his worldly artists, which made him a de facto expert on classical music competitions. He had deep European ties, bringing to the Cliburn Foundation a new and desperately needed source of international talent capital. He believed that musical competitions provided benefits to the majority of the artists they served.

Musical competitions had begun to receive criticism throughout the world as they searched for their winners. The complaint against

Sultanov and Cliburn visionary director, Richard Rodzinski. *University of Texas Arlington Library Photo*

the competitions was that they promoted a winner-take-all mentality, and the competitive environment didn't always suit each competitor. While each competitor had tremendous talent, one poor performance could damage their confidence or marketability. Due to the subjective nature of the jurors, oftentimes significant talent doesn't make it out of the first round. This subjectivity weighed heavily over a collection of worthy musicians and their respective career paths. The *Dallas Morning News* described the Van Cliburn Competition, prior to this year's competition, as something akin to a blood sport. Rodzinski's printed rebuttal outlined his belief that the Cliburn competition allows young pianists to measure themselves against their peers and allows them potential assessment of their performing career. His management style, though, was strict and often pushed his artists to extremes. Alexei felt uneasy in his presence. Richard's command of the Russian language and his ever-watchful eye made Alexei wonder if he was somehow a spy. Rodzinski had little patience with Alexei's rebellious nature, but he knew the tremendous talent he possessed and hoped it would benefit his competition. The two both craved control, and Alexei felt threatened by the Cliburn boss. The two would develop a tumultuous relationship that would come to a head years later. Rodzinski's leadership at the Cliburn competition, though, brought a swelling of international acclaim and validation to the already prominent piano event. Rodzinski and Jury Chairman John Giordano, in an effort to give competitors every opportunity to showcase their talents and get a sense of their respective marketability, toyed with a decision to open up the repertoire requirements for the Cliburn competition.

Denise Chupp, the artistic administrator for the Cliburn, who was tasked with researching all the major international competitions, found that most major international competitions were now moving in this direction and expanding their repertoires, which appeared to allow the artists to thrive. The previous Cliburn's repertoire requirements tended to penalize those competitors that performed relatively unfamiliar music. Rodzinski, Giordano, and Chupp went to Van's house to introduce to him this new idea for this upcoming Cliburn competition. Rodzinski posed the idea to Van and then threw it to Chupp to explain her findings. The nervous Chupp explained what she had discovered, then notably asked Van, "Maestro, consider what the Tchaikovsky Competition would have been like if they only allowed you to perform Mozart?" Her point seemed to hit its mark. Van chuckled at the notion and gave his blessing to open the repertoire for the next Cliburn competition. "Ok then, let's see who these competitors really are!" The excitement consumed the four of them, and the Eighth Van Cliburn International Piano Competition found a new and improved direction.[1]

15
The Draw

In 1985, shortly after the seventh Cliburn Competition concluded, the Van Cliburn foundation mailed out eight thousand applications to every corner of the globe. The result was 250 legitimate applications coming back. The Cliburn staff then buckled down and began the arduous task of vetting each of the potential competitors. Each applicant was asked to send in videos or recordings demonstrating their piano abilities. From these, the selection committee would personally visit those with the appropriate talent for the upcoming competition. After much effort, scrutiny, and much travel, the selection committee offered invitations to thirty-eight worthy individuals. The honor of being selected wasn't lost on anyone. The invitation to compete in the Cliburn was an honor in itself.

As the competitors arrived from all over the world and began their three-week stay, the many different moving parts of the competition were assembled in Fort Worth. Jury Chairman John Giordano, Cliburn Foundation Chairwoman Susan Tilley, and Executive Director of the Cliburn Foundation Richard Rodzinski would determine the focus and direction of the competition. The fourteen-member jury also arrived on the scene. Giordano had remained Cliburn jury chairman since 1973, when that year's chairman, Dr. Howard Hanson, fell ill the day before the competition. Hanson was directing the Eastman School of Music in Rochester, New York, and was a highly acclaimed composer, conductor, musical theorist, educator, and classical music advocate. His *Symphony no.*

4 brought him many awards, including the 1944 Pulitzer Prize. When Hanson took ill on the eve of the competition, Catherine Russell, the daughter of Cliburn co-founder Grace Ward Langford, called her close friend, Giordano, to ask for his help. Giordano, who had just moved to Fort Worth and was still unpacking, accepted over the phone. His previous jury experience in other competitions would serve him well. He would serve the Cliburn in this capacity for the next forty-two years. His upbeat personality and exceptional gift for music made Giordano a local favorite. Giordano had earned acclaim for himself early on as a concert saxophonist and later as a musical director and conductor for the Fort Worth Symphony Orchestra, where he served for twenty-seven years. He also founded Fort Worth's Chamber Orchestra. Giordano worked closely with Rodzinski and was involved with most major Cliburn decisions. Giordano cultivated relationships with people across the world who possess extraordinary musical skills and talents. His relationships nearly matched those of his boss Rodzinski. Giordano, after all, could call famed violinist Itzhak Perlman and legendary cellist Yo-Yo Ma close friends. Giordano's jury was charged with selecting the performer whose musical message spoke most eloquently. Every competitor, after all, had something to say.

Giordano's jury was given the freedom to vote based not simply on correct and incorrect notes but, more importantly, on the performers' interpretation of the music they were playing. The Cliburn jury was subject to rules set out by the World Federation of International Music Competitions, of which it was a member. Rules stated that at least half of the jurors could not be from the host country. The federation's aim here was to remove any bias or perception of bias from international competitions. A who's who of international music personalities filled this jury box. Each one picked not only for their recognized experience and fair mindedness, but also for their potential benefit to the Cliburn competition and its competitors. Such notables as the winner of the very first Cliburn competition, an American named Ralph Votapek, RCA recording producer John Pfeiffer, and the music director of the New Orleans Symphony—son of famous composer Dmitri—Maxim Shostakovich. Christina Ortiz from Brazil, who won the 1969 Third Van Cliburn Competition, and John Lill from Great Britain, who was the co-winner of the 1970 Tchaikovsky Piano Competition, were also on the robust panel of jurors. Each juror was paid ten thousand dollars for their three-week effort by the Cliburn Foundation.

Throngs of local and international media were present for the festivities. Guests included film director Peter Rosen, whose crew would be filming a documentary entitled *Here to Make Music*. Rosen went on to win the prestigious Directors Guild of America Award for his work capturing that year's competition. Journalists from New York, Los Angeles, Chicago, London, Rome, Tokyo, and many more made their way to Fort Worth. Media outlets of the Voices of America, *Vogue Magazine*, *Town & Country*, and CNN all sent representatives. Bernard Holland from the *New York Times* arrived to work on his introspective piece, "Playing to Win." Steve Cummins, a radio host from nationally syndicated WRR-FM, attended and even announced the preliminaries. Local radio station 88.7 FM KTCU broadcast the entire Cliburn contest with Rosemary Solomon's soothing voice. The Cliburn Foundation brought in Chicago-based radio station WFMT, the Fine Arts Network, to create a thirteen-part nationwide broadcast. The Cliburn Foundation even commissioned internationally acclaimed contemporary artist Robert Rauschenberg to design the Eighth Van Cliburn International Piano promotional poster.

On the night of the draw party, two days prior to the start of the competition, in the elegantly manicured backyard of a wealthy Cliburn supporter, the thirty-eight competitors gathered amongst a hoard of host families, Cliburn officials, and Cliburn supporters. This evening was centered around the draw, where the pianists took turns drawing numbers out of a bowl that designated their order of play. Alexei drew his performance order number with no real fanfare aside from the other competitors playful whistles: twenty-seven. The draw order generally was irrelevant to the competitors unless you were first or last, places everyone dreaded. The unpleasant distinction of playing first fell onto the shoulders of American David Buechner. Buechner had been an early exit from the 1985 Cliburn competition and now stared down the dreaded barrel of playing first. Twenty-nine-year-old Buechner had been a frequent invitee as well as a frequent exit from many of the competitions he competed in. He helped further the ongoing international debate suggesting that these types of piano competitions didn't always pluck the best talent but rather the ones who were most marketable. Buechner did have significant talent and had won on the international stage, but somehow that was not recognized at the Cliburn. He seemed to have a knack for always making the finals elsewhere, but his early exit four years prior weighed on his psyche.

    The cliquishness of the opening draw party was obvious to all. Any worldly party will find those who speak the same language in the same corner, just as a matter of convenience. These extracurricular events carried additional pressure on the host families to break the ice for those not comfortable doing so. The jurors and Van Cliburn competition staff made their normal rounds meeting each competitor, allowing certain time allotments for each. Jurors were careful to keep the conversation light and transparent. Everyone was to be treated fairly and equally. No awards would be handed out here tonight.[2]

16
Opening Round

A 1235-seat Neo-Georgian style concert hall on the Fort Worth campus of Texas Christian University, built in 1948, sat in the middle of Ed Landreth Hall. Born in Springfield, Illinois, and raised in Joplin, Missouri, Ed Landreth was a very successful oilman during the middle of the twentieth century. In 1918, Landreth's successful father sent him to Breckenridge, Texas, to sell machinery to the oil and gas drillers, a segment of the family business, Landreth Machinery Company, which needed a boost. There he peddled a leather-belted drilling motor long enough to realize the oil business was where he needed to be. After borrowing three thousand dollars from his brothers, Landreth would buy his first leases around Breckenridge and launch himself into the industry. After his first thirteen wells came up dry, he didn't lose hope, nor did his brothers, who loaned him an additional three thousand dollars, which he then turned into a string of twenty-seven straight producing wells and thus discovered the now legendary Ibex Oil Field. Landreth, an oil field hall of famer and long-time TCU trustee, left a legacy of overwhelming success, extreme generosity, and diligent community service that made him a pillar in the history of Fort Worth. Landreth Hall became the home for the inaugural Van Cliburn International Piano Competition in 1962, the same year Landreth passed away.

With the buildup now over and the competitors set in order, the sixteen-day grind (with two off days built in) began in earnest. The considerable number of competitors warranted two-part days during the opening round, spaced out to allow roughly six to seven performers per morning and afternoon slot for the first phase of round one. Every performance was treated equally with the utmost care and professionalism. Before the contest, the thirty-eight performers were each allotted an hour to come to Ed Landreth Hall to test out the eight available pianos in order to select the one they wished to perform on. The selection process took seven days to complete, with competitors selecting in order of their draw. The Cliburn Foundation owned two Steinways in the piano pool. The third was provided by the New York Steinway & Sons. The Kawai EX, which was one of ten concert grand pianos in the world, was made entirely by hand. The other pianos were a Baldwin SD-10, which was played by famed Cuban-born virtuoso Jorge Bolet on his tour of Japan as well as at Carnegie Hall. The Yamaha CG III was especially chosen for the piano pool at its factory for its debut at the Cliburn competition. Bösendorfer, which sent their Imperial Concert Grand, stood alone as the largest piano in the world. The Bechstein Model EN piano came complete with a full-page ad in the Cliburn program, in which each piano company participated, but Bechstein's ad contained quotes from Liszt, Wagner, Debussy, and Strauss, expressing their strong satisfaction with this brand of instrument. The American Steinway provided by the Cliburn Foundation bore a plaque honoring Van's mother Rildia Bee and had been utilized by competitors in the 1977, 1981, and 1985 Cliburn competitions. This same piano had accompanied Van Cliburn to the White House for his recital for President Reagan and Soviet President Mikhail Gorbachev in December of 1987. Each piano came along with a company representative and at least one piano technician charged with all maintenance issues. Most of the competitors chose the Steinway, which delighted their representatives. The Kawai piano company sent five piano technicians to the concert aiming to show the world the remarkable performance of their pianos. This brand display was indicative of the business side of music, which was clearly visible here. Sadly, none of the thirty-eight competitors selected a Kawai.

    As the competition kicked off, Maestro John Giordano opened the event with welcoming remarks, and he introduced the jury to the audience. Seating at Landreth Hall was unreserved for the preliminaries, so people showed up early to grab prime seats. The competition's initial performer, David Buechner, received added applause from the crowd for drawing first. Alexei's number twenty-seven put him on stage two days later. His time was spent practicing at his temporary home. The Wilcoxes made themselves invisible during his preparation. Their home, now a mini concert hall, was filled with long hours of Alexei's masterful tune-up. The days at Landreth Hall were busy and the music exquisitely rich. With so much on the line for these young prodigies, the crowd was always in for a treat whenever they attended. The initial day began at 9:30 a.m. and saw fifteen competitors before concluding at seven fifteen in the evening. The jurors would hear many sonatas by Scriabin, Rachmaninov, and Mozart, as well as more works by Bach, Chopin, Schumann, and Liszt. The jury members patiently made their confidential marks for each competitor. The media reported daily on the activity, and audience fervor spread quickly. Finally, on the third day—a Monday—Alexei's moment came.

This final day of the opening round consisted of twelve pianists performing from 9:30 a.m. to 6:00 p.m. with a short break for lunch. Alexei woke early, as he was the day's first performer, and clumsily dressed in a white turtleneck underneath his new dark suit. He looked to Susan and asked in his new language, "Is good?" wondering if his appearance was suitable. As Susan pondered her simple response, she used the old, tried-and-true method of pointing and shrugging. As masterful as Alexei was with a piano, he wouldn't have known the faux pas of wearing white athletic socks with his suit. When she pointed that out to him, he simply shrugged right back. He nonchalantly sought out Jon Wilcox to verify this dress code violation. As it turned out, Alexei, as per his culture, valued Jon's opinion more than Susan's. Jon confirmed the problem. However, Alexei liked how the socks felt and decided that this small wardrobe malfunction wasn't important enough to correct, so he walked out onto the Landreth Hall stage wearing his white socks. His socks received a hearty chuckle, albeit muffled, from the crowd. This wardrobe indiscretion would endear him to many of the people in attendance. As distracting as it was to the audience, his brilliance on the piano captured everyone. Susan and John sat in the first of two rows, which were reserved for host families and other competitors. The Wilcoxes were as close as Alexei would have to family for as long as he remained in this competition. They had their favorite and would support him every inch of the way.

The opening rounds found Ed Landreth Hall slightly over half full, with the bigger crowds arriving in the evenings and weekends. The opening performance was phase one of the preliminary round. The second phase of round one would begin in the evening at the conclusion of phase one. Phase two would entail two time slots for each competitor to play two twenty-five-minute recitals. Before the competition even began, each selected competitor had submitted their repertoires to fill the required time slots in the respective rounds. If jury Chairman Giordano or the committee felt a work wasn't conforming to the time requirements, they might make suggestions to help them. The committee would not suggest any works to play, but they would only offer advice to help them stay within the boundaries of time. The competitors were directed to select their own programs within the newly expanded repertoire without influence from the Cliburn.

During the preliminaries, the crowds were learning about these artists for the first time. Without much fanfare, the Cliburn emcee welcomed the audience to the day's performances, which included the opening performance by nineteen-year-old Alexei Sultanov from the Soviet Union. Alexei, white socks and all, took his seat at centerstage. He breathed deeply, then opened with the popular Bach Italian Concerto BWV 971, followed by a Haydn Sonata in E major, then the arpeggio-rich Etude in C minor Op. 25 no. 12 by Chopin, and concluded with Rachmaninoff's Etude in E flat minor Op. 39 no. 5. Alexei moved with the power and elegance of a much more seasoned performer. His lightning-quick hands blurred as his aggressive style of play and notable huge sound filled the hall. His compositions, modified slightly for time, hit their mark. The crowd's excitement was palpable, and it grew as he stood up upon completion, drawing a standing ovation.

After his initial recital was completed, Alexei joined the Wilcoxes backstage. They showered him with congratulatory remarks, which he shockingly brushed off, showing his displeasure with his performance. He politely thanked Jon and Susan for their comments, but his ravishing hunger now took over. He was whisked off to a Wilcox favorite, Sushi Arlington, on the corner of Green Oaks Road and Little Road. The Japanese American owner had worked with Susan at the YMCA and often took care of them when they came. Alexei discovered his love of sushi, mainly hamachi kama, which is the fatty and juiciest part of the yellowtail fish. He also especially loved the sake. Alexei's performance left him drained and far less animated at dinner. The subject of the performance came up during the meal. As would become customary, Alexei described his recent performance solely in terms of its shortcomings. Jon Wilcox used his Russian to carefully pull out every detail they could think to inquire about. Alexei was extremely critical of his performance when everyone else considered it a tremendous success. In his recital, he failed to grasp the magnitude of his performance and its reception, instead focusing solely on several unnoticed errors he allegedly committed.

Nonetheless, this initial performance marked the point in time when Alexei appeared on the Cliburn's radar. The audience questions ensued: "Who was this kid? What is his name again? Did you see his socks?" The media members noted their reactions. The major Soviet contender, Alexander Shtarkman, arrived as an early favorite to place, but Alexei had certainly made himself known to jurors. The preliminaries were often grueling for the jurors. After hearing several pieces repeatedly performed, Chopin turned out to be quite popular for these competitors, and jurors felt the associated weariness seep in. Phase two of the preliminaries was important for Alexei. He performed Mozart's Piano Sonata no. 10 (C Major K, 330), Liszt's Mephisto Waltz no. 1, and Prokofiev's second war Sonata no. 7 in B flat major Op. 83. His Mephisto Waltz performance left the audience with an unforgettable moment. As Alexei's face grew drenched in sweat, each sharp movement of his head sent sweat droplets flying everywhere. Alexei played the devilish dance piece with such gusto and power that, in the middle of the piece, a string snapped inside the piano. Alexei played on without missing a beat. Most patrons were none the wiser.

As Alexei concluded the Mephisto Waltz, but not yet finished with his entire performance, he abruptly stood up, bowed graciously, then took two steps back and pointed toward the piano, as if to acknowledge his partner. Alexei then quickly left the stage. The crowd was somewhat baffled, as he left the stage without performing his final piece, the Prokofiev Sonata no. 7. The audience's confusion was cleared up minutes later when the Cliburn emcee announced, "Ladies and Gentlemen, we have a broken string on the piano, and we are going to try and fix it." This elicited thunderous applause from the crowd; many of whom were now standing. Most had never seen a piano string snap during a performance before. After the twenty-minute impromptu intermission, the string was repaired, tuned, and Alexei returned to the stage for his Prokofiev finale. The energy from the crowd had not waned, and they soon became super charged as Alexei imposed his creative will upon the piano. Jurors felt the crowd's response, even when it was taboo to consider this while judging. People cried out and clapped loudly for their "Little Russian."

The sole Soviet juror was Sergei Dorensky, an active touring pianist and chairman of the piano faculty at Moscow's Conservatory, where he had been teaching since 1957. Alexei knew him well, as he had been a juror for the last Tchaikovsky competition in which Alexei had been expelled. Dorensky was asked by Chairman Giordano to abstain from voting for any of his countrymen. This was a common practice amongst international competitions to avoid ballot nepotism. Jurors were typically barred from voting for contestants if they had familial, teaching, or professional ties to them. This concept was at the center of Van Cliburn's fabled win in 1958, as the Soviet jurors rebuked the internal politics and awarded the prize to an American when the world expected quite the opposite. The term "block voting" had appeared in the years following Van's triumph in Moscow. Soviet jurors became notorious for their systematic predetermined voting practices, essentially rigging the votes in favor of the Soviets. Since jury tampering was still a possibility, the Cliburn Foundation made every effort to select jurors of good moral standing, coupled with a strict set of rules that ensured the fairest possible outcome. Giordano implemented a pass-or-fail voting system for the jurors. The competitors would receive, after each preliminary and semifinal round, a pass or fail from each judge that was allowed to vote. If a competitor received a pass from all the jurors, then they automatically moved on to the next round. After the unanimous selections were cleared, the competitors with the most pass votes would move on. The jury chairman, Giordano, would not vote except to break a tie. For the preliminary round, the top twelve competitors receiving a "pass" would move on to the semifinals. From there, six moved on to the finals with the same scoring system. The final count entailed jurors ranking the final six in numerical order, making the winner the competitor with the most first-place votes. Lastly, to hold the jurors accountable, they were required to sign each ballot they submitted.

At the end of the preliminary round, the jurors retired to the jury room to deliberate over the contestants' performances. Their difficult charge to select the twelve best to move onto the semifinal round was no small task. The loyal audience members loved to try to guess who would make it. Many had played so well that they all but staked claims with their performances to advance into the semifinal round. The audience all had their personal favorites. Alexei had performed beautifully, but he wasn't alone. Whispers around the hall seemed to quickly become uniform. People felt Alexei Sultanov was leading the pack as far as showmanship. His entertainment value was miles ahead of the others. He had, after all, broken a string during his second phase performance. People loved how they could see sweat flying off his forehead and landing upon the piano. There was something mesmerizing about the tremendous power coming from this petite teenager. The *Fort Worth Star Telegram* reporter for the Cliburn, Wayne Lee Gay, knew enough after the prelims to rank him as likely to make the finals. While Alexei was popular, he was far from winning, and he had impressive company around him. Nobody envied the difficult task of sending twenty-six qualified pianists home early.

After two hours of waiting, the remaining audience was lit up by the production lights on and near the stage, signaling the start of the announcement. It had been the television crew interviewing the jurors for the Cliburn documentary that caused the long delay. The thirty-eight contestants, all having returned, sat in the first two rows of Ed Landreth Hall. Van Cliburn opened the ceremony with several remarks about the quality of the competitors and the importance of what they were undertaking. Bernie Appel, the president of Fort Worth–based Radio Shack, took the microphone next, as one of the Cliburn's main financial supporters, and surprised each competitor with a brand-new, portable compact disc player. Van Cliburn then returned to the podium to call each of the thirty-eight competitors individually to the stage to receive their compact disc players, plus an envelope with a personal note from him that included a crisp one-hundred-dollar bill. Each competitor posed on stage with Van for a picture. Chairman Giordano retook the podium to make the official announcement of the semifinalists. Alexei felt good about his chances, but his experience taught him that anything could happen. He didn't have to wait long. The first Russian name was

Alexander Shtarkman. Alexei didn't have wait much longer. He was now a semifinalist. The Wilcoxes couldn't mask their huge smiles in their middle, orchestra-level seats. As the remaining names were called to the stage, the faces of those left in their seats grew somber as their reality set in. An early exit surely strikes a blow to one's confidence. Alexei was still surprised to learn that he wasn't going home just yet. As subjective as a jury can be, hearing one's name called brings with it a certain amount of surprise and relief. The Wilcoxes wouldn't have to resume their regular lives yet, which made them happy. The private concerts at home would continue.

As the final name was read, the radio, television, and newspaper reporters rushed to the stage to interview the new semi-final competitors resulting in a melee in front of the stage. Several of the early departures were later quoted as saying negative things about the process, the competition, and even the jurors. A snub in the first round always resulted in expected backlash from those clearly holding exceptional talent. The jurors selected eleven of the twelve semi-finalists unanimously. The twelve semifinalists were lined up on stage to take a group photo. Happiness was on display, but each knew what lay ahead. Three of the four Soviets made it through. American David Buechner, the first to play, was not called to the stage.[1]

17
Semifinal Round

Peter Rosen, the Emmy Award–winning documentarian, was here in Fort Worth producing a music documentary for the Cliburn, *Here to Make Music*, along with a tremendous team that would document every performance of every round, a monumental three-week task. This soon-to-be critically acclaimed documentary introduced the music of the Cliburn competition to a much wider audience, making Rosen a VIP in the Cliburn circles. Rosen, an avid classical music fan, loved Rachmaninov as much as Alexei. Rosen would later fuel the Alexei fire significantly when he shared with the world that Alexei's version of Rachmaninoff's Piano Concerto no. 2 was his favorite ever. Rosen became a vocal champion for Alexei, which helped further his career.

The semifinal round of the Van Cliburn Piano Competition called for the remaining twelve competitors to perform again in two parts. The first part was a one-hour solo recital of a selected work, which included newly commissioned work by William Schuman called *Chester, Variations for Piano*. William Schuman's commissioned work was orchestrated by none other than Van Cliburn himself. Schuman had been the president of the Juilliard School when Van attended school there. The two had met and initiated a lifelong friendship. Prior to that, Schuman had won the first Pulitzer Prize awarded for music in 1943 for Secular Cantata no. 2: *A Free Song*, an adaptation of several poems by Walt Whitman. Schuman then became the first composer to be commissioned by the United States government. He was fresh off receiving the National

Medal of Arts when he was approached by Van and his Cliburn Committee to compose a piece for this year's Cliburn competition. *Chester* was warmly received, and its popularity took off. Shortly after *Chester* made its debut at the 1989 Cliburn competition, Schuman went on to be honored by the Kennedy Center in Washington, DC, for his contributions to music.

    The second part of the semifinal round, played on a separate occasion, was a chamber music performance alongside the Tokyo String Quartet in which they would perform a piano quintet by either Brahms, Franck, Schumann, or Dvorak. The Tokyo String Quartet, one of the world's most well-known quartets, had played the chamber music portion for the Cliburn competition since 1977. Their brutal schedule called for each of the twelve semifinalists a ninety-minute rehearsal and their subsequent performance in the span of six days. Chamber music, which entails a back-and-forth interplay between the artists, is notoriously less stressful on the contestants compared to the remainder of the competition. The stress falls instead upon the Tokyo String Quartet who must learn the ins and outs of each performer's playing style along with the different pieces of music the competitors could choose from. High stakes had now grown for the remaining competitors. Hosts' homes were filled with the incredible sounds of preparation. These twelve competitors each wanted to taste the finals. The pressure intensified, as did the nervousness. Alexei spent his time furiously practicing at the Wilcoxes' Steinway. These increased stakes grew the audience larger, and the excitement followed suit. Alexei's solo recital program on day two of the semis gave the audience and, more importantly, the jurors a Beethoven *Appassionata* for the ages. This same *Appassionata* would one day change his life forever. He followed with Chopin's Sonata no. 3 in B minor Op. 58 and lastly the required *Chester*[1], by Schuman.

    Alexei's compact stature was lost on the crowd as he played with unshakeable ferocity, coupled with his full mop of hair waving around. The audience felt entranced with his passion, as he seemed to grow more excited as he played. His motions were so vigorous that he left sweat across the keys and upon the floor. He was rewarded with a standing ovation lasting nearly a minute. After his performance, Alexei collapsed backstage into a chair, huffing to catch his breath. Once he quenched his thirst with a glass of water and regained his composure, he found the Wilcoxes waiting near the backstage entrance and off he went. The Wilcoxes were giddy

Alexei performs with the Tokyo String Quartet. *Dace Collection*

with excitement over his performance. They now cautiously shared their praise with him, knowing he might not agree. They were correct. Alexei continued to find fault in his performances much to the chagrin of the Wilcoxes, who were privy to the buzz of the audience. Alexei's continual grumblings to the Wilcoxes about his performance seemed to escalate this fairytale that they were witnessing. Alexei seemed oblivious to the impact he was leaving upon the audience. Everyone increasingly wanted to talk to him and ask him questions whenever he showed his face at Landreth Hall. The restless media and people with access to Alexei pushed him for a story. This kid from the Soviet Union and his rudimentary, thickly-accented English became one of the media darlings. He, though, preferred to be at home with the Wilcoxes practicing the piano or playing Jon's Atari. He opened for a few people, including the competitors, but preferred those speaking his native tongue, which were few. His English had grown in a very short time to the equivalency of a six-year-old, making having a full conversation very difficult. Three days later, Alexei's turn at the Chamber Music segment provided the Piano Quintet in A Major Op. 81 by Dvorak alongside the Tokyo String Quartet.

Shtarkman gave the audience all it could handle in his solo recital with *Pictures at an Exhibition* by Russian Modest Mussorgsky, as well as his interpretation of the *Chester*. Shtarkman showed his complete mastery of the chamber music portion with the Piano Quintet in F Minor by Cesar Franck. A story would break that Shtarkman's knowledge of the Franck piece dwarfed the accompanying Tokyo Quartet's so much that he schooled them in rehearsal on how to correctly play along with him. His performance was tops for many in the audience.

Alexei's very impressive first two rounds made him the hot topic around the lobbies of Landreth Hall. He had tough company, though. Benedetto Lupo left a remarkable impression on the jury and earned vocal adulation from the audience. Jean-Efflam Bavouzet played the most memorable rendition of the *Chester*, which would earn him special considerations at the end. He accompanied that with stirring recitals of Ravel's *Gaspard de la Nuit* and Liszt's Sonata in B Minor.

The deliberation by the jurors over the potential finalists began immediately once the last semifinal performance concluded at around ten forty-five on the final evening of the semifinals. Most of the audience remained on hand for the announcement of the finalists. Many of the competitors had left town for home, as the disappointment was too much, or they had other affairs to attend to. The jurors' work now was increasingly more difficult, and their scrutiny was heightened. Their ballots were tabulated and certified after each round by Dr. Scott Cutler, a computer science professor at Rice University in Houston, as well as William Biggs from the accounting firm of Coopers and Lybrand. The audience was restless as they waited impatiently for word. After an extraordinarily long wait, the lights flickered in the lobby, signaling all back into Landreth Hall to take their seats, which didn't take long. Those snacking at the Cliburn Café quickly polished off their light fares and downed their champagne. Finally, at one fifteen in the morning, the film crew's lights were clicked on, illuminating the stage. The stage piano was gone, replaced now by a podium and chairs. The twelve remaining competitors smiled nervously each time Peter Rosen's crew flashed the camera lights in their faces.

The jury was now seated on stage for the announcement. Van Cliburn's night was just getting started, as he strolled elegantly to the podium. His comments covered the splendid performances from the remaining twelve competitors, and several remarks were aimed at the seventy-eight-year-old William Schuman and his *Chester*. His graciousness and charm grabbed everyone's attention. Each of the competitors were awarded high-end headphones for their compact disc players by the Tandy Corporation as semifinal gifts. The pleasantries and mounting suspense ended as John Giordano wearily reached the podium. He introduced the jurors once again and thanked them for their service and hard work for the Cliburn. The finalists were then unveiled. Shtarkman, as expected, had made it. He was joined by Tian Ying, Benedetto Lupo, Jose Carlos Cocarelli, and two Soviets, Elisso Bolkvadze and Fort Worth's newest sensation, Alexei Sultanov. Each name called brought with it a huge applause and some host family euphoria. When Alexei's name was read, the Wilcoxes joined the crowd's monstrous applause. Alexei had made it! His internal confidence now soared as he realized his unique situation. The Soviets were flexing their muscles here at the Van Cliburn, and the crowd certainly loved "the little Russian."

Faizul Sultanov had caught a signal several times on the Golos Ameriki radio broadcast but never in a way that tipped him off to Alexei's progress. In fact, the families would remain in the dark about Alexei for the duration of the competition. Dace yearned for updates from Faizul each day, as did his friends and family. Radios in the Soviet Union remained the primary source of news and electronic entertainment at that time for most people, so its value was high amongst Soviets. Faizul would spend hours carefully turning the tuning knob on the radio until he found a signal that carried the Cliburn. His efforts were extremely unfruitful. The inbound radio signal consisted mainly of white noise with off-and-on breakthroughs of the ongoing performances, which rarely lasted long enough to decipher the unfolding plot. Faizul's efforts on Golos Ameriki produced little aside from the crackled report that Alexei may have made it to the second round. In Riga, the Sultanov's owned a small and very crude radio. Janis inched carefully around the dial, hoping to capture its difficult signal. His efforts rarely brought forth much to hear as the signal remained tough to capture.

The next day, in Fort Worth, the six finalists were ushered to the Fort Worth Stockyards at the Cowtown Coliseum for each competitor's first rodeo experience. Afterward, they were hauled down the street to Billy Bob's, the country and western nightclub that boasts itself the World's Largest Honky Tonk.[1] This must have been a confusing scene for the six foreign finalists, who were experiencing country music, cowboys and their attire for the first time.

18
Final Round

The final round warranted a larger venue due to increased interest from ticket buyers. The Cliburn Foundation had arranged the move after prior Cliburn competitions had proven this to be useful. The new venue was the roomy JFK Hall at the Tarrant County Convention Center located in downtown Fort Worth. The convention center's gargantuan fourteen-city-block coverage, resembling a flying saucer, would stand in the shadows of an infamous former precinct of downtown known as Hell's Half Acre. This dusty half-acre block sprang up in the 1870s as a rest stop for cattle drives headed north to Kansas. Due to its boomtown nature, the downtown area quickly assumed a more devious nature. The bevy of saloons, brothels, gambling parlors, and hotels brought with it rampant lawlessness and violence. Hell's Half Acre became a known stop for the likes of Wyatt Earp, Butch Cassidy, the Sundance Kid, and Doc Holliday. After the violence reached unprecedented levels, the city was forced to shut most of the businesses down, including the White Elephant Saloon, known for its live entertainment and grandeur as much as its gun fights and sinister clientele.

One hundred years later, the JFK Hall welcomed the Eighth Van Cliburn International Piano Competition. The JFK Hall, in fact, was named after another notable event. On November 21, 1963, President John F. Kennedy would visit and sleep in the Hotel Texas, just feet from the future site of the Tarrant County Convention Center, the night before he was gunned down in his open-air motorcade in Dallas. This now re-commercialized convention center contained ample space for the heavily sought-after seats. The modern intimacy of the Ed Landreth Hall was replaced with a packed multi-purposed auditorium of around three thousand concentrated classical music lovers. The JFK Hall, which sat inside the convention center, contained continental seating, which meant no center aisle. This final round drew the classical music world's undivided attention in as much as the news media could broadcast. Without the invention of the internet yet, a multitude of radio, television, and news wires were utilized exclusively and extensively.

The finals were an honor in themselves, although these competitors weren't there for such trivial things. Performers of this magnitude knew what this victory could mean for their careers. It would open the door to a first-class section of performing artists. These doors, not previously available, would come flying open to whoever had the Van Cliburn winner tag to their name.

The championship round called for each of the six competitors to play twice over a three-day period. One performance entailed a concerto with the Fort Worth Chamber Orchestra and the second with the Fort Worth Symphony Orchestra. Polish American Stanislaw Skrowaczewski, from the Manchester Halle Orchestra, would conduct each performance. Skrowaczewski was a piano prodigy as a child but suffered a hand injury during World War II that ended his playing career and pushed him into a renowned career as a conductor and composer. The finals were a tall order for most with so much now on the line. Alexei had devised a hypothetical plan—months prior—should this moment ever arrive, and so the rehearsal at the Wilcoxes' home and at the hall went into overdrive. Alexei brought in Vladimir Viardo, the Soviet winner of the 1973 Van Cliburn Competition and current assistant professor to Alexei's professor Lev Naumov. As a very accomplished international pianist, Viardo came as a coach for Alexei and brought his outgoing demeanor with him. During the final rehearsal, Viardo made such a scene, commanding not only Alexei but also the entire Fort Worth Symphony accompaniment, that the conductor, Stanislaw Skrowaczewski, grew enraged and shouted at him to be silent. The pressure here clearly was heavy and palpable.

To win this competition, one must play inspired piano and move the jury. Mistakes would be noted but could be overlooked if their interpretive performance of the music was recognized as exceptional. Now was the time to pull out all the stops. The Cliburn scheduled a break in the action for the day prior to the finals. In place of the competition was a memorial concert honoring pianist Steven De Groote, who had passed away just a week prior to the beginning of this competition, due to multiple organ failure brought on by complications of AIDS. De Groote, a South African, had taken gold in the 1977 Cliburn competition, as well as winning Best Performance of a Commissioned Work and Best Performance of the Chamber Music, making him the only winner in the history of the Cliburn to take all three prizes. As an accomplished pianist, De Groote was named the artist in residence at Texas Christian University in Fort Worth. He was also an amateur pilot and, in 1985, barely survived a horrific plane crash with his instructor. Several former gold winners from the Cliburn returned to play at the memorial honoring De Groote. Van Cliburn gave a touching eulogy that remained fresh on people's minds and elicited many tears from the audience.

The finals began on Thursday with Alexander Shtarkman's Mozart Concerto no. 21 in C Major, K. 467, and secondly a technically proficient Prokofiev Concerto No. 3 in C Major, Op. 26, which surprisingly came off flawless but relatively unimpressive to the jurors. Next came Tian Ying, who performed his Chopin Piano Concerto no. 2 and Beethoven's Piano Concerto no. 4 to a much more receptive jury. Friday evening found Elisso Bolkvadze beautifully playing the same Mozart's Concerto as Shtarkman, with the chamber orchestra, and the Saint Saenz's Piano Concerto no. 2 in G minor Opus 22, with the symphony orchestra. Second on the night's schedule was the Soviet fireball. Alexei was so nervous, with so much at stake, that he struggled to sleep the night before. He spent several hours the morning of, sitting at the Wilcoxes' Steinway, touching up and imagining that night's performance in his mind. He got so caught up in his final preparation that he forgot to eat anything before he had to leave for his evening performance, which only added to his tension.

As his name was called, Alexei walked quickly on stage to his Steinway as the audience welcomed him. He adjusted his seat, upwards. He sat, paused briefly, took a deep breath, and began. His performance with the symphony did not disappoint. In a move reminiscent of Van Cliburn thirty-one years prior, and perhaps equally as apropos, Alexei chose a reliable friend, Mr. Frederick Chopin and his masterpiece Piano Concerto no. 2 in F minor Op. 21. Alexei flew around the keyboard with the dexterity of a surgeon, yet with the potency of a man twice his size. His uniqueness and style enthralled the hypersensitive crowd. He did, indeed, pass the first test.

When Alexei strolled to centerstage the next evening, in his tails for his chamber piece, his heart raced, and his senses acute. The crowd came prepared to hear the wonderkid play. His final piece, now well ingrained into his memory, was quite possibly his most impressive display of his talent. Written by Sergei Rachmaninov between 1900 and 1901, the iconic Piano Concerto no. 2 in C minor Op. 18 made Rachmaninov world famous. A piece so renowned that Objectivist author Ayn Rand's 1943 classic novel, The *Fountainhead*, cites the composition as a musical work capable of acting as a surrogate for a man's achievement. This piece allowed Alexei to showcase his distinctive heavy fingering style of power and skill. Alexei played not for himself that night but for his audience and the jury. As he played his eyes closed, fully enraptured by the music. His fingers seemed possessed; his creativity exploded upon his grand piano. The tempo was slightly faster than traditionally heard, but in Alexei's noted fashion. The audience quickly folded into his performance. The untrained ear could almost feel what Rachmaninov felt as he pulled himself out of a deep depression and returned into the joys of life through this work.

Alexei, that night with the Fort Worth Orchestra at his side, gave the attending audience and those capable of listening elsewhere, some through great difficulty, a moment in time of pure captivation. People purportedly were seen wiping tears from their faces. The juror box, which sat motionless, was no different. One member of the jury reportedly wept discreetly into her hand. She had her favorite. She was not alone. The acoustics of the JFK Hall were not especially excellent, given its design for a wide range of potential events. The large size of the venue, not built with acoustics in mind, benefitted those who played louder than others. Alexei stole the show and confirmed to all in earshot that he—not Shtarkman, not Lupo, not Cocarelli—was the best. The jurors could not overlook this moment even though they were trained not to be swayed by audience reaction. At his conclusion, the crowd launched from their seats in roaring applause that easily lasted two minutes. This audience yearned for more. Alexei stood, smiled boyishly, and bowed deeply at the attention and praise he was receiving. Relief and exhaustion settled over him. He knew they appreciated what he had done. In his characteristic manner backstage,

Alexei Sultanov performing at 1989 Van Cliburn International Piano Competition.
Dace Collection

Alexei fell into his critical self, as the Wilcoxes grabbed hold of him and pulled him close. They enveloped him in a huge congratulatory embrace. Alexei was visibly tired. His work was now done, and it was left to the jury to decide.

The Wilcoxes, buzzing with excitement, drove him home to rest and ponder what he had and hadn't done well enough. Saturday held the last two competitors. Cocarelli, a polyglot, gave the thirsty audience a wonderous Chopin Piano Concerto No. 2 in F minor Opus 21 and followed with a Brahms Concerto No. 1 in D minor Opus 15 performance played with the symphony orchestra. Final up was the tri-lingual Benedetto Lupo, whose sophisticated and romantic style upon his Chopin Piano No. 2 in F minor Opus 21, left the crowd incredulous. With his rendition of the Rachmaninov Piano Concerto No. 2 to round out the competition, he had given it his everything and left a serious mark on the jurors. The atmosphere was electric and tense with universal knowledge that a gold medal would be awarded on Sunday the eleventh at 5 p.m. during a special ceremony. Someone's life was about to change forever.

JFK Hall opened early at three in the afternoon on Sunday. The awards ceremony took place on the day after the finals concluded, making it an event of its own. The mood this day was noticeably anxious and excited, as the competition was now over, and the results were set to be released. There would be encore performances by the finalists, but the votes had been tabulated, and certified, and somewhere backstage, two accountants held the answer, but were unavailable to anyone. The hall was awash in activity as people, including Fort Worth mayor Bob Bolen, moved around everywhere: the music hall, the lobby, the bar, and even outside, where a few pulled on a cigarettes in the customary Texas heat. Those excited enough to return for this final moment found many of the competitors back in the building, sitting in the first couple rows, waiting cautiously for the ceremony to kickstart. The chatter around the hall continued, with most people talking with one another about who would win. People simply needed an outlet for their nervous energy. Seating opened to first come, first served, so people were free to move around close to the stage if they so wished.

The six remaining competitors were visibly exhausted from the brutal pace of the last three weeks, as was the stoic jury. Alexei had a slow morning and slept longer than normal since the pressure was gone. He chatted with several of his co-competitors and his undercover Soviet handlers but mainly counted the minutes, as did most of the finalists. Shtarkman and he had exchanged pleasantries about the days past, but both felt inside that they had defeated the other. Marina, the KGB chauffeur, sat behind Alexei to the left and cheered unreservedly for her countrymen like they were her own children. Her duties, nearly complete, had given her a guarded interest in the outcome. A celebratory party awaited everyone at the luxurious Worthington Hotel just down the street. This was the finale of more than twenty official Cliburn parties and easily the most celebrated. The jurors, competitors, patrons, staff, and supporters would finally let down their guard and revel in what had just transpired.

The results were announced live on stage with the Cliburn hierarchy seated to the right of the podium. Peter Rosen's lights and cameras were everywhere. The event was broadcast live on NPR. Cliburn executive director Richard Rodzinski opened the ceremonies with a bevy of thank-yous. He gave a genuine compliment to the crowd for sharing their lives with the Van Cliburn Competition. Then he thanked the jury for completing a most difficult assignment and doing it well. Next up was Cliburn Chairwoman Susan Tilley, the former Miss Dallas and Miss Texas runner-up, who offered up praise and thanks for the many important people who helped put this year's Cliburn competition together. Maestro John Giordano took the podium next to introduce the jurors, who were seated on the stage as well. He addressed the monumental task that they were charged with and thanked them profusely. Van Cliburn's turn came;

he shared some thoughtful remarks about this year's competition and the importance of classical music to the world. "For the potential audiences around the world, there are not even enough artists," Cliburn shared.

Then came the moment of truth. The winner's announcement came with its own special flair from wildly popular comedic actor Dudley Moore, of *Arthur* movie fame, which had been a huge box office hit in 1981. The Cliburn Foundation was in the habit of hiring notable celebrities to emcee the award ceremonies, and in this case, at a cost of ten thousand dollars. The emcee for the prior 1985 competition was F. Murray Abraham, who starred in the movie *Amadeus*. After Dudley stumbled around his script, written by Denise Chupp, thanking the people and humorously ridiculing himself for butchering their names, he took ten envelopes from Rodzinski. His reference to the competitors' exceptional methods of wrestling the black beast brought laughter from the crowd. Dudley, an accomplished jazz pianist and composer, utilized his time on stage to allow for maximum appreciation for each award.

The competitors all sat near one another and their host families. Alexei had snuck a glass of champagne into the second row beneath his chair, which made his Marina chuckle as she witnessed it. The new Steven De Groote Memorial Award for Best Performance of Chamber Music and a thousand-dollar prize went to several people: Jean Efflam Bavouzet, Jose Carlos Cocarelli, Kevin Kenner, and Alexander Shtarkman. The highest-ranking pianist from the United States and a thousand-dollar prize went to Kevin Kenner. The award for Best Performance of Commissioned Work and a gold watch went to Bendetto Lupo. The Jury's Discretionary Award for Non-Finalist along with one thousand dollars went to Pedro Burmeister, Kevin Kenner, Wolfgang Manz, and Andrew Wilde. Dudley then paused briefly, audibly exhaled, and smiled before he began.

"Sixth place in the Eighth Van Cliburn International Piano Competition goes to Elisso Bolkvadze." After the announcement, Elisso shuffled from her seat and to the stage to accept her prize. Each award invoked several minutes of clapping, hand shaking, congratulations, and photographs. "Fifth place is Tian Ying." Dudley Moore carried on, "Fourth place goes to . . . Alexander Shtarkman." An audible gasp was heard from the crowd. Rosen's crew filmed a look of shock on Alexei and several other competitors as the announcement sank in. Moore sensed the gravity of the moment and allowed extra time to settle the room. Shtarkman took the stage as Cliburn's face held expressionless. The moment, and its associated drama, lasted well past its intention. "Third place in the Eighth Van Cliburn International Piano Competition goes to Benedetto Lupo." Alexei's smile grew wider as Lupo climbed to the stage. Lupo, a crowd favorite, took pleasure in the adulation and additional time to get settled after. There were just two competitors left. JFK Hall fell completely silent. Every ear listened intently for any sound from Moore's microphone. "Second place of the Eight Van Cliburn International Piano Competition goes to . . . Jose Carlos Cocareli!" The crowd fed the substantial noise with their shouts and cheers, as they now knew. As quickly as it came, it left. The room again fell silent for Dudley. "The winner of the 1989 Van Cliburn International Piano Competition is . . ."

Alexei Sultanov being named winner of 1989 Van Cliburn International Piano Competition. *Dace Collection*

19
The Cliburn Kid

There was an immediate ignition of applause from the standing crowd. A scene reminiscent of any high-profile sports championship after a last-second victory. Alexei had won the hearts of the Van Cliburn audience. He had demonstrated superiority on his instrument and command of his pieces. His message and communication of his music left an indelible impression on the jury. Alexei—fists clenched and arms raised in a V shape over his head—jumped from his seat and bounded up to the stage. He wore a smile that one might perceive as epic. He accepted the handshakes from Van, Dudley, Rodzinski, Tilley, and many more, but this was a blur. He stood proudly on stage in front of his peers and now the world, as his life took on expedited momentum. The six-foot-four Van leaned down to hang the medal around Alexei's neck, who stood a foot shorter. He also handed him an engraved silver trophy denoting Alexei Sultanov as the grand prize winner of the Lankford-Allison Memorial Award. There was an extended intermission so that everyone could celebrate Alexei's marvelous victory. The film crew raced around Alexei and those that ventured close to him. After a long while, the exhilaration from the crowd calmed down, and everyone returned to their seats. Each of the six finalists played a short encore performance. Alexei concluded the competition by playing the Chopin's E-Flat major Waltz, and then treated the audience to the Etude in C Minor Op. 10. The Eighth International Van Cliburn Piano Competition was ceremoniously closed.

Alexei Sultanov, the nineteen-year-old Soviet prodigy, knew very well that his life would never be the same. The onslaught of hugs, handshakes,

Alexei signing autographs. *Dace Collection*

congratulations, interviews, and autographs were joyous events. The migration of the celebration to the Worthington took longer than planned, but few cared. A black tie after-party dinner, which entertained some fourteen hundred guests—basically everyone Cliburn—would be held in the hotel's Grand Ballroom. The dinner menu included suckling pork roast, fried catfish, black-eyed-pea relish, and tables of culinary sweets. The remaining contestants and throngs of people swarmed around the new champion. Being the center of attention was incredibly uncomfortable for him—especially crowds of this size. Alexei knew very few of these people but did his best to play the part of victor. Dace was not there to comfort him and tell him it was okay. The first trip to the champagne fountain seemed to be a release from all this unwanted attention. Alexei was then ushered on stage and to the podium by Cliburn's most important advocate, Martha Hyder. More champagne was opened, this time with a ceremonial saber. Alexei was handed a glass, and a heavy toast was offered in his honor. He downed the entire glass in one gulp to the amusement of the crowd. It wasn't long until Alexei became visibly intoxicated, prompting several comments from attendees, but given the circumstances, these were held in check, as this was surely just a young man enjoying his finest hour.

Alexei, after several hours of fraternizing, was finally free to leave the party. The ride home in the Wilcoxes' car took forever, but allowed Alexei time to ponder what had just happened to him. His mind raced with thoughts, mostly of Dace, who still had no idea. The car had barely made it into the garage around midnight when out jumped Alexei, sprinting inside to the phone. Alexei used the Wilcoxes' house phone—with a little help from Bell telephone service and its three-dollar-per-minute rate—to dial the Abele's Riga home in the neighborhood of Mezaparks, which was well into the morning routine, being eight hours ahead. At roughly eight in the morning, Latvian time, with the KGB agent monitors clicking in, Dace's aunt Aina answered the phone. She recognized the voice on the other end instantly. Dace was still asleep upstairs, recovering from a minor toe surgery she had the day prior. She shrieked in Latvian to Dace upstairs, "Dace, wake up! Alexei is on phone!" She only had to say it once. Dace, instantly wide awake, hopped down the stairs on one leg to the phone. As the phone reached her ear, she called out, "Alosha," her pet name for him. She could hear something different in his voice. "What has happened?" she demanded. In rapid euphoric tones, Alexei blurted out in Russian, "We are going to live in America! Our dreams are coming true! I have won the competition! Now I can bring you over to America to experience this place!" The news took seconds to soak in. As Dace processed his news, she squealed her congratulations, not fully understanding the magnitude of what she had been told. Just hearing the excitement in his voice alone sent her soaring. Her love bubbling up, along with her longing to see him. Dace interrupted Alexei to ask when he would be coming home. Alexei didn't yet know anything as far as his return, but promised he would hurry. He had to attend several meetings regarding the next steps, but he would be home at the earliest possible time. The animated call lasted around fifteen minutes as Alexei gave her further detail of what had happened. The Abele family had since gathered around Dace and came to learn that he won. Dace repeated out loud as much as she could to the family during the call. Her excitement and cheering infected everyone, and an impromptu celebration erupted inside the house. It only subsided because Dace was due back to the hospital early for a follow-up on her toe.

Everyone at the hospital that morning experienced a euphoric, crazy woman who continued to scream and shout out loud, telling all who could hear about what Alexei had done. She wanted to share the news with everyone. It wouldn't take long before the news spread throughout Riga. Back in Fort Worth, the two KGB chauffeurs would be meeting with the Cliburn Foundation in the morning to iron out Alexei's early schedule and outline for the future. It became apparent to Rodzinski and the Cliburn staffers that, aside from their KGB duties, these agents also had rank with the GosKoncert. The meetings quickly pivoted into how Alexei would be managed and to firm up the financial arrangements. The Cliburn contract called for two years of management, as well as a multitude of concert bookings. The GosKoncert needed their Soviet champion to play only recitals they deemed appropriate. When the KGB had their meeting with their superiors in two days' time back in Moscow, they would report that the Cliburn Foundation, and mainly Rodzinski, would have ultimate control over Alexei's management with little assistance from GosKoncert. Rodzinski had used his political pull to stave off any attempt by GosKoncert to intercept Alexei. The Cliburn was in charge, and Alexei would not be sidetracked from his Cliburn obligations.

 The second phone call Alexei made after phoning Dace early that Sunday morning was to a neighbor of the Sultanovs in the town of Ramenskoye, as the Sultanovs didn't own a phone. The neighbor quickly banged on the apartment door where Natalia and Faizul had been nervous wrecks for weeks awaiting any news. They opened the door and took the incredible news as any overjoyed parents would. Their son had won, and their hearts burst with pride. Inevitably, they knew and celebrated the fact that their son's life would now be forever better off. Natalia felt a satisfying peace come over her. This was the tangible proof that all their efforts had not been in vain. Natalia's early prediction of being a slave to this child perhaps now became vindicated. The third and final call Alexei made was to his professor Lev Naumov at his home. Alexei, having fun in the moment, called out as Naumov answered the phone, "Lev Naumov, did you order the gold medal? Well, you got it!" In the Soviet Union, and Latvia especially, good news often spread faster by word of mouth, as it could be trusted more. Slowly but surely, the cities of Riga, Ramenskoye, Moscow, and, shortly later, the entire Soviet Union learned of Alexei's victory.

 The gold medal award at the Van Cliburn International Piano

Competition came with a cash prize of fifteen thousand dollars, which, for Alexei, was more money than he had ever seen in his life. This money could impact the lives of many people back home in the Soviet Union, if he desired. Alexei was now able to repay the family friends who lent the Sultanovs money to finance his trips to see Professor Naumov in Moscow as an early teen. The real reward though was the unimaginable artist representation and management that guaranteed him concert bookings all over the world. These recitals would happen in the most prestigious halls the world has to offer, and they now provided a solid income for its winner. The Cliburn Foundation's Denise Chupp became the de facto manager for Alexei, and she excelled at placing him throughout the world. This tireless and thankless job began years before, when Denise would write hundreds of Cliburn letters to presenters throughout the world to offer up the Cliburn medalists. These presenters would decide if this offer fit their venue's needs. It very often did. Compiling a list of interested presenters early on would help Denise set a medalist's schedule. She would try to match the artists with the most appropriate type of performance needs or concert series. This included the other finalists typically in descending order of desirability to presenters.

As per Cliburn's rules, Alexei would embark on a dizzying two-hundred-concert tour, which would last the next two years and would net him close to a quarter of a million dollars. Alexei was expected at recordings, interviews, music camps, performances, talk shows, radio broadcasts, and the ever-uncomfortable dinner parties. His social awkwardness, tiny stature, wild hair, and passionate style of playing made him a very marketable musician. A disagreement arose early between Richard Rodzinski and Denise Chupp over how best to manage their young gold medalist. Richard felt he was ready for the demand that was out there. He wanted to load up Alexei's performance calendar. Denise felt strongly that Alexei was too green and needed time to develop as a performer, thus having a softer schedule. Alexei's popularity and demand prevailed, so Denise was tasked with booking him all over the world. He would ultimately visit forty cities in his first six months under Cliburn management.

20
Victory Lap

Dace always believed that Alexei had wanted to move away from the Soviet Union to escape the familial and musical pressures that were thrust upon him at such an early age. He disliked practicing the piano immensely, but under his parent/teacher guidance that was all he ever did. Leaving the nest would likely give him his life back. The idea of living in the United States didn't seem like such a crazy idea now that he had some basis. He could play piano on his own terms and perhaps rekindle his love of the instrument that seemed to be waning as the years stretched on.

Immediately following Alexei's win at the Van Cliburn competition, he was thrust into the international spotlight. His name was broadcast across the global media. The pronunciation of his name was consistently butchered around the United States. His calendar became immediately full because of the efforts of his new manager, Denise Chupp. She received a multitude of invitations for Alexei to appear on national talk shows. Alexei's return to Moscow would be delayed until his waiting public was satisfied. Alexei flew to New York the week after winning the Cliburn for an appearance on the *Today Show*. Host Jane Pauley interviewed him briefly with the help of an interpreter. Alexei was able to answer her questions sufficiently enough with his primitive vocabulary. Then, his music was introduced to the national audience with a rapid snippet of a Chopin Etude—all jam packed into a two-minute segment. The unfolding scene must have been confusing to watch on television, as time would not allow Alexei anything but a flurry of hurried pianistic fragments. Alexei then flew to Washington, DC, on

June 17 for his scheduled performance at the John F. Kennedy Center for the Performing Arts. He headed to California three days later. Alexei was booked in Burbank the next day on *The Tonight Show Starring Johnny Carson*. Alexei opened his segment with a quick cut of a Chopin Etude and then took a seat next to Johnny's legendary desk for a little back and forth. Carson wore a curious smile, as if to mock a performance that had been so short and furious.

Carson began the conversation by asking him if he had learned any American phrases since he's been here. Alexei replied, "Mostly, I learn I need more practice, and I like Texas very much." This comment elicited some applause from the audience. Then Carson followed with, "Let me ask you, I'm sure you get asked this a lot. Now, you're nineteen and you're a good-looking young man. How about the American girls?" Alexei sheepishly grinned and replied, "Ummm, nice! I like them, but I didn't meet anybody because no time." The audience chuckled. Carson followed with, "Did you find America the way you wanted it? Any surprises in America?" Alexei responded, "Ahh, yes! For me surprise is anything, no, everything. The biggest surprise for me is winning the competition." While he was not smooth, Alexei managed to follow along nicely. Carson then closed with, "Well, I can see why you won it! You're marvelous!" Then as quickly as it began, it was over, with an appreciative applause from the audience. The next day he was scheduled to give his American debut recital at the Pasadena's Ambassador Auditorium. He showcased his wide-ranging, and nearly demonic playing style with several sonatas by Mozart and Beethoven. This new performing schedule would keep Alexei on the move for years to come.

Three weeks after claiming victory in Fort Worth and having finished up the preliminary business of playing a few necessary recitals, Alexei finally boarded a plane for Moscow. He was armed with a two-year contract, plenty of awards, fifteen thousand dollars, and an international piano competition title. He had not seen Dace in nearly two months with very little in the way of communication, either. Having completed his obligatory champion showcase performances and interviews, Alexei longed to see her. The eleven-hour flight was especially grueling for him, but he knew Dace would be there waiting for him. His anxiety grew with each passing hour. The alcohol they served him on the plane was the only thing that seemed to calm him. Faizul had made the required call to the KGB to alert them to Alexei's return. Dace had taken the long overnight train from Riga to Moscow, where she barely slept, to welcome Alexei home. Faizul met her at the Sheremetyevo International Airport in Moscow, obviously anxious to see him, too. Dace bought flowers for the newest Soviet hero. As the scheduled arrival time came and went, the flowers began to wilt.

The delayed flight landed several hours later, and tears burst forth as he finally appeared at the plane's door. Dace ran straight to him and jumped into his arms. The welcome home embraces lasted for five minutes with happiness aplenty. After his much-improved baggage was collected, the three headed to the Sultanov apartment in Ramenskoe. The reunion time was wonderful for all in the cramped apartment. After Alexei shared his tremendous tale, answered all the questions, and showed off his hardware, he produced some gifts he had brought back for them. He had bought an Apple II series computer complete with its floppy disk drive in the United States for Faizul, just so that he might resell it in Moscow. Computers could be sold for exorbitantly high prices in Moscow, as they were exceptionally rare and thus expensive. For Dace, Alexei oddly brought her back a green and gold bikini, which he shelled out a whopping one-hundred-thirty dollars for at Neiman Marcus. Bikinis were hardly a fashion item in the Soviet Union. He strangely didn't like when she wore it as it showed off more of her than he thought people should see. Even more peculiar was that Alexei failed to bring anything back for his mother, which caused her to get upset with him.

The visit home was fast and furious and lasted only two weeks, as he was booked at the Schleswig Holstein Musik Festival in northern Germany. Sadly, Dace would not be joining Alexei back in America just yet, but during his visit, her options were weighed. Alexei reaffirmed his intention to bring her to the United States with him, permanently if possible. Alexei had little interest in living back in the Soviet Union. Alexei's touring schedule was to begin immediately within the US, and he wasn't capable of stringing together a tourist visa for Dace in a short time. Leaving her behind was difficult, especially knowing the plan to move her would need time to implement. As the plan took shape, Alexei would travel back to Moscow to see Dace eight times between winning the gold in June 1989 and September 1990—mostly on his own dime.

Dace, in Alexei's absence, still studied in Moscow at the conservatory. She had been handpicked by her professor Fedorchenko to play in the Moscow Conservatory Symphony Orchestra. The conservatory orchestra's schedule had been taking her around Europe as one of the five orchestral cellists, which warranted Dace having a passport and visa. Dace's work with the Moscow Conservatory Symphony Orchestra afforded her a look outside the Soviet Union, which opened her eyes to the world. Soviet musical instruments also required a passport to travel. Dace's constant sidekick, Mr. Cello, was no exception. Soviet officials created a certain blue passport for Mr. Cello, which contained photos of each of his four sides. He had more documentation than she did. Mr. Cello's passport received the traditional entry/exit stamps for each foreign country they visited. With proper documentation in hand, Dace and the Moscow Conservatory Symphony Orchestra visited Belgium, France, and Spain, where she experienced many unique customs previously unknown to her. This was her first time outside the Soviet-controlled borders. Alexei's friendly rival and fellow Cliburn finalist, Sasha Shtarkman, had joined the conservatory orchestra at several stops as the piano soloist. The two conversed about the Cliburn and, more importantly, the wonders experienced in America. The visit to the Chapelle Notre-Dame-de-Pitie Church in the coastal town of Sanary-sur-Mer in the southeastern region of France further stoked her thirst for travel and adventure after she witnessed her first outdoor Christmas lights. She was enthralled with the idea of decorating the exterior of a building. Dace was ill-prepared for orchestra life and hoped her music career, wherever it went, kept her close to Alexei.

In the initial meetings to discuss his two-year contract, Alexei asked Rodzinski and the Van Cliburn Foundation to help him procure a working visa for Dace, allowing her to come to the US. The twenty-nine-year-old Denise Chupp headed up this difficult political maneuver. As Cliburn artistic administrator and now Alexei's manager, Denise handled most of the grind for the Cliburn artists' bookings. Things were never easy when dealing with so many different personalities maneuvering around the globe, but the unshakable Denise kept the machine humming along. Alexei, though, would test her limits. As difficult as he often made her job, Denise would later describe Alexei as the smartest person she ever met.[1]

21
Meeting God

On July 18, Alexei embarked on a three-concert, five-day tour of Michigan, followed by a trip to Pittsburgh to perform at the Great Wood Festival alongside the Pittsburgh Symphony Orchestra with that year's Cliburn conductor, Stanislaw Skrowaczewski. Next, on July 27, the prime-time television trifecta found Alexei in New York for the *Late Show with David Letterman*, where he again played a furious snippet, this time of Prokofiev's Seventh Piano Sonata, third movement. The scene on David Lettermen's taping was especially awkward. Alexei's performance was barely forty seconds in length, leaving many watching confused as to what just unfolded. Letterman's back and forth banter with Hal from the control room seemed to reduce Alexei's tuxedoed performance to a side show bit, which quickly disintegrated into Letterman's top ten list of ways he was going to lower his cholesterol. Tom Frost—the seven-time Grammy Award–winning senior executive producer for Sony Classical and Deutsche Grammophon—set the appearance up with help from Chupp. Frost had produced Vladimir Horowitz's recordings from 1963–1973 and again from 1985–1989, as a trusted friendship had blossomed between Horowitz and Frost. As a violinist by training, Frost would also become a long-time juror for the Van Cliburn competition.

Instant celebrity can be a hard pill to swallow, and Alexei had immediately been force-fed a horse pill. He was ill prepared for the attention he elicited, but there were a few perks that he enjoyed. Back at the hotel that evening, after the Letterman debacle, the phone rang, and Denise answered. Tom Frost was on the line and informed her that a limousine would be arriving shortly to pick up her and Alexei. Tom told her it was a surprise and to make sure she and Alexei were in that limousine. The two took the elevator to the ground floor at the prescribed time that evening and waited a few minutes by the curb. When the limousine arrived, Alexei and Denise were driven to one of the tall buildings in Manhattan where Tom Frost arrived simultaneously. Frost greeted them warmly and asked them to follow him inside the building. The three arrived at a high-rise apartment door where Frost looked at Alexei, smiled, and knocked on the door. A member of the household staff greeted them and welcomed them in.

Upon entering the apartment, there in the living room on a large couch watching a Spanish soap opera sat the greatest living pianist in the world, Vladimir Horowitz. Alexei's and Denise's jaws dropped. Frost, who had worked and recorded with Horowitz for nearly fifteen years, asked casually, "Maestro, what on earth are you doing?" The eighty-six-year-old Horowitz responded quite sharply, "Learning Spanish." Almost immediately, Horowitz's gaze turned toward Alexei, eyeballed him for a few seconds, and then launched into a rapid Russian dialogue with him. Alexei's nervousness was obvious to all. Denise and Tom stood by watching this entire scene unfold and both valiantly fought the urge to smile. Then minutes later, without warning, Horowitz motioned toward his living room. There it stood! Sitting in front of Alexei was Horowitz's world-famous concert grand Steinway. Alexei could not believe what was happening. Horowitz told Alexei in Russian to play for him. Alexei felt the weight of the moment instantly. Denise had never seen him so nervous. Alexei would admit later that this moment was the most terrifying of his life. He took a seat at the legendary Concert D #503 and carefully began to play Prokofiev's *Piano Sonata no. 7*, a piece that both pianists knew very well and that had been tortured that same day on the *Late Show*. The Letterman television audience of millions had nothing on his current audience of three. As Alexei played into the second movement, Horowitz, who had since walked over beside Alexei, stopped him amid a wildly chromatic part of the piece. Then, Horowitz waved Alexei to the side, sat down in his place and continued the piece. The small awestruck crowd couldn't contain their joy at what they were witnessing. Here, in front of just them, was a musical icon for the ages, Vladimir Horowitz, playing Prokofiev on his iconic Steinway, which had accompanied him across the world. In fact, each time he performed, a crane was required to remove the piano from his apartment. The hair on Denise's neck stood up and chills covered her body. Horowitz still performed with his trademark intensity and focus.

Alexei stood by, entranced by what he was seeing. Horowitz didn't stop at the end of the second movement. He powered into the third movement, the Precipitato. The scene that was unfolding left the room spellbound. After the conclusion, Horowitz and Alexei conversed some more in Russian, ignoring Denise and Tom for most of it. Alexei was asked to play more Prokofiev as the two bonded over their mutual love for him. Before the night ended, Alexei shared with Horowitz his incredible encounter from the rooftop of the conservatory in 1986 when he saved Dace from falling, which gave Horowitz a great laugh. The entire meeting lasted nearly two hours before it was time to get back in the limousine. Alexei couldn't speak on the ride back to the hotel. Overcome with joy, he had little to say. Finally, Denise pried Alexei to share some of their conversation. Alexei breathed deeply. He paused and softly told her that Vladimir Horowitz asked him to carry on the musical legacy that he had created. He seemingly had passed the torch to Alexei. This request deeply touched him and made this evening the most special of his entire life.[1]

Vladimir Horowitz's style of playing was remarkably unique and beloved throughout the planet. His style was enhanced by his extremely long fingers, which afforded him wide range and use of the keyboard. He was a notorious perfectionist and even had his piano obsessively tuned to his exact specifications by the German-born Franz Mohr, who also lived in New York. Mohr's exceptional ear and trusted tuning abilities earned him the respect of the most notable pianists with whom he worked. Mohr worked with Horowitz, Cliburn, Rudolph Serkin, Glenn Gould, and Arthur Rubenstein, to name but a few. Arthur Rubenstein famously traveled the world playing his personal Hamburg-built Steinway grand piano. The efforts to transport the thousand-pound Steinway were incredible until one day in New York when Rubenstein—prior to an upcoming performance—sampled one of Mohr's finely tuned alternative pianos. He credits Mohr for opening his eyes to using other pianos, appropriately tuned of course, thus ending his huge transport costs as he continued to travel the world. Mohr recalled Horowitz's fascination with the young Van Cliburn and his similarly sized hands and style of play. Mohr would go on to become close friends with many of the pianists he tuned for, including Van Cliburn. He would regularly fly to Fort Worth to tune the reported fifteen pianos Van kept throughout his large house. The actual number was closer to eleven or twelve. After Horowitz's death, Mohr was asked by Steinway to accompany Horowitz's piano on its tour around the world, as other pianists of acclaim would play the famous Steinway for recordings and concerts. Once in 1968, Mohr was accompanying Horowitz to his recital in Chicago's famed Orchestra Hall. Mohr had the piano tuned perfectly to Horowitz's specs and was invited to sit in the box with Horowitz's wife, Wanda, to finally enjoy his famed client's performance from the audience, which was a first for him. He was so nervous as Horowitz played his Haydn Sonata that his enjoyment of the moment was ruined. During the intermission, he received notice that Horowitz was furious backstage and needed to see him immediately. Mohr raced backstage to the pacing Horowitz. Fearing the worst, Mohr approached Horowitz, wondering if the piano wasn't tuned correctly. Horowitz snapped that it was not the piano at all but rather the bench that was too high and thus caused him to miss many notes. Mohr was sent out to the stage to lower the seat by three fingers, as Horowitz had instructed. As Mohr walked onto the stage, the crowd, initially sensing he was Horowitz himself, opened up with a raucous applause. Mohr raced to the bench, lowered it per instruction, took a quick bow, much to the amusement of the crowd, and exited the stage. From this point on, Mohr would keep himself relegated to the backstage areas during his client's performances. Horowitz maintained a wild temper throughout his career. He was prone to temper tantrums over the slightest details. Mohr's history with Horowitz taught him precisely how to prepare his piano every Sunday he performed.[2]

The Cliburn Foundation had strict rules regarding the concert schedule they set forth and how their artists should follow them. Cliburn winners were required to perform at all concert bookings during the two-year sponsored tour. Every performance would showcase Alexei as the winner of the 1989 Van Cliburn International Piano Competition, furthering the prestige and influence of the competition as well as garnering Alexei much prestige. The Cliburn Foundation wished this schedule to begin in earnest once the smoke had cleared from his victory. Alexei met with Richard Rodzinski and Susan Wilcox the day after he won gold. Alexei made his intentions known to Richard, saying that he would be calling Fort Worth his home base and would need a permanent working visa, ensuring his legal status. Richard had the influence and power to make this happen. Soon after, Alexei requested an additional visa for Dace to come live with him. He desperately wanted to be reunited with her. Those three weeks of silence had been tortuous for him, and he didn't know how he could manage without her. Richard told him that he would work on it and would get it done. Alexei took him at his word. This would prove to be very problematic later on. Richard then asked Susan Wilcox point blank, with Alexei sitting beside her, if she and Jon would allow him to continue living with them for the next two years, or until such time as Alexei could earn enough to warrant new accommodations. Susan, being put on the spot, felt compelled to accept the offer.

With his career now in hyperdrive, Alexei found himself whisked off to Europe for a bevy of recitals and concerts in places like France, Switzerland, England, Poland, Finland, and Germany. Alexei's triumphant return to Fort Worth wouldn't come until several months later, on October 3. His highly anticipated return took place at a familiar locale, Ed Landreth Hall, and not a seat was left empty for the event. Alexei performed his Cliburn-conquering Rachmaninov *Piano Concerto no. 2* again for the eager crowd, and this time, instead of chairing the jury, Maestro John Giordano conducted the Fort Worth Symphony Orchestra accompaniment. Those in attendance bragged about the evening for months. Two months later, on Sunday November 5, the news broke of the passing of Vladimir Horowitz in New York at the age of eighty-six from a heart attack.

The spring of 1990 was a whirlwind for Alexei as his travel found him performing across the globe in locales known to the most sought-after artists. The situation of getting Dace to Fort Worth continually weighed heavily on him. Alexei believed that Rodzinski was leveraging political pressure, but at the same time he was increasingly frustrated by the Cliburn's lack of progress in obtaining Dace's visa. Then the call came in from Denise Chupp that Alexei's presence was requested personally by then President George H. W. Bush to play a recital at the White House, an honor bestowed on precious few. Alexei was indeed excited by the opportunity to play in this famous residence and workplace. Days prior to the event, Alexei surprised everyone when he promptly canceled his appearance due to Dace becoming ill back in Moscow. Her sickness wasn't serious, so everyone involved was shocked when he flew home to check on her well-being. The president would have to wait. Dace needed him more.

Alexei was back in Moscow in late September 1990 to visit his family and Dace. He had hoped then to bring her back with him to America. Cliburn had booked him as a headliner for the renowned Linz Festival in Vienna, Austria. In the middle of the night, the phone rang in the Fort Worth apartment of Denise Chupp, destroying what had been a sound sleep. On the other end of the line was the organizer of the Linz Festival in Austria who had contracted Alexei to perform during this significant time slot. The Linz Festival had brought in their chamber orchestra to accompany Alexei, making this a very sought-after ticket. A screaming and furious man interrupted Denise's sleepy answer. He curtly shared that Alexei had missed the plane to Vienna from Moscow. With her slumber now ruined, Denise scrambled to get answers. She then got on the phone to find Alexei somewhere in Moscow. Her first call was to the Moscow Conservatory dormitory, where he stayed when in Moscow. It being the middle of the day, a woman who spoke, not surprisingly, only Russian, answered the phone quickly. Denise, having only English to work with, began name-dropping Alexei Sultanov or Dace Abele's name as if to alert the woman to go find them. After she spent more than an hour on the line waiting, Alexei's voice came over the line. Denise, in a moment of a pent-up desperation, unloaded onto Alexei. She informed him in no uncertain terms that he had made a terrible career mistake not showing up for the Linz Festival. The tongue-lashing found its mark as Alexei recognized the carnage he had created. He explained rudimentarily that his absence was due to the failure of the Cliburn organization to procure a visa for Dace, which they had promised him. He was essentially calling their bluff and would not play until this part of the deal was met. He would not be appearing in Vienna. Denise could not convince him otherwise, and her return call to the Linz Festival organizer was heavy. The organizer even offered to send a private jet to Moscow at exceptional cost and difficulty to pick up Alexei, but to no avail. The damage had been done. The prestige and locale of the Linz Festival should have been enough to pull Alexei from hiding, but his steadfastness over the visa issue held.

Several European concert managers and conductors who would be in attendance at the festival to inspect this boy wonder for future performances would strike him from their list of candidates once the story broke, which crippled his future European bookings. The event was also scheduled for television broadcast, so the exposure would be high. For an artist on the way up, this was a very foolish move. Denise was desperately in need of a European manager for Alexei, and his actions had undermined the possibility of finding one now. Denise learned that Alexei felt the Cliburn Foundation was not taking his repeated requests for a visa for Dace seriously. He felt they were playing games. The Cliburn, as it turned out, had done its job, and the visa had been waiting at the US Embassy office in Moscow for Dace to pick up. Someone in the chain of command had relayed this information poorly. Alexei had made up his mind that he had been lied to. Many at the Cliburn Foundation discovered a side of their champion that they had not expected, and it concerned them deeply. This would turn out to be a tremendous professional blunder that would come back to bite Alexei. Denise took much heat back at the office due to Alexei's misgivings. This would not be the last time either.

A thirty-day tourist visa was indeed ready for Dace to pick up, which she did that same day. A ticket for Dace and Alexei waited for them at the airport a few days later. The Cliburn had to get Alexei home regardless of their sour feelings, as his next booking awaited him here in the States. There was even an extra ticket included for Mr. Cello, who could not be subjected to the uncertainties of the underside luggage compartment of the plane. She carefully buckled her cello in the seat next to her and lay back for her long first voyage west. Her mind was awash with excitement to experience America. Alexei had talked it up so much that she couldn't wait to land. Was America as wonderful as Alexei described? She could not have known she wouldn't see her family again for more than two years.

22
Together at Last

On September 30, 1990, Dace arrived in Fort Worth armed with her new thirty-day tourist visa. She wanted to spend every second exploring America with her beloved Alexei. Upon her arrival, she experienced the same firsts that Alexei had. Dace entered through customs unable to speak a single word of English. Everything she experienced was at once shiny, new, and overwhelming. America, the land of excess and corruption, as she had been schooled, came with its assortment of challenges for any new visitor. Dace not only wanted to be by Alexei's side, but she was also helpless without him due to her language barrier. She was introduced warmly to the Wilcoxes and their home where she would live during the extent of her visa. Her time was spent enjoying the fruits of Alexei's recent labors. He had become an overnight celebrity in Fort Worth. Media personnel from across the world were always in search of a story on him. Alexei knew that he must buckle down on his concert schedule, which he hoped would undo some of the damage he had caused. He was audacious but far from stupid. Dace traveled with Alexei for several concerts but not all, so she frequently remained at home with the Wilcoxes. The next thirty days were a sensory overload for her. She experienced her first visit to an American restaurant, and Mexican food quickly gained favor. Dace's arrival in Fort Worth lasted only a few short days before she was whisked off to the Hawaiian Islands with Alexei for a second concert series. The first stop was a recital at the same Kahilu Theatre where he had played eight months prior. Two days later, Alexei and Dace boarded a puddle jumper to Maui to play the Rachmaninoff Concerto no. 2 with the Maui Symphony Orchestra at the Marriott Hotel Concert Hall. The tickets for the event had sold out weeks before the event. The two enjoyed each other's company and the beautiful landscape of Hawaii. Alexei shared with Dace that he finally felt accomplished in his life. His finances were substantially improved, and he felt free from everything that once pained him. He had achieved everything he ever thought possible.

Dace's thirty days passed in a flash and inevitably her time had come to return home. Alexei had decided sometime back during the competition that life in America was markedly better than that in Tashkent or Moscow. He loved the life he enjoyed here in Fort Worth and knew Dace now felt it too. But moving Dace to America permanently proved much more challenging than Alexei imagined. Alexei asked Jon Wilcox to help him. Jon found him an immigration attorney in Dallas to work with. The legal process had begun for a working visa for Dace, but her thirty days only gave them enough time to scratch the surface. The process had much red tape to battle and given her legal circumstances, coupled with no real employment here in the United States, her options were few. Defection was something she even considered. Dace's time was indeed running out, and the Soviets would be needing her home. Alexei had every intention of playing by the rules to get her to the US, as he himself could easily lose his newly acquired working visa if he strayed from the course. He knew the American government would have little problem deporting them both back to the Soviet Union, permanently. The couple, wild as they were, always followed the script when dealing with the requirements of the Soviet government. Alexei knew that the Soviets had far-reaching tentacles, and he was playing a game that he could ill afford to lose. He needed to get Dace here permanently but how? Every time Alexei went home, he took added risk going through customs due to his unsatisfied duty to the Red Army. The Cliburn influences had offered him some respite, but never was it assured. Alexei made the decision not to return to the Soviet Union. A decision that remained in effect for the next four years.

Alexei on stage accepting the grand prize golf medal. *Dace Collection.*

Draft papers from the Red Army would often arrive at his vacant Moscow dormitory, alerting him to report for his call-up. Faizul would pick them up from time to time and forward them to Alexei's address in Fort Worth. This bolstered his decision to stay away from his home. Now, he must solve Dace's problem.

Since Alexei had used his Cliburn connections to get Dace to the US, he was now faced with her impending departure. Her visa, which was sponsored by the Wilcoxes, gave her only thirty days of freedom, but her reliance on Alexei and the certainty of a return made her very nervous. Since she only spoke Latvian and Russian, Dace was very limited in her ability to move around. She relied heavily on Alexei to do most things. The language barrier kept her out of public and desirable places, as she was afraid of the unknown. Was the KGB waiting for her? Would the police arrest her and send her back to Latvia when they discovered her? Would she get lost and never return to Alexei? These thoughts plagued Dace. Alexei treasured every minute he shared with Dace in Fort Worth, but he dreaded losing her. Nothing was certain anymore, and not knowing when he would see her next deeply troubled him. When she was home in Riga, his life felt lonely. He wanted desperately to find a way to keep her here. He didn't think he could live without her. As his immigration lawyer needed more time, Alexei looked to the Wilcoxes for help. Jon Wilcox, after talking options with the lawyer, suggested an idea that would fix this problem, but it would involve major concessions by Alexei. Alexei had been against the idea of marriage from early on. The couple both considered marriage inconsequential. They didn't need a piece of paper to prove they loved one another. In their minds, they already had everything marriage could promise them.

Jon explained why it might make sense. If he would marry Dace, then legally she could remain in the United States with Alexei, which the lawyer did indeed confirm to Alexei.

On October 18, nearly four months after Alexei had claimed gold, Peter Rosen's documentary, *Here to Make Music*, was nationally broadcast on the PBS network. The final product lasted ninety minutes and was critically acclaimed by a large audience. Rosen would receive further honor for his film in March of the next year by winning Best Director in Television Documentary/Actuality by the Director's Guild of America.

As Alexei continued his American education, he was earning far more now than he knew what to do with. Alexei sought the assistance of Jon Wilcox with his finances. He trusted Jon, and more importantly, knew very little about balancing a checkbook. In fact, he had never had enough money to warrant having one, until now. Overnight, he had become the most successful Sultanov ever, and he was still a teenager. Alexei knew but one thing, the piano, and the efforts required to ensure financial security were of no consequence to him. The money wasn't important to him anyway. What mattered was the freedom he now appeared to have and wanted to share with Dace. This child prodigy essentially became a college dropout the moment he won the Van Cliburn International Piano Competition. Alexei felt as though he had spent his life learning and preparing for a moment such as the Cliburn victory. Now that he had achieved it, he saw little use in continuing his education. He had reached the top, and his ambition for more waned. This moment marks the time when Alexei Sultanov abruptly stopped regularly practicing the piano. Alexei had jokingly nicknamed the piano the black coffin. He would now practice when he so desired and play when he was ready. He would play the required performances and travel the world on his own terms, seemingly.

In September 1989, Denise Chupp had booked Alexei through the legendary British management duo, Ibbs and Tillett Company, to record an album with the London Symphony Orchestra, conducted by Russian Maxim Shostakovich, for the Teldec label. She had made the arrangements with managing director Richard Apley to pick Alexei up at Heathrow Airport in London upon his arrival. Denise had received some push-back from Alexei about going, so she was nervous that it would happen at all. She knew Alexei was capable of anything when his mood wasn't right. He had continued to ruffle a few feathers at the Cliburn Foundation by arriving late to scheduled meetings, no-showing at a few scheduled appearances, and causing logistical problems for Denise. She had learned the lengths to which Alexei would go when he wasn't feeling cooperative. Denise knew this was a big opportunity for Alexei, even if he didn't, and she wasn't going to risk it. Denise drove Alexei to the Dallas Fort Worth International Airport and even walked him to his plane. In 1989, airport security hadn't yet evolved to its current form, so Denise was able to walk Alexei all the way to the gate. She wished him well and, for reassurance, watched the plane take off. A sense of relief fell upon her as she drove back to the office.

These days her schedule was so hectic she often left her apartment before sunup and got home well after dark. Dealing with Alexei's uniqueness only added to the hassle. Long hours were nothing new to her or the Cliburn staff. The competition alone required a Herculean effort by the entire company to pull off what most patrons take for granted. The final week before the actual competition typically became an exercise in keeping oneself from mental and physical breakdown. Denise, at one point, made the decision to purchase new underwear in lieu of doing her laundry, just to save a few minutes of her severely limited time. Now, with the competition behind her and a full plate of artists to manage, she soldiered on and thrived. That evening, after Denise had finally made it home from the trip to the airport and her bevy of office duties, the house phone rang about the time Alexei's plane should have arrived at Heathrow Airport. Richard Apley, from Teldec, was on the other end asking where Alexei was. Denise cringed with confusion and disbelief. Richard had waited for Alexei near the baggage carousel with a placard bearing his name. After no one appeared matching Alexei's description, Richard tried paging him on the airport intercom, but still with no luck. Denise racked her brain for an answer, then it hit her. She advised Richard to check for the next flight back to DFW Airport and go to that gate. Richard wasn't clear why, but he did as Denise instructed him. When he walked up to the gate, there waiting to board in forty-five minutes was his artist. Richard was somehow able to convince Alexei not to fly home but instead to come with him. Alexei was driven to the Snape Maltings Concert Hall, located on the edge of the Alde River in Snape, Suffolk, England. This exquisite hall is best known for its annual Aldeburgh Festival held each June. The Aldeburgh Festival was founded in 1948 by iconic composer Benjamin Britten, who had lived in Snape years prior. There, Alexei recorded the classic Tchaikovsky Piano Concerto no. 1 and Rachmaninoff's Piano Concerto no. 2 conducted by Maxim Shostakovich, the son of the great twentieth-century composer Dmitri Shostakovich. Maxim, as it turned out, had developed a tremendous appreciation for Alexei, as he had served as a member of the jury for the Eighth Van Cliburn Competition. After Van Cliburn had won the 1958 Tchaikovsky competition, Maxim, alongside conductor Kiril Kondrashin and Fritz Reiner, recorded these same pieces. Maxim Shostakovich and the Ibbs and Tillett management group came up with the idea of leaving us with an incredible comparative album of the two artists. Both styles of play are easily discernable. Cliburn's album saw tremendous success. Alexei's rendition, while less popular than Cliburn's, still remains today as one of Teldec's most popular classical recordings.

In January 1990, Alexei played for the Keyboard Artist Series in Carmel, California. This annual event included a standing reservation for the Cliburn gold medalist after each quadrennial competition. Alexei's performance met with some harsh criticisms from the local music critics. His style of play, they suggested, didn't honor the music properly. Alexei wasn't experienced enough to fully understand the music he raced through. His unique style, coupled with his youth, sometimes received unfavorable reviews from seasoned music critics. The event promoter easily explained away these criticisms when it was revealed that Alexei's standing ovation at intermission was the first ever in the concert hall's eleven-year history.

23
The Plan

The last day of October 1990 finally arrived. It was time to return Dace to the airport, as her tourist visa was expiring. The prospect of defection seemed stronger than ever, but the likely problems it would entail for the Wilcoxes, their sponsors, and Alexei were too risky. The United States deported people caught with expired visas. The political pressures of the time could easily undo such a plan. The car was packed with Dace's things, new and old, as the scared couple sat in the back seat of the Wilcoxes' sedan and headed off for the airport. Susan was behind the wheel and felt the nervousness of the young couple. She hated to see Dace leave and knew how hard it would be for Alexei. She felt helpless, and it broke her heart. Dace, sensing the inevitable, began asking questions to which Alexei had no answer. An argument broke out due to the stress and confusion of the situation. Alexei panicked over the thought of Dace leaving him. He knew the challenges he faced in getting her back once she left. He nervously fidgeted in the back seat and began to sweat profusely.

As the car drove past their favorite spot, Six Flags, near the DFW airport, Alexei caved to his fears and pleaded with Susan in English to instead take them to their immigration attorney in Dallas. Dace, not understanding a word of their conversation, sensed something was wrong. Alexei calmed her with unrelated talk. Their attorney had seen this situation before and outlined for them a solution, if Alexei really could go through with it. He told Alexei that he needed to drive straight to the courthouse in Fort Worth and summon a justice of the peace. Susan then drove them back to Fort Worth and led the Sultanovs to the Fort Worth courthouse. After a short search, a justice of the peace was located. Alexei and Dace were presented to the acting judge and a service was quickly under way. They filled out the proper documentation and somehow the sympathetic judge waived the normal three-day waiting period. Susan Wilcox, fully aware of what was transpiring, had coached Dace just minutes prior on how to say the word *yes* when the judge looked to her and asked her a question she would not understand. This simple word—along with hello, goodbye, and thank you—was now the extent of Dace's English.

Dace patiently waited, oblivious to the situation, as the judge and justice of peace talked to them. Occasionally, she nodded with a smile, feeling as though she needed to. Dace did not know what was taking place. The couple stood side by side and proceeded with an impromptu ceremony. The marriage ceremony was short and sweet and completely foreign to Dace. Susan was the required witness to the ceremony. Dace stood by Alexei quietly and in complete bewilderment, as a man well past his prime sat behind a judicial bench in his black robe and read off a paper that had no meaning to her. She feigned interest, as surely Alexei knew what he was doing. When her moment arrived, the judge looked at her and asked her if she took this man to be her lawfully wedded husband, and not quite realizing her cue, gave the judge a toothy smile. Alexei gently nudged Dace to get her attention. She looked toward him only to be reminded in Russian to "say yes, say yes." The communication landed perfectly. She retuned her glance to the judge and responded "Yes!"

She had, on October 31, 1990, unknowingly consented to become Mrs. Alexei Sultanov. Her return to the Soviet Union, now paused, still needed to be handled through the courts, which took time, but Dace could now remain indefinitely in the United States with her brand-new husband. Dace only learned of her new arrangement a few minutes later when Alexei shared the good news. The newlyweds celebrated over a bottle of champagne back at home with Jon and Susan. Jon, who had missed the ceremony, learned of the news over the phone at work. They continued their celebration, attending their very first Halloween party, where Dace became thoroughly intrigued by her first dry ice encounter.

The Halloween anniversary would, from then on, entail dressing up and satisfying their sweet tooth in lieu of dinner and flowers.

Dace grew close to the Wilcoxes during this time. Susan filled the motherly role that Benita had filled over five thousand miles away in Riga. The Wilcoxes' two cats were Dace's first encounter with household pets of any kind, and she became enthralled with them. Life began in earnest for the new couple as they were now safely together in America.[1]

24
Boo Si Ness

Dace's new life living under the Wilcoxes' roof started with the Wilcoxes signing her up for beginning English classes several weeks later at Texas Wesleyan University. The class time wasn't easy for her, but now that she was settled, Alexei set off to fulfill his engagements across the world. Dace's new English immersion fell onto the shoulders of a woman named Beverly Archibald. Beverly, a high school English teacher, arrived in Cairo, Egypt in 1981 alongside her defense contractor husband and quickly found work teaching English to the hotel employees where she lived, which was designated for American visitors. Her arrival in Cairo went smoothly enough, until four days after her arrival on October 6, 1981, the Egyptian President, Anwar Sadat, was assassinated. Sadat, a 1978 Nobel Peace Prize winner, was gunned down during a national victory parade. Sadat's efforts to pass the Egypt-Israeli Peace Treaty ultimately led to a fatwa against him by Abdel Rahman, also known as the blind sheikh, who would be convicted fifteen years later for his role in the 1993 World Trade Center bombing. Sadat's funeral was attended by three former US Presidents, as well as his close friend, Israeli Prime Minister Menachem Begin, with whom Sadat shared the Nobel Peace Prize. After things calmed down, Beverly again resumed teaching the hotel employees. She became, in short order, the foremost expert in teaching English to hotel employees, a highly valued position. Her teaching connections led her to compile a list of valuable contacts to help further her career. Her expertise in teaching English to hotel employees in foreign countries, coupled with these contacts, led her three years later to Saudi Arabia, following her husband, where her services were even more valued. She now oversaw the English program for most of the hotel managers. She became widely loved by her students and those she oversaw. Her reputation grew throughout the Middle East hotel industry as one of a warm and caring teacher who empowered her students. Her sought-after talents, and again her husband's work, finally led her to two highly influential years in Turkey. Beverly's husband regularly worked long periods of time away from her and began to grow distant. Beverly, who was home in Fort Worth on leave from Turkey with her husband, got warning that he had met a twenty-two-year-old Turkish girl and that their marriage would not last. Those thirty-three years imploded seemingly overnight. This was very traumatic to Beverly, so much so that she would never marry again. She became very independent, which would allow her to carry herself proud for the remainder of her life. She threw her efforts and passion into those she taught. Her life reset after she telephoned an old friend who ran Texas Wesleyan,[1] a small college in her hometown of Fort Worth.

She was offered a job and rented an apartment with her son close to the college. Beverly began teaching basic English to people new to the community. The work was easy yet extremely fulfilling. This transition period and easy teaching gig allowed Beverly to spend more time enjoying things that were previously unavailable. She became enamored with the Fort Worth Symphony and the abundance of talent they had collected and displayed. Many a night was spent at Ed Landreth Hall, emotionally captured by the heavenly arrangements that filled her with joy. When a friend invited her to her first Van Cliburn Competition one afternoon in 1989, she was instantly hooked. She especially enjoyed the Rachmaninov Etude she heard from a young, wild-haired Soviet named Alexei Sultanov. Little could she have known that afternoon in May that their paths would eventually meet.[2]

The 1989 competition still rings in Beverly's memory. Days later, after an obligatory Cliburn recital, Alexei had impressed her and the locals further by giving a short lecture on music and his background at the conservatory, which showcased his rapid grasp of the English language. So, when Alexei showed up at her class one day, it was a special moment. Alexei, though, was not there as a student. He was accompanying his new wife, Dace, who lacked any basic English abilities. His attendance was sporadic but always made the classroom of around fifteen livelier. He would often tease Dace when she had difficulties with pronunciation. Beverly recalled Dace trying to mimic Beverly's lips as the word business was being taught. Dace could manage simply *boo-si-ness*, much to the chagrin of Alexei, whose roaring laughter infected the classroom. Even Beverly managed a semi-approving smile. One of the class assignments was to visit a restaurant and order from the menu. Dace broke traditional protocol and invited Beverly to join. Beverly knew she couldn't miss this dinner. She would have to remind Dace when ordering dinner that she wasn't yet technically old enough for wine. Alexei, the consummate playful gentleman, often carried Beverly's books to her car after class, perhaps trying to grease the wheels for Dace's education. Dace's lack of substantial support base in Fort Worth made Beverly an easy pick as a companion. Dace invited her over for dinner several times for Latvian cuisine, which Beverly enjoyed immensely. Beverly loved these events, as she was often the recipient of a private concert between Alexei's piano and Dace's cello.

As Dace's English improved, so did her circle of friends. As Alexei traveled, he took Dace along with him as often as he could afford to. Texas Wesleyan had a strict policy regarding absences. Due to the short time span of the introduction to English class, a student could have no more than three unexcused absences. Dace quickly accumulated enough misses, and even though she had grown to love Beverly, was asked to drop the class as per school policy. Dace had a rudimentary understanding now of basic English, which was strengthened greatly by watching television. The age barrier and her unassuming nature caused Beverly not to push the friendship further, so they lost contact for a long time. Beverly privately felt Alexei's control over Dace may have been the real culprit. Beverly thought of them often but always wanted to be respectful of their lives. She had seen first-hand how people would glom onto Alexei and Dace because of his celebrity. She would be there if they needed her, but she would not think of inserting herself in their lives just for her benefit. Friendship in her mind had to be a mutual thing. Beverly, after all, would get her updates from her oldest son and Fort Worth Police officer Paul Archibald, who worked security on his off hours at the Blockbuster video store that the young couple frequented, looking for entertainment. Paul knew of Alexei from his mother and would always say hello to the couple.

It was during this time living with the Wilcoxes that Susan made note of the strange habit Alexei had. Her memory of Alexei not valuing her opinion on his choice of white socks during the competition made more sense now. He didn't seem to listen to Susan when something of importance came up. Alexei would seek out Jon's opinion even when Susan was clearly in the know. He had the same attitude toward Dace. Dace didn't seem to have much of voice in their relationship when a meaningful subject arose. Susan believed this a cultural thing that went back to his upbringing in the Arabic-based city of Uzbekistan. Women in this region of the world were not looked upon as equals to men. Alexei showed little regard for women's equality or their beliefs. Susan described it as an Arabic characteristic in which women were considered second-class citizens. Alexei seemed to make all decisions for the couple, and Dace rarely had a say. This would prove to be more problematic as time went along.

Eventually, Alexei's earnings began to grow in the Bank of America account Jon had set up for him, another first for Alexei. Jon had to explain the American method of banking to Alexei. Alexei had never even seen the inside of a bank until he arrived on US soil. He told Jon that, "In the Soviet Union, people either have little money or they have no money at all." The Soviet state bank called, Gosbank, morphed in 1990 under Gorbachev's Perestroika Program into the Central Bank of Russia with several subsidiaries. The Central Bank's stated role was to protect the stability of the Russian currency. The Abeles, as well as the Sultanovs, and the overwhelming majority of the Soviet population lived paycheck to paycheck, so banks held little value to them. Savings accounts consisted of little more than money hidden in the sock drawer. People kept their rubles, if they had them, hidden away at home. The money Alexei was now making would have put him in the top one percent of earners in the USSR.

With their marriage the Sultanovs had bought themselves time to remain together in the United States—indefinitely, they hoped. The immigration attorneys had smoothed everything out with their working visas, allowing them to live in relative peace. The Wilcoxes floated the idea that it was time for the Sultanovs to find a home for themselves. They needed a house in which to start their new lives but hadn't a clue how one accomplished this. Jon and Susan offered advice as it was needed. They were careful not to interfere too much so the couple could learn together how to operate in the US. They often showed them the way and then let them handle as best they could. The concept of owning a home, buying insurance, using a credit card, and visiting a doctor's office were all new and exciting activities for them. They succeeded in finding a small house in November, a mile away from the Wilcoxes', that was purchased with money earned from Alexei's Cliburn prize and worldwide engagements. The new house fit them perfectly, but something was missing. Susan, as a belated wedding present, gifted the Sultanovs two cats. Their family grew once again with the addition of a pet iguana. The family continued to grow even while Alexei traveled the globe. Dace loved to adopt stray cats whenever they found their way into her backyard.

Alexei had begun drinking at an early age, to dull the enduring pain of his childhood and his chronic loneliness away from Dace. His new wealth offered him more opportunities to indulge. Even at home, he would find alcohol an increasingly constant companion. When the Sultanovs moved to their first home, Alexei had no one to oversee him on a daily basis, so drinking became a regular thing. Their move to the new home meant returning the loaned Steinway and Sons piano back to Danny Saliba. Now without a piano on which to practice, they paid a visit to Luke Wickman's Pianos, who had been a dealer for Saliba, where they purchased a fifty-thousand-dollar Yamaha Concert Piano for half price.

The Sultanovs celebrated their very first Christmas together in their new house. The Wilcoxes took them to a Christmas Eve service at First United Methodist Church in downtown Fort Worth. Dace fell in love with the building and its kind people and thus would develop deep roots here. Her first visit found her lost for most of the Christian service, but it all came together when the lights dimmed and the congregation stood holding candles and sang *Silent Night*. Dace sang along to this popular Christmas classic in Latvian and joined the crowd caught up in the moment, as tears welled up in her eyes. She felt comfortable in this not-so-strange land.

Alexei's schedule on the road was brutal, to say the least. He played forty-five concerts in the year after winning Cliburn gold after receiving one hundred twenty requests to perform. For the first twenty weeks since his win, Alexei had traveled to and played twenty times in places like Finland, France, England, the Netherlands, Poland, Switzerland, Germany, and the United States. He was rarely home and often far away. Dace would accompany him when Alexei could pull the right strings, but usually it was quite expensive and unreasonable for her to join him. She made three sizable trips the first year along with a multitude of events within the Wilcox driving distance.

Alexei's celebrity was applauded throughout the world. He received standing ovation after standing ovation from the public and adulation, acclaim, and criticism from the hypersensitive critics. His travels after the initial twenty weeks acquired steam and took him to the major music capitals of the world like New York, Berlin, Frankfurt, Milan, Osaka, Zurich, Washington, DC, Seoul, Hamburg, Helsinki, Athens, Taipei, and Nagoya. Alexei loved his orchestral engagements. He received many invitations: Royal Philharmonic, Japan Philharmonic, Rochester Philharmonic, Royal Concertgebouw, Moscow Philharmonic, Warsaw Philharmonic, Philadelphia Philharmonic. Alexei also played alongside the symphonies of Pittsburgh, Detroit, Milwaukee, New Orleans, Dallas, and Atlanta. Fame was thrust upon Alexei, but it did not sit easily for him. The pressure it carried was more than he bargained for. Alexei felt the tremendous pressure to perform for the throngs of fans he now constantly encountered. He did not want to disappoint them and thus gave his audiences maximum effort. Alexei was never one for pretentiousness, so he played his heart out each time. His trademark pounding upon the keyboard and rapid finger work gave crowds consistent awe-inspiring performances. He always stayed after and signed every autograph that was requested of him. While Dace would only accompany Alexei internationally on occasion, she made each of his concerts within the United States. She especially loved arriving in a new, unexplored city. People of all sorts welcomed them to town for his concerts. The fans abroad, though, had a level of rabidity rarely seen inside the United States for classical music. Each stop in Europe, and especially Japan, would find thousands of fans offering flowers, cookies, homemade gifts, and themselves to Alexei. His hosts, upon his arrival, did not always recognize him, so he would have a bit of fun at their expense. Alexei would arrive wearing his typical off-duty t-shirt, jeans, and a head of long wild hair, which often threw the hosts for a loop as they were expecting a more conservatively dressed individual. Alexei loved to give the hosts fits in finding him at the airports. The panicking hosts would search frantically for him, as his attendance or lack thereof could mean their jobs. They often were forced to page Alexei over the public address system.

The fallout from the Cliburn victory would further add to Alexei's growing popularity. The audio recordings from his victorious month at the Van Cliburn Competition, aptly titled, *The Winners*, by Teldec Classics, was a two-disc masterpiece that covered the globe in its popularity. Alexei's popularity brought him opportunities to record solo piano sonatas by Prokofiev, Rachmaninov, and Scriabin, along with several works by Chopin. His Japanese popularity soared, inspiring two live performances recordings in 1997 and 1999. He recorded in Tokyo the *Fantaisie Impromptu*[3] and *Sultanov plays Chopin* which were released by Arts Core Corporation to further global adulation.

25

Mr. Cliburn

Winning a musical competition of the Cliburn magnitude brings with it many perks. Alexei's status on the world stage leapt to the top overnight after his win. People now knew who he was, wanted to meet him, take a picture with him, get his autograph, and hopefully book him. This was before social media and cell phones, so photographs and autographs held tremendous weight amongst decerning fans. In Fort Worth, there was no bigger celebrity than Van Cliburn himself. A few days after his remarkable victory at the 1989 Cliburn Competition, Alexei received a phone call from Van inviting him and Dace to dinner, once Dace arrived in town. Van Cliburn's palatial eighteen-acre manor in the heart of Fort Worth's most exclusive neighborhood, Westover Hills, was nothing short of jaw dropping to the Sultanovs. After all, opulence like this was rarely seen back in Russia. Alexei, always the cool customer, kept his awe in check. On a tour of Van's walk-in refrigerator, Alexei commented to Van that his refrigerator was bigger than his parents' apartment. Dace, on the other hand, wasn't quiet with her astonishment at the grandeur of the place. Everywhere they turned, she ooohhed and awed with amazement. Her feedback caused Alexei to become uneasy. His A-type personality was extremely sensitive, and watching Dace's joyous reaction to Van's wealth elicited feelings of jealousy and insecurity. Alexei had developed over the last year a fear of losing Dace, even under ridiculous circumstances like these. These feelings of inadequacy stirred in him an underlying distrust of Mr. Cliburn. Alexei jokingly later asked Dace to wear a Burka, an outer garment traditionally won by Muslim women that covers most of the face and body, so as to keep her out of the eyes of all other people. This jealousy would follow Alexei around the world whenever Dace accompanied him. Dace exuded everything Alexei lacked. Her inquisitiveness and openness made her an inviting target to anyone interested in the couple. She always welcomed the opportunity to converse with a complete stranger. Her friendly intentions were always sincere but were often considered unnecessary by her jealous husband. Dace's piercing green eyes, from time to time, engaged in some playful yet harmless flirting, which enraged Alexei.

The visit to Cliburn's house for dinner would spur future invites, as Van became quite fond of the young couple, and they would spend many hours at his house. Van's hospitality was always exceptional and overwhelming. Van, the consummate night owl, often awoke in the early afternoon to begin his day. His nights typically ended well into the next day, almost as the sun peeked over the horizon. Cliburn's fascination with flowers was no secret. His home was often adorned with large displays of flowers, and many of these arrangements were no longer living. The dead bouquets gave Van as much joy as the living arrangements and were left around the home for his continued pleasure. Van's grand home was an homage to his mother Rildia Bee and to her son's worldly accomplishments with photographs, memorabilia, and gifts from across the globe. His travels around the world were so extensive that he filled two rooms with his collection of accumulated luggage. Van loved the Sultanovs and especially favored the young piano prodigy. He regularly encouraged him and tried to advise him on many issues. He suggested Alexei cut his long hair and repeatedly offered his personal hairdresser to work with him. The invitations agitated Alexei. He was not interested in making a fashion change and took the invitation as an insult. Van's attempt to help his young prodigy occasionally felt like more than mere guidance. Van's focused attention often made Alexei uncomfortable in their one-on-one encounters. While Van threw lavish gifts and parties at the Sultanovs, Alexei felt increasingly uneasy in his presence. Although Dace found Van quite mesmerizing, Alexei quietly stewed.

Jon Wilcox attempted to help manage Alexei's money with extreme care, but Dace's world-wide accompaniment, their new house, the new apartment for Alexei's parents outside of Moscow, a new violin for

Natalia, a new cello for Faizul, and a much-needed car for the couple quickly ate into the developing nest egg. All this newfound wealth was uncharted territory for Alexei. After all, Alexei never desired to live lavishly and even preferred simply to be at home playing video games with Dace. The concept of paying taxes, keeping savings accounts, and future planning were completely lost on him. Despite his incredible talent, he seemed to be permanently stuck in teenager mode. On the road with Alexei, Dace witnessed first-hand the fervor that her husband could instill in people with his performances. Dace, who was never the jealous type, often saw women throw themselves at Alexei. She knew Alexei found this uncomfortable and hated the attention he garnered. Dace secretly felt uncomfortable watching these women fawn over him. Just before he walked out, he would often scour the crowd from the edge of the stage to find Dace, whenever she was with him. Her playful attempts to hide herself amongst the crowd brought a smile to his face when he spotted her. Alexei had always been extremely protective of his Dace. He had even once punched out a classmate who was attempting to flirt with her back at the conservatory. Adoring fans seemed to come at every stop, but outside the United States, the fans seemed far more brazen. The culture surrounding classical music was more powerful in Europe and Asia. Japan would be the extreme case. The Japanese people treat classical musicians as rock stars of the highest order. The female audiences abroad asserted themselves significantly more than those here in the States.

Life on the road also found Alexei drinking more—perhaps a mask for the absence of Dace during those long periods away. His professionalism suffered because of it. A habit began forming within Alexei that drew sharp criticisms from the Cliburn. Alexei increasingly canceled concerts across Europe for reasons lost on the promoters. His reputation for not honoring his commitments began to spread the globe. He grew his hair to shoulder length based on the advice of his hairdresser, Melinde. Alexei came to believe that his hair contained certain powers, much like the biblical superhuman Sampson, who derived his strength from his long locks. The uber-confident Alexei took great pleasure visiting Melinde and came home often with new ideas for his appearance. As Alexei's concert schedule progressed, he increasingly found ways to upset his Cliburn managers. Even with his impressive popularity, his continual push-back against authority made his opportunities begin to dwindle. Promoters had tagged Alexei as a booking risk, and even a contract in place with him held no guarantees. He was worth the risk to many as his audiences remained significant, but increasingly these bridges caught fire. His reasons always were of a personal nature, but they usually weren't legitimate. This proved to be quite a sticking point for his managerial team back at the Cliburn. As promoters began losing faith in his ability to show up, his disappointed fans also began to slowly turn on him. His erratic and unpredictable professional behavior had confirmed the Cliburn's initial worry that he was not mature enough for such a high-pressure schedule. Alexei seemed to be on the road to a professional burnout. He hadn't learned to be a professional, and he hated the effort it asked of him. Alexei's ambition seemed to have hit a roadblock. He had worked his way into the world's spotlight and had the talent to become one of the greats, but this Mozart in the making seemed to be comfortable just getting by. Alexei felt that his impact on the world had plateaued, and periodic maintenance was all that was required of him. His one constant was Dace.

Her complete loyalty and subservient nature found her at his beck and call—not a sharing partner in a marriage. Nothing the couple ever did together was Dace's suggestion. They did as Alexei dictated. He called the shots, and Dace's naiveté kept her in the dark. Dace unknowingly was enabling Alexei's behavior, and she was powerless to push back. Alexei remained her knight in shining armor, and always would be. She continuously chose to overlook the obvious and be the wife he so desperately needed. Dace's spotlight had yet to shine as a cellist, and she remained in the shadow of her husband.

26
Carnegie Hall

The Carnegie Hall website tells a joke. Famed violinist Mischa Elman and his wife were leaving Carnegie Hall through a backstage door one day after a rehearsal when they were approached by two tourists looking for the hall's entrance. The tourists noticed Elman's violin case and surmising that he might know, asked, "How do you get to Carnegie Hall?" Without looking up and continuing on his way, Elman tersely replied, "Practice." The joke is now well-known and befits one of the world's most prestigious concert halls. The great honor of playing this grand hall suggests to the world that you are in the company of world-class musicians. Whether or not one is truly a musical great, merely playing here is an honor of a lifetime as the Carnegie joke intimates. Carnegie's storied history boasts performances by Vladimir Horowitz, Artur Rubenstein, Benny Goodman, Duke Ellington, The Beatles, Led Zeppelin, and the Rolling Stones, to name but a very small few. It hosted the last public lecture of Mark Twain as well as one by Booker T. Washington. The Hall was constructed by steel magnate and philanthropist Andrew Carnegie and opened officially on May 5, 1891, with a concert conducted by none other than legend Pyotr Tchaikovsky.

Carnegie Hall sits on Seventh Avenue in Midtown Manhattan, across the street from the Steinway Hall. Steinway Hall, a registered historic and cultural landmark, contains in its basement an exclusive collection of Steinway and Sons concert grand pianos, which select Carnegie artists can use for live performances or studio recordings. When pianists get the special invitation to play Carnegie Hall, they typically are offered a visit to Steinway Hall to select a piano to play during their performance. Every available piano comes with it a storied past as well as a who's who list of famous users.

Alexei entered the Steinway Hall a day before his scheduled Carnegie Hall performance with Faizul Sultanov, Denise Chupp, and Jon and Susan Wilcox in tow. Alexei sat down to test out the pianos belonging to and played by the likes of Irving Berlin, Benjamin Britten, George Gershwin, Cole Porter, and Sergei Rachmaninov. After playing each available Steinway instrument, Alexei shockingly announced that he wasn't satisfied with any of the pianos he had tried. The manager expressed confusion, as this wasn't the typical response he received. Alexei, never being the one to follow protocol, looked around the place and finally motioned towards a piano over in the corner sitting in the shadows. "Can I try that one?" Alexei asked. The manager paused briefly before responding, "Let me make a phone call first." After several minutes, he returned with confirmation. Alexei sat down and began running through the keys. It took but ten seconds before Alexei had made up his mind. This was the one. A pained smile crossed the manager's face as he then shared the piano's provenance. The manager's phone call had been to Wanda Toscanini, the second daughter of world-renowned Italian conductor and musician Arturo Toscanini. Toscanini was arguably the most acclaimed musician of the nineteenth and twentieth centuries and three times graced the cover of *Time* magazine, an unmatched accomplishment for any musician. The piano in question belonged now to Wanda Toscanini and was her late husband Vladimir Horowitz's most cherished piano. The incredible coincidence was lost on no one.

The light tuning of the strings required required gifted agility of its player, not found in most pianists. It required extraordinary dexterity to play powerfully, but with a delicate touch. Alexei had chosen an extraordinary instrument that wasn't normally available to all who played Carnegie. This same piano had traveled to Moscow on that rainy afternoon in 1986 for Horowitz's glorious return to the conservatory when Alexei and Dace gazed from the rafters above. His visit to Horowitz's New York apartment after his Lettermen's appearance came rushing back. Now that Horowitz was no longer living, this connection to him touched Alexei deeply. Alexei's excitement to play Carnegie was exceeded only by his excitement to play his hero's favorite piano.

Alexei's entourage took their seats alongside the director of Carnegie Hall in his private box. On May 3, 1990, sitting at Steinway Concert D 503, Alexei played an inspired sold-out performance in the Main Hall for the 2,804 ticketed patrons. The program included Mozart's Sonata KV 330, Beethoven's *Appassionata*, Scriabin's Sonata no. 5, Prokofiev's Sonata no. 7 and Liszt's *Mephisto Waltz*. The audience sat mesmerized as the passionate music poured out. They properly celebrated him at the conclusion with a standing ovation that was deafening. The crowd cried out for an encore. He gave them three, with Chopin's Waltz E flat major Op. 18 and a *Revolutionary Etude* as well as Rachmaninov's Etude-Tableaux Op. 39 no. 5 in E flat minor. The night's performance was topped off with an elaborate reception at the famous Metropolitan Club on fifth and sixtieth street thrown in Alexei's honor by none other than Wanda Toscanini. The celebration found many of New York's musical patrons on hand, including fifteen members of the International Friends of the Van Cliburn competition. The notoriously critical *New York Press* gave the performance mixed reviews with his youthful inexperience again being the biggest critique. How could Alexei truly know this music and what it means to play it at his age? The *Fort Worth Star Telegram* music critic Wayne Lee Gay made the event and pronounced the performance exhilarating. Peter Goodman from *Newsday* described Alexei's performance as "perfumed lightness in pianissimo passages." Patrick Stearns from *USA Today* wrote, "Delicious incongruity between Sultanov's diminutive stature, boyish stage presence, and thunderbolts he unleashed at the keyboard." Whether the reviews were positive or negative mattered little to Alexei. The three encores and standing ovation at Carnegie Hall told him all he would ever need to know. Alexei could now answer the age-old question of how does one get to Carnegie Hall?

The next day, May 4, Alexei flew to Washington, DC, to prepare his Rachmaninoff Piano Sonata for a special evening on May 5 at the Kennedy Center for the Performing Arts. His newly acquired fame was never more apparent as the sold-out crowd was filled with many of the nation's leaders and musical elites.

27
Pupil, Pedagogue, Legend

Alexei had become a world-class concert performer due in part to the tireless efforts of his longtime teacher, Tamara Popovich. Her methods were so rigorous that Alexei ultimately grew to despise practicing. Popovich's strict tutelage found vindication with Alexei's gold, but the success of her prodigy fueled his backlash. His childhood or lack thereof was consumed by his time in front of the keyboard. A prodigy without question, but never equipped with the life skills he needed to make the transition from adolescence to adulthood. Popovich represented to him the childhood he never had. Yet his relationship with her was one of complete trust and understanding. If Alexei would trust Popovich and do as she said, then Alexei's talent would be realized. He listened to her and obeyed. Perhaps he might really be mentioned in the same sentences as Mozart. Popovich was structure and guidance to Alexei's immature gift. The freedom he gained back from his Cliburn win, however, did not end his relationship with Popovich altogether.

When his preparation for an important or tough upcoming recital required, he would fly Popovich to America to smooth out the rough spots. No one ever, including Dace, knew Alexei's musical idiosyncrasies as did Popovich. As much as Alexei despised practice, he had discipline enough to know her guidance was critical, although he was still absolutely terrified of her. He followed her instructions as closely as possible.

This tiny woman had his undivided attention and never failed to get the best from Alexei. Popovich wasn't hard to convince to fly to the United States. Popovich cherished each of the three visits she made to Fort Worth to coach Alexei. Alexei enticed her with the promise to see America and possibly spend time with her beloved Van Cliburn. Each stay lasted roughly a month, and Alexei spent the time carefully listening, learning new compositions, and fine-tuning his craft. Her visits always magically fell around times that Van was hosting dinner parties to which the Sultanovs were invited.

Since Alexei had become a favorite of Van's, he would ultimately visit his home nearly a dozen times. Van loved showing him off at the piano to other guests. Popovich was enamored with Van and loved just being in his presence. Popovich was from the older Soviet generation, which considered Van some type of pianistic deity. His legendary 1958 performance at the Tchaikovsky Competition had become part of Soviet folklore. He had endeared himself to the Soviet people and become a hero with a vast following. Her love for this man was remarkably apparent at their first meeting when Alexei witnessed Popovich do something he had never seen. Popovich smiled. She opened up and expressed her admiration for him, showing a tender side few ever saw. Dace half expected her to die from happiness after receiving a hug from Cliburn. Van always gave the biggest hugs. Like any unbending hardnosed instructor, she never let her students stray off course and had plenty of unorthodox methods to keep them toeing the line.

Popovich's strict Soviet style appeared at the second party she attended at Van's magnificent home. Shortly after arriving and receiving her highly prized hug and a few minutes of pleasantries, she changed gears abruptly. She told Alexei that she appreciated the party, but the time had come to leave, as practice time beckoned, even though they had only arrived fifteen minutes prior. Alexei somehow soothed Popovich into staying late into the evening, even after the concert party came to its end. This concession though did come with its price.

Early the next morning, at around six-thirty, Alexei and Dace were awakened with a sharp rap at their bedroom door. Popovich was awake, focused, and ready to begin his training. Upon Alexei's refusal, Popovich offered him the option of soapy water in his eyes if he didn't comply immediately. This method had been effective before, and this time was no different. Alexei, with a hangover in tow, crawled from bed to begin his practice. On another more lighthearted occasion, the Wilcoxes invited the Sultanovs and Tamara to the Fort Worth Petroleum Club for dinner. The evening was as uneventful as a fancy dinner with a hard-core communist piano teacher lacking the comforts of the English language could be. The awkwardness wasn't lost but rather embraced as the table enjoyed the slow and easy back and forth. John was able to utilize his Russian much to the delight of Popovich. The highlight for the Wilcoxes' night came when they ordered a bottle of champagne for dinner. The champagne was of the brut variety with a dry, less sweet taste, which wasn't quite what Popovich had in mind. Thus, she opened two sugar packets and dumped their contents into her glass. Due to the chemical reaction, the champagne bubbled out of Popovich's glass all over the table. This brought much laughter to the table and the evening.

28

The Sultanovs

On January 18, 1991, the Sultanovs finally had their official wedding party at the prestigious Fort Worth Petroleum Club, hosted by none other than Van Cliburn himself. The visits to his house had endeared Alexei to Van, who wanted to help the fledgling couple. Van learned early of the couple's impromptu marriage ceremony at the courthouse and immediately wanted to throw them an appropriate Texas-style celebration. The date was set during a small lull in Alexei's schedule. Van Cliburn contributed much to the occasion. The newlyweds were unaware of the customs of marriage, and thus, when the wedding date was announced, they were shocked at what came next. Several months prior to the party, a volunteer from the Van Cliburn Foundation picked them up and took them to Neiman Marcus to register. The entire scene made the couple's heads spin. Dace discovered that she loved the fancy dinner plates. Alexei was dumbfounded to learn that one of the plates she admired came with a price tag of one hundred fifty dollars. As per instruction by their Cliburn staff guide, they selected many high-end things, not quite understanding how the process works. Alexei could not believe that Americans would buy someone just one plate or one saucer for a wedding gift. He had an even harder time explaining this to Dace. Weeks before the wedding party, Van Cliburn noticed only a few items from the registry were being purchased for the young couple, as they knew very few people in this part of the world. So Van bought all the remaining unpurchased

The Sultanov wedding with its benefactor, Van Cliburn. *Dace Collection*

items for them. With a few days remaining before their celebration, Susan Wilcox learned Alexei planned to wear jeans and a t-shirt to the celebration, so she stepped in. She again drove him to Neiman Marcus, splurged, and bought him an eight-hundred-dollar Armani suit, which instantly became his favorite suit.

The wedding celebration day finally arrived and was a marvelous affair filled with many people who had never met the Sultanovs and just wanted to see and meet the new Cliburn champion. The venue was adorned with the most beautiful flower assortments and tables of delicious fare. There were fountains of shrimp, mountains of food at every turn, several bars with constant lines, and a live band. Alexei and Dace met and thanked most of the attendees at their wedding party for the graciousness they showed. Dace honed her thank you skills that evening. On the very morning of the party, Alexei took Dace to the West Loop Mitsubishi dealership, where they found and fell in love with a year-old red 1990 Mitsubishi Mirage. They bought the car for seven thousand dollars, and it was named "Little Tomato." The license plate was ordered with Alexei's pet name, Alosha.

Life at home for the Sultanovs was simple, which was the complete opposite of Alexei's life on the road. Alexei increasingly disliked the demands his concert schedule put on Dace and him. He always preferred being at home with Dace, where he could be himself without the constant pressures of life on the road. The couple loved to eat out at their favorite restaurants. Eating out was part of the appeal of America. Local mainstay restaurant Bella Italian became a weekly venue for Dace, with or without Alexei, so much so that the owner would put Alexei's picture on the wall for his most treasured customers to see. Home life remained easy whenever Alexei had time to be there. The couple spent endless hours playing video games and watching movies as Alexei reveled in perpetual childhood. The couple bought season passes to Six Flags Over Texas theme park, where they spent many long hours of their free time.

Dace loved to work in the yard and often felt most at home around the abundant plants and flowers that she coddled in the Texas heat. With endless time on her hands, she read often when she wasn't practicing her cello or raising her animal family. Learning English was no easy feat for Dace, but she credits her grasp of the American culture and overcoming the language barrier to *I Love Lucy*, which remains her favorite television show. Her short stint at Texas Wesleyan with Beverly created in her a desire to keep learning the English language. The television gave her the immersion her education needed. Alexei's travel schedule kept the couple separated often. Whenever Alexei was able, he would take Dace on his longer international trips. Alexei's typical absence lasted four to five days of each week. Alexei arrived home from one of his trips with a new Nintendo game system, and home competitions were never quite the same. Dace loved *Super Mario Brothers*, *Tetris*, *Zelda*, and *Final Fantasy*. Christmas time also became a special moment for the couple. They, after all, had few people to dote on. The act of gift giving took on a substantial role in their home. During the Christmas shopping experience, Alexei coordinated his shopping list for only one person: Dace. So, Dace had to shop for everyone else. When Alexei arrived home from his shopping excursion, he requested Dace disappear so he could empty the car of his newfound treasures. Dace donned her winter coat so she could sit on

At home with the Sultanovs. *Dace Collection*

the back porch, giving Alexei the privacy he needed. Alexei spent hours wrapping the assortment of gifts, which were all for her. When she was finally allowed to come back inside to thaw out, the entire Christmas tree was engulfed in a wonderful concoction of gifts wrapped in the crudest fashion. He was a talented musician, but details such as gift-wrapping didn't come to him easily.

Alexei's control over the couple's life kept Dace at home and without a real purpose of her own. He wouldn't allow Dace to work, as he seemingly earned enough for them both. He didn't want her to get into any trouble outside in the city. Those interested in communicating with the couple via the telephone often had difficulties. The home phone was never very important to the Sultanovs, and the message recorder would often be full and unable to accept new messages. When the Cliburn Foundation or concert promoters could not reach Alexei, they typically sent someone to their house to discuss any pertinent business matters. The Wilcoxes often would assist with bookings so that Alexei didn't miss a concert. Alexei and Dace found comfort in each other's presence so much so that the outside world lost interest. When they were together, nothing else mattered.

In the Soviet Union, the business side of music offered substantially fewer options than in America. Finding talent was never in question, but the managerial control that affected all Soviet imports and exports could be problematic. All Soviet musicians were managed by an organization called GosKoncert. Gos is the Russian abbreviation for government. The communist-run state agency was in command of its country's entire music empire. This agency was reportedly rife with corruption, as it handled the business side of the vast Soviet music empire. As a reward for exceptional talent, the GosKoncert took a substantial percentage of each artist's income as its managerial fee. As Alexei performed all over the world under his Van Cliburn contract, the Cliburn Foundation sent as much as 90 percent, depending on the prearrangement, of his performance income from Van Cliburn-sanctioned events to GosKoncert. Rodzinski felt obligated to honor the agreement the Cliburn made with GosKoncert. Alexei asked Rodzinski several times to skip sending his money to the Soviet agency, but Rodzinski, who had labored hard to keep GosKoncert out of the way of Cliburn interests, ultimately honored the contract he worked so hard to create.

As Alexei earned his substantial income under US income tax rules, he was also paying the GosKoncert tax. So, when he received a letter from the Internal Revenue Service with a tax notice for sixty thousand dollars, Alexei paid a visit to Jon Wilcox. A tax attorney was found who determined little could be done. Alexei was advised to send the IRS their money to avoid contaminating his residential status in Fort Worth. Alexei was extremely upset with this and sought to end this double dipping into his money. His answer would come with the expiration of his Van Cliburn contract in 1991. Denise Chubb's wonderful patience and exceptional sacrifice to keep Alexei booked ran out with the conclusion of his Van Cliburn contract. His career management then transitioned to Columbia Artists, where he stayed until 1998. This agency, the oldest brand name in the record business, was owned by music behemoth Sony, which took a twenty-five percent management fee for its efforts.

As Alexei and Columbia were joining forces in 1991, the Soviet Union was collapsing. It was during this public crumbling of the communist empire that Latvia stood up against the Soviet Union to ultimately regain its independence. Latvia finally resurrected its national pride as its sons and daughters united, rose against Soviet oppression, and fought to repair the country's severely damaged culture. The Soviets sent in tanks in response to squash the rebellion. The tanks were met by hundreds of Latvians who formed a human wall to block them. The media coverage of the event brought the world's discerning eye and subsequent support to Latvia. Soviet leader Mikhail Gorbachev bowed to the international pressure and backed off, thus opening the door to the new Latvia. Tens of thousands of Latvians quickly volunteered to join the new Independent Latvian Army, including the now middle-aged Janis Abele. Janis had risked his life to stand firm as Soviet tanks churned toward him. His participation in the human wall represented the fervor of all true Latvians to regain their independence. Everyone wanted to fight for their country's return to independence. Men and women felt compelled to offer their services to their precious Latvia in any way they could. Latvia finally could make its own mark on history. May 4th marks this historic Independence Day for the country. Latvia was now free.

In February 1992, Alexei was returning home from a nine-day stint in Berlin, recording another album for Teldec Records at their studio. This time he performed several Chopin works including four *Scherzi*, *Ballade no. 4*, and a *Grand Polonaise*. The work was easy and financially rewarding for him, but he experienced sharp pains in his abdomen during the recording, which grew as he finished the project. Tamara Popovich had recently come to Fort Worth by request and awaited Alexei's arrival back home to begin practice. Alexei was preparing for an upcoming European tour and needed her help with some fine-tuning. The flight back from Germany was excruciating for Alexei, with every slight movement sending horrible waves of pain shooting through him. Upon his arrival at DFW International Airport, Dace, who was awaiting his return at the gate, realized his situation was serious and called Jon Wilcox from an airport phone. He directed and met them at Harris Southwest Emergency Room.

The doctors quickly determined Alexei's appendix had burst, requiring immediate surgery. Alexei was put to sleep under anesthesia, and the procedure was performed with precision, saving his life. When time came to awaken Alexei from the surgery, the situation turned critical. Doctors discovered no pulse and immediately went for the defibrillators. They placed the paddles upon his chest and shocked his stopped heart. One shock was all it took as Alexei's heart popped back to life in text-

Tamara Popovich on one of her several trips to Texas. *Dace Collection.*

book fashion. Dace, who had grown exceptionally nervous during the surgery, snuck back behind the waiting area and found herself outside the surgical area. She had mistakenly stumbled onto the scene of the doctors shocking Alexei back to life. He quickly stabilized, and doctors felt he would make a full recovery. Alexei was released from recovery the next day, but Dace, who had taken custody of him, was never officially informed of the life-saving measures utilized on Alexei. The next morning, as Alexei rested comfortably in his bed, he was awakened early by a sharp rap at the door. Popovich, fully aware of his medical situation, was ready to begin Alexei's practice. Alexei, who was clearly unprepared and unfit for the task, could barely talk her down. Popovich would have to wait this time.

On May 15, 1992, the Fort Worth Chamber Society proposed a concert that featured both Alexei at the piano and Dace on the cello. Dace was relatively unknown for the talent she possessed. The overshadowing by her famed husband kept her talent out of the public's eye, although Dace had on occasion accompanied her husband on the cello. This event

The playful Alexei pushed Dace into a pool. *Dace Collection.*

at the Kimbell Art Museum finally brought her into the limelight. The duo performed to an enthusiastic audience of Fort Worth's elite chamber music patrons. Dace and Mr. Cello introduced themselves to the city while Alexei's draw power brought the masses. Alexei opened with Beethoven's Sonata in C Minor alongside Society president and accomplished violinist, Robert Davidovici. When Dace appeared, the crowd looked on in wonder as this beautiful blonde walked onto the stage. Alexei at times ripped through several arpeggios, letting everyone know who was in charge, but he did give way to Dace's deep rich cello for the second part of the evening with Beethoven's Sonata no. 2 in A Major for cello and piano, a composition dedicated to Joseph Haydn. The unpolished Dace and Mr. Cello stole the show that evening as her perfect accompaniment hit its mark. The third and final part of the evening found the couple and Davidovici performing the Beethoven Trio no. 3 in C Minor, Op. 1, which delighted the chamber music crowd as the cello, violin, and piano filled the room with the rich sounds of the trio.

29
1993 Van Cliburn Competition

The 1993 Van Cliburn International Piano Competition arrived on schedule, four years after the previous. The Soviets were now referred to as Russians as of January 1, 1991, as the Soviet empire was now re-imagined. The Russians sent an arsenal to this Cliburn competition, eager to showcase their repurposed country's talent on the world stage. Alexi's role as past champion morphed considerably for him. Tradition dictated that previous competitions' winners were to return to Fort Worth and be part of the ceremonies to encourage, excite, and promote the competition and competitors. Alexei, as the past competition's winner, was the celebrity of record—next to Van Cliburn, of course. Part of Alexei's Cliburn responsibilities were to attend these official engagements, where dinner and drinks were often served, and possibly speak or even play at the gatherings. The functions seemed endless, but funding for this competition was born from these events.

This year, though, the Sultanovs played an additional role as well, as hosts. Their home became ground zero for the Russian competitors and their entourages. Dace would soon learn what the Wilcoxes already knew, that playing host is a remarkably difficult and thankless job. Dace entertained, cooked, cleaned, and chauffeured these Russians for the duration of the three-week stretch. And their required presence at the Russian performances during the competition kept them racing around.

Additionally, one of Alexei's longtime Russian friends from back in the conservatory days, Sasha Korsantia, was entered in the Ninth Van Cliburn International Competition and was an early favorite to make the finals. Alexei knew his level of talent was significant enough to take him far in the competition. Sasha grew up in Tbilisi, the capital city of the Soviet Republic of Georgia. He had followed a path not dissimilar to Alexei's. Everyone would discover their favorites, and Sasha was certainly Alexei's.

The first round went off without a hitch. The talent on display was evidence of the masterful ability of the Cliburn to find and attract incredible talent from all over the world. Crowds and media alike gushed over the new Cliburn class. Korsantia indeed performed wonderfully, or so Alexei thought. Then time came for the announcement of the semi-finalists from Maestro Giordano. When Korsantia's name wasn't called to the stage as a qualifier for the second round, Alexei became visibly irate, loudly admonishing the jurors from his seat, and he stormed out of Ed Landreth Hall. Korsantia, after all, had won the 1988 Sydney International Piano Competition, so surely he was good enough to make the second round at the Cliburn. The jurors felt differently. In Alexei's mind, backstage politics, aimed directly at the jurors, had seeped into this competition. This marked a point in Alexei's life when pianistic competitions no longer felt subjective, but instead rather prejudiced. His disappointment quickly developed into disdain for these types of competitions, especially the very one that launched his career. How could a jury really pick one pianist and say he was better than all the others? How could a jury say one pianist was fourth or fifth best, when they all have such exceptional talent?

Author Joseph Horowitz (no relation to Vladimir), who attended the entire 1989 Cliburn when Alexei claimed gold, wrote a book based on research about music competitions. Horowitz described competitions negatively, and pointed out the negative impact on performers who don't win. The book, titled *The Ivory Trade*, struck a nerve in Fort Worth for its in-depth depiction of the Cliburn's means of selecting a winner. His book received critical acclaim for its detailed depiction of the Eighth Van Cliburn International Piano Competition and his harsh criticisms of the entire international piano competition environment. Horowitz's feelings, now shared by Alexei, were further strengthened when Korsantia, two years later, took first prize in the Arthur Rubenstein Piano Master Competition in Tel Aviv.

Now, at the 1993 Cliburn competition, Alexei felt as if he was being swept under the rug. He sensed he was being utilized by the Cliburn organization to promote the image of the Cliburn rather than the spirit of competition. To him, the competition was more akin to a sports game than a showcase of talented pianists. The Cliburn, to be fair, never shied away from its highly competitive stance, knowing that some of the world's best talents don't always showcase well and often get eliminated early. Alexei felt like an underling, which made watching the competition very painful for him. As for the overall pulse of the 1993 competition, it had continually grown in popularity and had plucked another sensational field of competitors for its finalists. The Van Cliburn International Piano Competition was known throughout the globe for its premier competitors and stood toe to toe with any piano competition in the world. Simone Pedroni, playing the most inspired music and winning the hearts of the audience and jurors alike, took home the gold medal. Another Russian, Valery Kuleshov, took second place in splendid fashion.

Dace was left exhausted by the constant hosting efforts thrust upon her. After the daily barrage of events, she typically was called upon to drive the Russian competitors to their respective host homes, as they had no cars. She regularly climbed into bed well past two in the morning. No one was happier to see the Ninth International Van Cliburn Piano Competition come to an end than she.

As the second and third rounds of the Cliburn competition were unfolding, Alexei spent the time with Korsantia and another early exit Russian, Sergei Tarasov, away from the competition at the Six Flags of America theme park. Alexei's pent-up anger subsided as the three pianists reveled in the childish freedoms they were now afforded. Alexei and Korsantia quickly developed a blossoming friendship. On their visits to each other's homes over the years, they would squeeze as much activity as possible into the time they had. Very rarely did the topic of music come up in the course of conversation, even though it soaked their daily lives. Alexei would make a tremendous impression on Sasha. They shared an incredible talent on the piano, although Alexei displayed his personality when he performed. His electrifying style of playing attracted other virtuosos in some sort of spiritual fraternity. These friends developed a strong bond, which made their time together so much fun. Alexei would introduce Sasha to the joys of playing Nintendo, where the two spent countless hours together. Even without its former champion's blessing, the 1997 Cliburn competition was by all accounts a raging success. Record crowds, prizes, performances, and bookings spewed forth. Whether Alexei liked it or not, the Cliburn was thriving, and the world was watching from the edge of their seats.

On August 3, 1994, Fort Worth was hit with the death of one of its most beloved music teachers. Van Cliburn's mother Rildia Bee passed away at age ninety-seven at Fort Worth's All Saints Episcopal Hospital, leaving a gaping hole in her son's heart. She had been living with Van for much of her senior years. She had birthed and groomed one of piano's legendary performers, and Van never took this fact for granted. She was cared for at every turn by her fiercely loyal son. Nearly until the day she passed, Rildia Bee loved to recount her ninety-fourth birthday party that Van had planned in her honor. It was a glorious social event, so much so that it made mention in the *New Yorker* magazine. It was on a Sunday evening, October 14, 1990, at the prestigious Fort Worth Club, where six hundred guests convened for the occasion. When Rildia Bee arrived, Maestro John Giordano and the entire Fort Worth Symphony opened up with *The Star Spangle Banner* followed by several Richard Strauss's *Der Rosenkavalier Waltzes*, her favorite. Roberta Peters,[1] the New York operatic legend, then appeared and sang a few powerful opera favorites of Rildia Bee's.

When Rildia Bee's cake was wheeled into the room, she broke down in tears. Her subsequent speech grew into lovely sermon that energized all her guests. Her passing hurt Van deeply. Van's affection for the Sultanovs resurfaced when the Cliburn Foundation called to ask Dace to play her cello at Rildia Bee's memorial service. The honor was flattering to Dace, but when she told Alexei, he had a markedly different reaction. He had lost his appreciation for the Cliburn and its politics. Sadly, he told Dace that she was not to do it.

30
The Help

Ask most concert pianists and they will surely tell you that their piano technician is as critical to their performance as they are. The concert piano is an ever-changing instrument, requiring constant technical maintenance. Vladimir Horowitz's tuner, Franz Mohr, was anywhere a performance by Horowitz was taking place. The two could not operate without each other. Piano technicians, the good ones at least, endear themselves to the performers they keep happy. Mohr worked for and appeased the likes of Horowitz, Elton John, Artur Rubinstein, Van Cliburn, Rudolf Serkin, Glenn Gould, and Emil Gilels, to name but a few.[1] James Williams, who came to be employed by Steinway and Sons, would study under Mohr, but his beginnings made him uniquely different.

Williams aspired to be a drummer from an early age. His dreams behind the drum set moved to the back burner when the oil patch came calling. His father toiled tirelessly at the now defunct but largely successful Sun Oil Company (Sunoco) and Sun Gas for most of his career, and it just made sense to James to follow in his footsteps. His first fifteen years would find him across Texas and California with Sunoco and then finally for the Hunt Oil Company. He likely would have succeeded in this dream of one day becoming a known drummer had it not been for his good friend, Richard Theisen. Theisen was a classically trained pianist who found fame when he wrote *Rock 'N Roll Me*, an electropop hit made popular with its inclusion on the 1984 *Original Beverly Hills Cop* movie soundtrack, where it achieved gold then double platinum status. It was Theisen who introduced Williams to his piano technician, Leon Spear, who taught Williams the business of piano maintenance. Williams's extensive training as an engineer in the oil business gave him the foundation for his future career change, but the change wouldn't come for many years, so he spent years as a roughneck. In 1977, Williams was transferred from the Permian Basin near Big Springs, Texas, to the coastal venue of Ventura, California, where Sunoco has just completed installation of an offshore drilling platform named Hillhouse. The Hillhouse Platform sat six miles off the coast of Santa Barbara and one mile east of Union Oil's infamous Platform A. Platform A made world headlines back in 1969 for a blowout emergency during drilling operations which resulted in the largest oil spill in US waters at that time. The environmentally disastrous blowout now ranks third after the Deepwater Horizon (2010) and the Exxon Valdez (1989) spills. The Santa Barbara Oil Spill resulted in a reported one hundred thousand barrels of crude spewing from the ocean floor into the Santa Barbara Channel.[2]

A decade later after the Platform A blowout, Williams, through his hard work and dependability, worked his way up to platform operator on the Sunoco-owned Eugene Island 380 platform off the coast of Texas in the Gulf of Mexico. His role often found him grinding out grueling twelve-hour shifts. Often the mountains of paperwork stole away his time. It was a routine shift change during a frigid February in 1979 that changed the course of his life. As the Bell 212 helicopter arrived to airlift Williams and his departing team members off the platform, the copilot seat was offered up to Williams, the most senior member. Pilots of these fifteen-seat helicopters, manufactured in Fort Worth, Texas, were typically assigned to Vietnam vet pilots, who flew them as if on combat missions and typically with more than their five-thousand-pound cargo limit, as if normal flying conditions weren't challenging enough. The second acting platform operator on duty that day took his seat behind Williams in the cabin amongst the twelve other passengers.

Several minutes after liftoff on the one hundred eighty-mile flight back to the mainland, Williams realized he had forgotten to grab a handful of paperwork he needed to deliver to headquarters. He turned suddenly to his right to ask the second platform operator if he had picked it up. The quick movement propelled his knee into the secondary cyclic stick (joystick) which moved between his legs and knocked it free from the pilot's controlling grasp. The helicopter rolled sharply onto its side and nosed down toward the biting sea just below them. Panic ripped through the cabin as they grabbed for something to hold onto. The expert pilot was able to pull the chopper from certain disaster mere seconds before the helicopter crashed into the sea. He launched into a screaming tirade at Williams at his inexcusable blunder and told him in certain terms to sit still in his seat and not move an inch. Williams sat in silence for the remaining two hours of the flight, contemplating the tragedy that nearly unfolded because of him. As the helicopter touched down, Williams's decision had been made. The gripping thought of nearly killing fourteen people was more than he could bear, and he walked away from the scene and his career, never to return. Williams, haunted by the events of that day, never again would board an aircraft, opting instead for car or boat travel regardless of distance.

Opting now for an office gig, Williams spent a few years in an office at Hunt Oil, resigning after a fifteen-year stint in the oil patch. It was around the time that Alexei Sultanov was competing in the 1989 Van Cliburn Competition that Williams set upon a new path where he would become one of the most coveted piano technicians in the United States. Williams discovered that his engineering skills were perfect for the complex work of fixing and tuning pianos. The work was long and grueling but much safer in the long run. Williams went to work for Tyson Piano and Organ Company in 1990. The Tyson Company was at the time a respected Steinway & Sons piano dealer. Williams also began a home piano restoration business that brought him close to his early technological mentor, Leon Spear. It wasn't long before Williams became the on-site piano technician for the El Paso Symphony Orchestra. The El Paso Symphony Orchestra was preparing for a concerto performance from famed Russian American pianist Vladimir Feltsman.

Feltsman's career launched after he won the Grand Prix at the Marguerite Long International Piano Competition in Paris in 1971. With his concert bookings soaring, his confidence also grew. But in 1979, after he applied for an exit visa, Feltsman was banned for eight years from recording or performing publicly by the Soviet state-run music agency, GosKoncert, after he publicly shared his discontent regarding the Soviet Union's strict artistic policies. After eight years of performance exile, he was finally granted permission to leave the Soviet Union, which he did in earnest. He was quickly embraced by the United States and performed his American debut concert at the White House for then President Ronald Reagan. Critics consider him a wonderful talent as well as the master of reinventing himself. He was also known for his virulent temper. It was during his rehearsal in El Paso that the tempestuous Feltsman flew into a rage, as the piano he was set to play didn't sound right to him. With the entire El Paso Symphony Orchestra on stage watching, Feltsman screamed and cursed Williams for his perceived poor tuning of this piano. Then he moved on to Gaye Brown, the president of the Orchestra, where he stood inches from her face, publicly berating her, with spittle flying everywhere from his mouth. He proceeded to grab his crotch and suggest that this piano needed a set of balls. Williams dusted himself off and drove the piano back to his shop in Fort Worth after the repugnant Feltsman performed the following day and then quickly left town. Williams worked the piano over with a fine-toothed comb and then returned it to El Paso for its next concert engagement. The next scheduled performer would be a much better encounter.

The symphony brought in a young Soviet pianist living in Texas who was the winner of the Van Cliburn Competition back in 1989. Alexei Sultanov was well received as he performed beautifully. He stunned the El Paso audience with his lightning-quick hands and spellbinding ferocity, earning him several encores as the crowd expressed their sincere pleasure. Alexei found the piano tuned very much to his liking and even expressed his pleasure to Williams. Williams developed into one of Steinway's most qualified technicians in the country. Williams's work and subsequent training from Steinway & Son's chief concert technician emeritus, Franz Mohr, opened many doors. Mohr eventually introduced Williams to his most important client, Vladimir Horowitz. Williams's keen ear and exceptional mastery of the interior workings of the piano translated into instant rapport with celebrated artists such as Stephen Hough, Yefim Bronfman, Olga Kern, Barry Douglas, and many more. He also became the de-facto tuner for the Cliburn Competition, the Fort Worth Symphony Orchestra, and the Dallas Symphony Orchestra.[3]

# 31
The Chopin

In 1995, Alexei, feeling the effects of several professional blunders and his snubbing of the Cliburn organization, decided he needed to restart his career. His star power dimmed as his reputation for a stale repertoire and, more importantly, unreliability spread. Alexei felt ready to test his talents again against the world's best and thus sent in his application to the Chopin International Piano Competition in Warsaw, Poland. Founded in 1927, this piano competition remained one of the premier competitions in Europe with only the Tchaikovsky Piano Competition in Moscow receiving heavier acclaim. The Chopin competition is unique in that it is held every five years and requires from its hopeful one hundred thirty-nine competitors works only from its namesake. Alexei had begun to feel more and more irrelevant as the newest Cliburn class was making its mark on the international scene. Alexei felt winning this competition would show the world he was still relevant and viable. The Van Cliburn Foundation and Richard Rodzinski were against this move but had little sway over Alexei these days. A pianist of Alexei's renown shouldn't need a piano competition victory to boost his career. He needed to expand his repertoire to make himself more appealing to promoters and secondly, to show up. Alexei was not moved by the advice of those he owed so much. The Chopin competition remained a lifelong dream for him. He always had a special place in his heart for the music of Frederic Chopin. Chopin, a composer of Polish descent, was a piano virtuoso whose technique for the piano made him a legend for all eternity. He wrote over two hundred thirty compositions, and his massive accomplishments before his untimely death at the age of thirty-nine left an indelible mark on the Romantic period.

The application process required a video of each applicant to be reviewed by the Chopin selection panel. Alexei needed help creating a video and sought the assistance of Dr. Tamas Ungar, the highly acclaimed professor on Texas Christian University's piano faculty. Dr. Ungar was also against the idea of Alexei playing in the Chopin, but realizing his determination, helped him nonetheless. Dr. Ungar, with borrowed video camera from the University and a key to Ed Landreth Hall, set up Alexei to record. It was two o'clock in the morning when Dr. Ungar began recording in secret Alexei's performance of Chopin's Etude No. 18, which showcased his talents on this most incredibly difficult piece. Dr. Ungar also filmed Alexei playing the *Revolutionary Etude* and Polonaise No. 6 *Brillante*. The recording was mailed to Warsaw where it was quickly accepted by the Chopin competition selection panel. Dr. Ungar's secret plan was somehow discovered, and he received a call from the Dean of the TCU Music Department. After a stern lecture and a slap on the wrist for using school property after hours for unrelated business, Dr. Ungar waited for the results of the competition. The Chopin competition and its three weeks and four rounds of competition now became Alexei's measuring stick against his successful peers. Chopin's music to him was about freedom and life. The stress exerted by playing the music of Chopin on a pianist's ring and pinky finger tended to test those not up to the technical challenge. The strength and dexterity of these two digits are pivotal to play exceptional Chopin, and only many years of practice could prepare a pianist's fingers for such stress.

The excitement of Alexei's arrival spurred a Polish television station producer, Aleksandra Padlewska, to create a documentary entitled *Point of View*, which showcased Alexei Sultanov at the Thirteenth Chopin competition. Alexei opened as the early favorite due to his noted ability and aging popularity. This four-part documentary aired later throughout Europe.

Alexei prepared mightily for this competition and showed up ready for gold. Playing the selected Steinway no. 90, he wowed the international audience with his own interpretation of Chopin's classic B Minor Sonata. He felt he had played exceptionally. Alexei did not disappoint and easily earned high juror marks. His talent was a crowd favorite, but there was a host of others that performed inspired Chopin. The third week of the competition, Alexei had qualified for the finals along with five others and joined up with the Polish Symphony Orchestra as per the requirements. He rewarded everyone with his interpretation of the classic Chopin piece Fantasia A Major, Opus 13. The audience offered deafening applause before he even took the stage for his much-anticipated final performance. This piece had been privately renamed *Maljuk*, after the Sultanov couple's family cat they purchased from Fort Worth's Hulen Mall pet shop. His grey coat matched the pants Alexei was wearing that day, which resulted in the impulse buy. As they would learn, Maljuk, the cat, was indifferent to Alexei's music at home, except when he played Chopin. This romantic kitty would come running to Alexei's side only when Chopin was played. He was visibly entranced by Fantasia, which led Alexei to rename the composition. The crowd, also entranced, soaked in every note and leaped from their seats as he concluded. Richard Rodzinski, who had made the must-see trip, joined in the appreciation. He knew from the crowd's reaction that the competition was Alexei's.

The crowd applauded him in a way that seemed to anoint the champion, reminiscent of his Cliburn final performance. He raised his arms victoriously as he rose from his bow. He exited the stage as the applause grew louder. Alexei, feeling the power of the applause, paused just behind the curtain. He knew he shouldn't but felt compelled to return for only an encore bow. The renegade in him yearned to bend the rules. The Chopin competition officials blocked his return to stage, as it was strictly against competition rules. The applause continued for an unheard-of ten minutes, which only reaffirmed what he had done. The jury convened, after the remaining finalists performed, to their jury room. Alexei knew that he was up against the similar hard-lined jurors that had robbed him of the Tchaikovsky gold early in his career. The audience was restless as they waited, each having an opinion needing to be validated. When the jury returned after their lengthy discussion, the chairman, Jan Ekier, a recognized authority on Frederic Chopin, took the podium for the announcement after the pleasantries were completed. When he read the verdict, the anxious audience gasped loudly with shock.

The Thirteenth International Chopin Piano Competition would

have no winner, but instead a much less coveted double second-place award. Alexei would share the award, much to his chagrin, with French pianist Philippe Giusiano. This was an outrage to the sensitivities of Alexei and even tainted the audience award that Alexei had won as well. Alexei felt he had earned and deserved this outright win and thus was in no mood to converse with the press afterwards. The Associated Press reporter, when he asked Alexei to share his thoughts, was told bluntly, "Leave me alone!" Dace, always the shoulder to lean on for Alexei, felt the severe damage done to Alexei's psyche. Alexei refused to attend the post-competition Gala concert the next day, where each of the six finalists were asked to play a fifteen-minute solo work. The noticeable decline in enthusiasm at the event due to Alexei's absence wasn't missed by anyone. One of the jury members was overhead complaining that the "winner's concert was the most inconsequential thing" he had ever seen. The Chopin organizers, in order to salvage the competition, somehow convinced Alexei to play at the second post-concert reception. He begrudgingly agreed on the condition that he was not to be referred to as the co-silver medalist. He performed his fifteen-minute solo recital along with the other five finalists but was singled out by the audience with their continued and sustained applause, resulting in an extra thirty minutes of encore performances. The Polish Minister of Culture, Kazimierz Dejmek, publicly blasted the jurors for "effectively destroying the Chopin Competition's reputation" for not awarding a champion in the last two of their quinquennial events. Piotr Wierzbicki—Polish radio presenter, popular DJ, and tour guide—made matters worse when his widely read review of the Chopin competition described Alexei Sultanov as the greatest Chopin pianist in history.

In his mind, Alexei had utterly failed himself. All the suffering he endured as a child at the piano amounted now to a complete waste. Alexei felt so strongly about his Chopin victory that the alternative result crushed him. Alexei later told the press, "I was not angry because I got second place, but I was unhappy that the prize was shared!" "I wanted to show the difference between me and the five others (finalists), who played like nice, polished, proficient, college students." Alexei then abruptly left Warsaw to return to Fort Worth, only to withdraw into a shell of disgruntlement. As perhaps the most controversial young pianist in the world, Alexei went back home rattled to his core. From this moment on, Alexei refused to travel outside Fort Worth without his Dace by his side. His bitterness was apparent, but a spike in concert bookings erupted after the Chopin debacle. He would consequently perform in Milan's Teatro alla Scala, regarded as one of the world's most important opera houses, as well as back in Warsaw, then Poznan, Hamburg, Athens, Santiago, Zagreb, Berlin, Taipei, Helsinki, Osaka, and Tokyo. Each performance found a sold-out venue. He rode this new popularity, and his mood seemed to improve for a bit. But as his resurgence in popularity calmed as the year progressed, his bitterness ensued.

Alexei began to intermittently question his parents by telephone as to why they had made his childhood so unbearable. Natalia would always deflect this line of questioning as a common occurrence for any child prodigy. She refused to find fault in her rigid methods of teaching and structure. Alexei's anger began to boil over again, and this time he lashed out at the perceived source of his unhappiness—his parents. He found tremendous fault in his parents for subjecting him to a tortuous childhood. He felt his talent was on par with the great ones. His hero Horowitz, after all, had passed him the torch. His career mishaps and self-diagnosed sufferings were not supposed to happen, not to him. These things didn't happen to the greats. It would take extraordinary efforts by Dace to get Alexei's head back in the game. He did still have a career to think about. Mild relief again would find him, and this time from the Alexei Sultanov Fan Club in Tokyo, Japan.

After the Chopin competition, Alexei's luck had another rough patch on the international side. He had sought to get a new passport as his current one was inundated with stamps from his travel. He ran into strong resistance from the new Russian republic. He was denied a new passport as officials determined he was clearly not Russian, but rather Uzbeki due his country of birth, Uzbekistan. The Uzbekistan officials also denied him as well, due to his time living in Moscow when the Soviet Union was breaking up in 1991. He was essentially a man without a country. He could not confirm citizenship with any country. Alexei utilized a U.S. State Department permit to allow him to travel for his musical bookings.

Dr. Tamas Ungar would, weeks after the Chopin competition, receive a case of vodka as thank you from Alexei after TCU discovered his misconduct in creating the video for his application. Dr. Ungar, a music prodigy in his own right, recognized Alexei's special gift and consulted him whenever he could.

Later in 1995, Dr. Ungar arranged a concert performance by the world-renowned Russian pianist, Lazar Berman, who was his admitted pianistic idol. Susan Tilley, who had chaired the Van Cliburn Piano Competition for many years, had become the manager of Berman's son Pavel, who was an accomplished violinist and conductor. In 1990, young Berman won the Gold Medal at the International Violin Competition of Indianapolis. Tilley's connection helped Ungar book Pavel's famous musical father to Fort Worth for the TCU/Cliburn Piano Institute recital series. One of Lazar Berman's conditions for performing was that he must have a Fazioli Piano from its plant in Sacile, Italy to play. Dr. Ungar painstakingly arranged for the exclusive two hundred-thousand-dollar piano to be shipped to Fort Worth by airplane, where it arrived at Fort Worth's Meacham Airfield. The concert event on June 15th, 1995 was highly anticipated by the city. Lazar's arrival and public comments to the press about Americans were not positive in nature and subsequently would damage his local reputation. Berman's disparaging remarks about Americans not understanding music and being over eager for everything left many angry with this musical great. Local Fort Worthians Heywood and Harriett Clemons hosted a dinner party for ten people after the conclusion of the recital at Ed Landreth Hall. Dr. Ungar, feeling the need for friendly company at the dinner, invited Alexei and Dace. Van Cliburn needed no invitation and joined his friend Berman and the group. The dinner quickly went sideways as Alexei became intoxicated and indulged in conversation with Berman that included hurtful remarks regarding the Cliburn Competition, Americans' understanding of music, and musical competitions in general, within earshot of the entire table. Dr. Ungar's repeated requests to calm down were ignored, which sadly ruined the affair for all, including the very disppointed host family. Dr. Ungar was highly embarrassed by the entire ordeal.[1]

Lazar Berman was many people's musical idol. The Russian classical pianist was worshipped for his large and thunderous technique, which made his Liszt and Rachmaninoff especially poignant, and he was sought after by promoters. He was only ten when he made his debut playing Mozart's Piano Concerto No. 25 with the Moscow Philharmonic Orchestra. In 1941, his music school was evacuated to Kuibyshev, a city on Europe's longest river, the Volga, because of the threat of invading

Lazar Berman having dinner with Van, Alexei, and Dace. *Dace Collection.*

Nazis. The living conditions were so miserable that Berman's mother cut the fingers off his gloves so he could practice the piano without freezing his hands. His fifth-place finish in the Queen Elizabeth International Competition in Brussels in 1956 opened the world's eyes to this extraordinary prodigy. His short marriage to a French national earned him a spot on the Soviet no-travel list for seventeen years. He lived in a tiny two-room apartment in Moscow, with one of those rooms completely filled by his grand piano. His reputation still thrived inside the Soviet Union, but the state-run GosKoncert ignored any and all outside concert requests. When GosKoncert finally caved to international pressure in 1975, Berman was allowed to embark on an American tour. His *Transcendental Etudes* by Liszt during his New York debut at the 92nd Street Y launched him to super stardom. Seemingly overnight, Berman's recruitment by major record labels Deutsche Grammophon, EMI, and CBS jumped him to the world's stage. Berman performed and recorded throughout the globe with wild success and was given the unofficial American moniker, "The Mohammed Ali of the Keyboard." When he returned to Moscow from a concert in 1980, customs officials discovered a Soviet-banned book by an American author in his luggage, resulting in his passport being revoked. One of the world's most popular living pianist was now to be a prisoner in his own country. Ten years later, as the Soviet Union was in its downward spiral, Lazar made his way to Italy, where he became a citizen, performed internationally again, taught, and ultimately died in 2005.

Nineteen ninety-five was also an eventful year for Alexei's longtime conservatory friend, Sasha Shtarkman. His pianistic talent was well known, but he needed some catalyst to move his career forward. That event came in the small mountainous Italian town of Bolzano, Italy where the Ferruccio Busoni International Piano Competition had been held since its creation April 12, 1949, the twenty-fifth anniversary of its namesake's death. The Busoni competition's original stated goal was to bolster the reputation of the city and its conservatory as well as to repair the cultures of Italy and Germany after the Second World War through a high-profile international music competition. Ferruccio Busoni had been a renowned Italian pianist, composer, and teacher whose exile from Italy for five years during the first World War led to his monumental works of the Bach-Busoni Edition, compositions of his Turandot and Arlecchino, and the beginning of his grandest work, an opera called Doktor Faust. Busoni's pedagogic legacy was far reaching throughout the world before he died at the early age of fifty-eight.

Shtarkman, with his final round performances of Beethoven's Fourth and Rachmaninoff's Third, accompanied by the Haydn Orchestra of Bolzano and Trento, took the grand prize at the 1995 Busoni competition. The top prize came with it several valuable rewards for Shtarkman. The first and most obvious was the honorable distinction of winning the Busoni, which awarded a trove of recognition, money, a new Kawai concert piano, and a heavy list of engagements. Secondly, Shtarkman, unlike Alexei, was able to put an end to all future piano competitions for himself. The tremendous pressure to perform, especially at the competitive level, had been finally relieved for him. Shtarkman subsequently moved to New York, where he began his obligatory concert schedule, propelling his name to new heights. Shtarkman credits the Busoni victory for his success. Shtarkman would go on to become a distinguished recurring jury member for the Busoni.

32

Pinprick

Alexei confidently walked into the beautiful Kioi Hall in Tokyo, Japan, on a perfect Tuesday evening on April 2, 1996. He was not originally scheduled here, but after the quick sell-out of the Tokyo Metropolitan Theatre five days prior, Alexei was quickly booked. A concert in Osaka on April 30 kept Alexei on the move in Japan. The first performance on March 31 only included works from Chopin. The second performance at Kioi Hall provided more variety. This exquisite music venue was opened the year before by Nippon Steel Company to commemorate their twentieth anniversary. This Japanese-style music hall designed in a shoebox layout exudes intimacy for its eight hundred engaged and connected patrons. The architect desired closeness between audience and performers. The elaborate wood finishes and tall ceiling enhance the full and rich acoustics. The price tag for such opulence was just shy of the equivalent of fifty million US dollars. A Steinway New York concert grand model D piano, handmade of possibly the finest collection ever assembled of wood, glue, felt, buckskin, paper, steel, iron, and copper glimmered on stage, awaiting Alexei. Japan Arts Corporation, a well-seasoned management corporation founded in 1976 and based in Tokyo, set up Alexei's trip to Tokyo. Surprisingly, Japan Arts had found him during his recent Chopin Piano Competition and booked him for a Japanese tour. Japan had a rabid fan base that truly loved their classical music and included a devout following of everything Alexei.

Alexei's short walk out on stage was met with welcoming applause. He bowed deeply and smiled to the crowd as he always did. He quickly readjusted the piano bench with a slight turn of the knob. The eighty-eight shining keys waited, as if they knew what was to come.

When the box office for the event was opened, it sold out that day. Tickets were expensive. This engagement earned Alexei five thousand dollars, which was a substantial amount for a classical musician at this time. Beethoven's Piano Sonata No. 23 in F Minor Opus 57 was ready and waiting in his memory. Most refer to this piece as the *Appassionata*, meaning passionate in Italian. Ludwig Von Beethoven composed this piece between 1804 and 1806 and dedicated it to Count Franz von Brunswick. This piece is dear to classical music lovers and critics alike due to its elegant composition and technical difficulty. Considered one of the greatest and most tempestuous piano sonatas in Beethoven's works, this composition frequently uses the deep and dark tone of the lowest F key on the piano, which was as far left as Beethoven could travel on his new modern Erard concert piano ivories with its noted heavy action. This is the likely reason Beethoven chose the F Minor key in which to play *Appassionata*.

Beethoven never earned much money during his life. He composed as any eccentric genius might. His extreme depression was understandable, as he was the offspring of a violent alcoholic father. The composer began losing his hearing at age twenty-two and by forty was completely deaf. The majority of his masterpieces came during this "late" period. Beethoven's legacy began early on, when Mozart, upon hearing Beethoven play at age seventeen, declared, "Watch this lad. One day he will force the world to talk about him."

As Alexei's first finger touches down into the middle "C" the audience snaps to attention. Alexei, for this moment in time, acts as the voice of Beethoven himself. Due to technical limitations of the time, no recordings exist of Beethoven performing. As *Appassionata* begins, a window opens into the soul of a man who composed timeless arrangements for a nearly a decade without the ability to hear.

33
Light the Fuse

Alexei Sultanov grew to love playing for the Japanese people. Their intimate knowledge of his musical stylings and profound appreciation for classical music made playing in their country a sought-after venue. He was in a country that loved and celebrated him, and his Dace was with him. Dace sat purposely and quietly in the middle rows, where Alexei could easily find her. She wore her elegant long dark-green dress, which had become a favorite among a collection of six concert-worthy dresses purchased for her by Alexei. Tonight, though, was different. From the moment he walked on stage and commenced his two-hour performance, Alexei sensed that something wasn't quite right. As focused as he was, he wasn't fully there. Decked out in his white tie and tails, he began performing while noticing a strange feeling inside which he hadn't felt before. As the playful and ominous dance of *Appassionata's* first movement began, his right hand tingled and went numb. He began to feel a loss of control of his hand. This feeling wasn't apparent to anyone in the audience except himself. His powerful strokes and swift fingers had since captured his audience.

This first movement, *Allegro Assai*, typically is performed in ten to eleven minutes. Alexei regularly completed it in fewer than nine. When the *Allegro Assai*, referencing its very fast tempo style, reached the forty-seven second mark, Alexei's pinky finger on his right hand misfired on the high G note. One solitary note he missed. He was the only person who noticed. As training and experience teaches the pianist, mistakes will be made, and you must always play on regardless. The likelihood of anyone noticing is exceptionally minute and, in this case, completely absent. Alexei continued on with no further mistakes to speak of. After concluding *Appassionata* and its three movements, he rose to bow to the extraordinary delight of the crowd at Kioi Hall. As he stood for the night's first intermission, he was bombarded with a standing ovation from the wildly appreciative Japanese crowd.

He exited stage left to meet his wife backstage. Dace, who had been witness in the crowd, joined Alexei in his backstage room to share in this moment. When he entered, she reached out affectionately to her *Alosha* for a hug. Instantly, she could tell something wasn't right. Dace asked him what was wrong. She had no inkling that Alexei was troubled until she saw him that instant. He kissed her as she smiled in congratulatory style. Everything had been perfect, and Dace confirmed it. She knew this piece by memory as well. Listening to Alexei practice was the norm in the Sultanov household. Dace was a devoted young wife who understood her role in Alexei's performance world. But Alexei's look this time told a troubling story.

This moment seemed different from the rest and not just because of what he said but because of the look in his eyes. It was one of fear and concern. With a pained look, Alexei peered at her with discerning eyes. "I think I had a stroke!" Dace laughed slightly and thought he was kidding, but no smile emerged from her husband's face. He quickly explained how he missed the high G early in the piece of *Appassionata*, a mistake he never makes. He was the only person on the planet privy to the minuscule error, but as hugely prepared as he was for this recital, the error loomed large for him. Every note he knew by heart and the fact that his finger missed its intended target on one solitary key amidst the swirl of a rapid series of notes trumped the night's first wildly applauded performance, but only for Alexei, a known perfectionist. Simply put, he did not make this type of mistake. Alexei fretted. He sensed something terrible internally and now became completely convinced that his life clock had begun an expeditious countdown.

He knew something was wrong but could not possibly know the true nature of his fate. To all in attendance, the piece was played with his beloved passion and gusto. Alexei calmed himself with a drink of water, then sat for a few minutes to review the upcoming Chopin in his head for the second half, but he couldn't escape from that missed high G note. Chopin remained one of the most requested pieces in his repertoire and remained at the ready even though Alexei possibly wasn't. The intermission quickly passed, and Alexei headed back out freshly hugged and encouraged by Dace.

Whatever problems Alexei was experiencing, his second half performance never exhibited anything but pure mastery of the music. The power and creativity he displayed left many in the crowd occasionally wiping their eyes. The Japanese crowd sat mesmerized by Chopin's Ballade no.4, Op. 52 and Scherzo no.3, op. 39. Then he launched into Scriabin's Piano Concerto no. 5, Op. 53. He concluded with Rachmaninov's Piano Sonata no. 2, Op. 36. He then jumped to his feet. Alexei gave them his traditional deep bow, smile, and appreciative clasped hands overhead, which empowered the sustained ovation, something he never tired of. He then made a quick exit stage left. He stood out of view of the crowd for a good thirty seconds, for effect, and then returned for an anticipated encore. The audience fueled his return to stage even though his mind was swirling with concerns over the missed note. Alexei gave them Chopin's *Revolutionary Etude*. This sent the crowd into a rabid frenzy. At its end, he stood, grabbed the corner of the piano, and bowed once again. He briskly walked off stage out of view. Alexei knew he was not quite finished, even as exhaustion consumed him. Thirty seconds later, as the unified crowd begged for more, he headed back to the piano. He again rewarded them with more Chopin, this time the *Minute Waltz*, which he condensed into three minutes. The scene repeated itself once more as Alexei stalled backstage this time for forty-five seconds for added flair and concluded his night with a third Chopin encore lasting four minutes. The audience was thoroughly satisfied and poured out their adulation.

His bow and final exit ended backstage in his dressing room as he collapsed into a chair drenched in sweat. Dace was there waiting as he caught his breath. Exhaustion aside, Alexei seemed distant now. Even as Dace embraced him, he was lost in thought. There had been no missed notes after the intermission. Perhaps everything was fine. Perhaps there was no reason to worry. He was convinced that a stroke had occurred when reasonable logic would find this self-diagnosis unlikely. He was acutely aware that something negative had transpired in his brain.

After Alexei finished signing autographs for the throngs of Japanese fans who waited for him, he and Dace were ushered to a waiting car and the post-party where they crossed paths with another visiting artist. Van Cliburn had just concluded his own recital at Suntory Hall and the managers of each artist decided to combine the post-performance receptions. Van was overjoyed to see his young friend Alexei and Dace so far from home. The celebratory party lasted long into the night. The musical prodigies conversed for some time and caught up since last they saw one another. Van spent the majority of his time with the Sultanovs. He inquired about the status of Alexei and Dace's respective families. He always seemed especially interested in Dace's father, Janis, back in Riga. The evening concluded and the performers flew home days later, where Alexei's concerns were just beginning.[1]

34

Appassionata Explained

Several weeks after Alexei returned from Tokyo, the concern over his self-diagnosed stroke consumed him. A Japanese doctor had examined him extensively before he departed from Tokyo but found nothing. They had administered a round of acupuncture before his final performance to alleviate whatever was troubling him, but to no avail. Back in Fort Worth, he spoke to several people he knew and visited a bookstore to read up on strokes, his mind made up. He took himself to the emergency room at Fort Worth's Harris Hospital, where hours later they sent him home with a clean bill of health. A few days later he drove to the Fort Worth Osteopathic Medical Center ER, where he would receive the same diagnosis. His paranoia got the best of him, and he returned days later to the Osteopathic Medical Center to get a second opinion. After completing his full examination, the on-duty doctor ordered Alexei upstairs to the psychiatric ward on the sixth floor. Alexei voluntarily checked himself in and was given a concoction of psychiatric drugs to relax. He was diagnosed with symptoms of a burn-out and and prescribed a regimen of rest and medication. Alexei knew he was not burned out nor crazy, and flushed the drugs down the toilet.

He tried to leave but was convinced to remain for the week. Dace visited by day but left at night as per hospital rules. There happened to be a piano on the psych ward floor, which made Alexei an instant attraction to the other patients. After a week, he was released and sent home with no real progress. The doctors continually found nothing medically out of the

Alexei pointing out the missed 47th note of Beethoven's Appassionata, when his self-diagnosed stroke occurred. *Dace Collection.*

ordinary. The Sultanov's did though receive a bill from Osteopathic Medical Center for forty thousand dollars for his weeklong stay. A week later, Alexei showed back up, demanding to see a neurologist, as his personal research from a purchased medical book seemed to point in this direction. Dr. Ed Kramer was on duty that day. He listened carefully to Alexei and gave the impression that he cared about what Alexei was telling him, thus endearing himself to Alexei. Dr. Kramer studied the numerous brain scans and other related cranial tests that Alexei had undergone since the perceived incident at Kioi Hall. The previous doctors hadn't noticed anything of concern and began to think Alexei might be some sort of nut case. Dr. Kramer's steady eye and careful work finally found something on the MRI scan that no one else had. He discovered a pinhead-sized spot in the grey matter of his brain tissue. This spot was indicative of a collapsed or clotted blood vessel and the surrounding dead brain tissue, which qualifies as a mini stroke. Dr. Kramer also diagnosed Alexei with high blood pressure between the beats of his heart, or medically, low-grade diastolic hypertension.

Alexei, as it turns out, had remarkably been correct about his mini stroke that night in Tokyo. According to Dr. Kramer, Alexei was not expected to suffer any long-term impairment, but still he threw himself into researching his situation further. He read as many articles as the sluggish dial-up Internet and medical books found for him. He became obsessed over his medical condition and even penned a detailed analysis of what he was sure was happening to him. He felt increasingly sure that the death he had prophesized for himself as a teenager at the conservatory would come for him. This mini stroke was only the beginning. His demise was certain regardless of what the medical profession could promise him.

35

Doctor Onboard

Alexei and Dace lifted off from DFW airport during the fall of 1996 en route to Frankfort, Germany, aboard Lufthansa Airlines. A new European tour was underway due in part to several forgiving concert promoters still believing Alexei was worth the risk. Reliability was always the most warranted concern. Several hours into the flight, the couple was comfortably engaged in their assortment of mini board games and their new Nintendo Gameboy. Dace always found time on long flights to read books in her Latvian tongue. Suddenly, their playtime was interrupted as an announcement crackled over the intercom. The captain's voice measuredly asked if there was a doctor onboard the flight and to please press your call button. A long silence ensued as the call buttons went untouched. The news circulated that a woman in the rear of the plane was in serious pain and needed medical attention. Alexei had been carrying his own blood pressure monitor with him ever since that finger stroke at Kioi Hall in Japan was officially confirmed by Dr. Kramer. Alexei's paranoia about his own health had systematically worsened over time and thus he read voraciously about strokes. Through his research, he had inadvertently picked up some useful medical information and knowledge of minor medical procedures. Alexei leaned over and whispered to Dace that he thought he could help her. Before Dace could muster a logical response, Alexei stood up and approached the flight attendant, "My name is Alexei Sultanov, and I've heard someone needs some help." The flight attendant glanced down at the diminutive long-haired stranger in front of her and replied, "Well, Dr. Sultanov, we have a girl who is very sick in her seat, and she needs some help!" The freshly anointed Dr. Sultanov, armed with his over-the-counter blood pressure monitor, followed. The young woman he was shown was in such tremendous agony that she continually moaned out loud. She painstakingly shared her symptoms with Dr. Sultanov, which entailed a sharp pain in her abdomen and exceptional nausea. He felt her head and discovered her temperature highly elevated. He was instantly reminded of these same symptoms he himself experienced five years prior. He had required emergency surgery for a ruptured appendix to save his life. He checked her blood pressure, as this was the only thing he was remotely qualified medically to do, and found it slightly above normal. His concern to help was sincere, and acting on a whim, he announced to the watchful flight attendant that "This plane needs to land as soon as possible for this girl has appendicitis!" The attendant retorted, "This is not possible, and you must speak with the captain." So, the twenty-seven-year-old musical savant stood face-to-face outside the cockpit with the captain of the Lufthansa 737 and confidently demanded, "This girl is in great danger, and her life is in your hands! You need to land the plane as soon as possible!" Alexei explained to the captain that he has the power to save this girl. The captain pondered this for a few seconds and returned to the cockpit.

Moments later, Dace and the passengers heard the stern announcement over the intercom that the plane was turning around to make an emergency landing in Montreal. The concerned passengers sat still, quietly looking around as preparations were made for an unscheduled landing. As the plane touched down, the ambulance was already waiting. Passengers were all asked to remain in their seats. Paramedics entered the plane and gingerly escorted the ailing girl, out of the back to a waiting ambulance. The situation was over quickly as the passengers were put back through takeoff protocol. As the plane taxied around toward the end of the runway for takeoff, the flight attendant returned to tell Alexei, "Thank you, Dr. Sultanov, for saving that girl." The paramedics confirmed to the captain via radio relays shortly after the plane was back on course that this lady was indeed suffering from acute appendicitis. Her odds of survival would have been greatly hampered if not for the quick actions of Dr. Sultanov and his trusted blood pressure machine.

Alexei wore a smile for the remainder of the flight. He looked at Dace and coyly said, "I told you so." Dace could only stare at him in disbelief. The excitement of the plane trip dwarfed that of the concert tour he was to embark on. Alexei met with the German Orchestra and its conductor Justus Frantz to begin a hellacious twenty-day tour dubbed the Philharmony of the Nations. Frantz, a conductor, pianist, and close friend of Leonard Bernstein, made his name performing pieces mostly of his beloved Mozart. The German Orchestra and Alexei were scheduled to perform the famed Tchaikovsky Piano Concerto no.1 a total of nineteen times during the twenty-day tour. This brutal schedule would challenge even the most seasoned performer, mainly because of the monotony of repetition. Alexei found unique ways to liven up the days, as he would change the tempo of each performance with Frantz's blessing to spice it up a bit. The crowds filled each performance across the small section of Europe they toured, and each night was as magical as the previous one.

Tchaikovsky's Piano Concerto no. 1, while played into the ground by Alexei and the German Orchestra, still holds a special weight with multitudes of music fans throughout the world.[1] Van Cliburn himself had won the 1958 Tchaikovsky First International Piano Competition in Moscow with his moving performance. His rendition was recorded by American record label RCA Victor and attained platinum status, the first classical recording ever to do so, and it earned Van a Grammy. In fact, this recording still holds as one of the world's most beloved classical music recordings of all time.

Shortly after the exhausted Alexei had finished his German tour, he ran into a music manager backstage that knew a close conductor friend of his. The manager asked Alexei in English the whereabouts of their mutual friend. Alexei replied that he was on his tour with his *"whore" (the Russian word Alexei was using is the Russian word XOP, which pronounced phonetically sounds like "whore")*. The manager was shocked by what he heard. Seconds later, Alexei realized what he'd done. The word *XOP* in Russian meant choir. His conductor friend was on tour with his choir. The two burst into laughter.

36

The 1997 Van Cliburn Competition

The 1997 Van Cliburn International Piano Competition arrived as scheduled. The buildup to the competition had begun, as per tradition, shortly after Simone Pedroni had received his gold in 1993. The behind-the-scenes work amounted to nothing short of a herculean effort by a small, dedicated staff who scoured the world for the next batch of worthy amateurs. Alexei, now with his mind focused on his medical situation and his performance obligations, dreaded the impending 1997 Van Cliburn International Piano Competition. His international reputation suffered greatly due to his chronic cancellations. People loved him nonetheless, but everyone has their limits, and Alexei continually pushed them. The Cliburn Foundation remained guarded in all dealings with Alexei, who now came ready with a medical alibi. Alexei's name as a former champion, however, was still used and promoted regularly by the Cliburn. Now that 1993 champion Simone Pedroni had succeeded him, there was less pressure on Alexei to conform to the Cliburn appearance demands. There were plenty of people at the Cliburn events that he no longer wished to see. As a former gold medal winner, Alexei still had star power, since the public loved him. The opening reception for the 1997 Van Cliburn Competition still required his attendance, if nothing else for the encouragement of the incoming class. For support, he brought along Dace as well as his brother, Sergei, who was in town for the competition. The incoming class of competitors included several Russians who knew Alexei and emulated the former winner. He had done what so many back home aspired to. At the conservatory, Alexei remained a living legend. Alexei was asked by the Cliburn to make nice with the incoming competitors, a task that pained him. The Cliburn tradition required the past Van Cliburn winners to be in attendance and to participate in the festivities. The opening party was held again at the luxurious Worthington Hotel, built in 1981 on three city blocks that once encompassed the famed Leonard's Department Store on the west side and the Striplings Department Store on the east.

All the dedicated patrons were again in attendance, decked out in tuxedos and dark suits. The setting was awash with smiles, small talk, and introductions. The sit-down dinner allowed the Cliburn executives to take the stage and thank the appropriate people, who were many. Van Cliburn held court over the evening while he gave each competitor a piece of his time. When he finished encouraging everyone, he repeated the performance with the patrons, former champions, and Cliburn VIPs. Cliburn remained graceful through the entire event. Competition executive director Richard Rodzinski was beaming as his event unfolded before his smiling donors and peers. Richard remained lost in conversation with the new class and valuable patrons. He would not have noticed the three glasses of red wine that Alexei had consumed, nor would he have believed his incredibly low tolerance. Richard also would not have noticed the growing fire inside Alexei's mind. Everyone took their seats for dinner and the formal proceedings began. The Cliburn execs covered the crowd with praise for efforts put in. Van Cliburn made a short speech and captured the everyone' attention. Simone Pedroni made some impressive remarks regarding his time as incumbent champion. The competitors listened intently, at least the ones who could understand him. At last, Alexei was ushered on stage by Van Cliburn's right-hand woman and former chairman of the Cliburn Board of Directors, Susan Tilley,[1] to great fanfare, where he was asked to say a few words. Susan had been Van Cliburn's manager in 1987 and had orchestrated his comeback from a nine-year hiatus from public life. She had used her wits and southern charm to arrange Van's first return performance on December 8, 1987, which took place in the East Room of the White House during a summit meeting between President Ronald Reagan and Soviet General Secretary Mikhail Gorbachev. She also accompanied Van on his 1989 performing tour of the Soviet Union.

Alexei during a trip to Greece. *Dace Collection.*

Susan, acutely aware of Alexei's propensity for trouble, was praying Alexei would describe how wonderful the competition was for him and for his career. It wouldn't take long before Susan and others, noticed his slurred speech and loose composure. It was clear to all he was inebriated, and Susan quickly regretted her decision. Alexei proceeded to embark on a ramble for five painful minutes. He began slowly but quickly gained steam. Alexei hinted to the crowd that he didn't like the way the contestants were treated by the Cliburn organization. Susan's cheery smile quickly dimmed. Contestants, according to Alexei, were forced against their will to perform at private parties in private homes alongside patrons' wealthy friends, much like shiny little toys. Then Alexei turned his attention to Rodzinski, whose blood pressure had risen. Rodzinski felt his face flush. Alexei shared that Richard had tried to control him ever since he had won. He told the crowd that he would not be controlled. He referred to the Van Cliburn competition as a circus. He could not and would not fit into the box that the Cliburn Foundation society had created for him. He again would not be controlled. The room was deathly quiet, Susan playfully tried to retrieve his microphone several times to no avail. Dace, sitting with Sergei at the table, found herself petrified at what was transpiring. She wanted to disappear. She knew he was speaking the truth from his heart, but she also knew that his message was not being delivered correctly. Everyone stared in disbelief, feeling helpless to stop what had begun.

Alexei's volume increased as his excitement boiled over. Alexei concluded his rant with a rousing admonition that described the three supreme beings in the classical music world—the late Vladimir Horowitz, the great Van Cliburn, whom he motioned to, and himself. Jose Feghali, the consummate gentleman and Brazilian winner of the Van Cliburn Competition four years before Alexei's victory, attempted to coax him off the stage. After several attempts, his friend Feghali succeeded in wrestling the microphone away. As Alexei concluded his impromptu speech and exited the stage, he missed the second step and tumbled down the staircase, crashing to the floor to an audible gasp from the concerned crowd. Van Cliburn held his gracious composure, as only a man of his supreme elegance could, but was clearly uncomfortable, and days later would reveal to close friends how utterly embarrassed he was at that moment. Rodzinski was overheard saying later that evening that Alexei was banned from all future Cliburn events. The Sultanovs departed the scene immediately, leaving the wake of trouble behind them. The damage control at the party went into full effect. Apologies flowed forth from the Cliburn leadership. Those nervous competitors each forgot about their worries for the time. Several competitors sat mesmerized by the spectacle as it unfolded.

Alexei awoke the next morning with the pain of a hangover and, even worse, tremendous remorse and embarrassment. Dace, Sergei, and Alexei visited the Fort Worth Zoo that day, mainly to satisfy the couple's cravings for animals. Alexei donned sunglasses inside and out the zoo property to hide himself from the public he so much wished to avoid. He seemed to fully realize that he had severed any ties to the Cliburn and the competition that helped create him. The Van Cliburn competition had indeed washed its hands of its prize gold medalist. As Alexei's new Cliburn-less reality set in, his management group, Columbia Artists, decided that he was no longer a suitable client for them. Profitability was certainly at the core of the decision, but there had been several instances where Alexei had accepted bookings through personal contacts that weren't run through Columbia, which violated the terms of his contract. Simply put, Alexei's unpredictable and irrational behavior coupled with a reputation for unreliability made him a liability too great to manage. Columbia officially cut ties with Alexei after seven years.

The 1997 Van Cliburn International Piano Competition went off with tremendous success, crowning American Jon Nakamatsu as its newest champion. Nakamatsu received the increased prize of twenty thousand dollars for winning gold. The Stanford University graduate then quit his job teaching high school German to embark on an incredible career as a soloist and chamber musician. The San Jose, California product recorded thirteen CDs for Harmonia Mundi (USA) and was being honored as the jury chairman for the First Cliburn International Junior Piano Competition in 2015. Nakamatsu's talent would also entertain President Clinton at the White House. The Cliburn competition remained in the upper echelon in the major competition circuit as its worldly influence soared.

37
Riga

Latvia was a favorite visit for Dace and Alexei. He loved Dace's family and of course Skujinas. Alexei's music was widely known throughout Dace's home country. He had built a tremendous following amongst Latvians and performed many times in the country. The years after Alexei successfully brought Dace to the United States, a void developed in the couple's lives. Their fear of returning to their home countries and not being able to get out was real. Their working visas allowed them to remain in the United States, but did not grant them all the rights full citizenship did. All their dreams and future now belonged in the United States, and the Russian political system could quickly ensnare them, blocking a trip home. Alexei was still technically in violation of his required conscription to the Red Army. This risk was too great. They did not return to the Soviet Union/Russia after Dace arrived in the US in September 1990 until the summer of 1996, when safe passage back was assured. Alexei's age, career, and now possibly his medical condition mitigated his risk of arrest. The first visit back was just that, a visit. Alexei did not perform there again until the 1998 Tchaikovsky competition. He filled this absence by purchasing a small but exclusive Moscow apartment for his parents on well-known Begovaya Street for thirteen thousand dollars. While he wasn't able to see his parents in Moscow during his hiatus, he used his concert travels throughout Europe to arrange reunions with them and the Abeles. He was able to see his parents many times outside the Russian borders.

On the left, Alexei's Fort Worth family, Susan and Jon Wilcox. *Dace Collection.*

They especially loved to meet up in Greece for his performances and subsequent vacation.

The scheduling of all Alexei's travel, without the aid of a management team now, fell onto Dace's shoulders. At that time, the Sultanovs owned a typewriter which Dace used to handle the business end. Once she took over for Denise Mullins and the Cliburn, she quickly discovered the tremendous efforts required of a manager. One evening as Alexei was dictating a letter to Dace on the typewriter, he became enraged at the numerous spelling mistakes she was making. He demanded that she retype the letter, over and over again, until there were no mistakes. Dace's frustration boiled over as an expletive-laced shouting match ensued. Alexei, reaching his wits end, grabbed the typewriter, raised it over his head, and smashed it down onto the floor, ending its usefulness. For Dace's birthday later that year, Alexei replaced the problematic typewriter with the family's first computer and its highly sought-after spell check feature.

38
Tchaikovsky

His paranoia mounting over his health and severed business ties, Alexei set out again to jumpstart his career in the fleeting time he felt he had left. He didn't fully realize that his career troubles stemmed from his own lack of commitment and tired repertoire. He believed he needed to win something significant to prove to himself and the world that he still remained a premier concert pianist. The 1995 Chopin competition debacle had helped salvage his sinking career, so perhaps the 1998 Tchaikovsky International Piano Competition was his next chance. Dace, his new manager, entered twenty-eight-year-old Alexei into the Eleventh Tchaikovsky International Piano Competition. Alexei, now by all measures a seasoned veteran, albeit an ailing one, would now compete against ninety-four of the world's best pianists aged sixteen to thirty-two in what was arguably the top musical competition in the world. Alexei's reputation preceded him, and he was again an early favorite to win. Alexei put in the work and trained hard at home for the competition. He arrived well prepared and cast his powerful spell over the audience, which quickly made him the centerpiece of the contest. The talent at the competition was plentiful, but there was no one who whipped the crowd into a frenzy like Alexei did. His style of play was unique to him, and his style stood in high contrast to that of the others. In Moscow, he was playing on his home turf for many of his former professors and friends. His parents Faizul and Natalia were on hand to witness it all. The Russians much anticipated Alexei's return to the Grand Hall at the conservatory. Alexei's grand homecoming was as controversial as it was anticipated.

Alexei opened the competition with a stirring and magical performance of Prokofiev's Sonata Number 7, which left the crowd standing screaming for their storied hometown hero. The powerful technique and skill he exhibited reminded those in attendance of what made Alexei so special. A storm surged through the crowd and seemed to spill outside, as reported by the *Moscow Times*. A literal thunderstorm erupted outside the conservatory as he concluded his first-round performance. The audience was deeply moved by his performance, but his wasn't the only one that was well received. British pianist Freddy Kempf, along with two Russians, Denis Matsuev and Vadim Rudenko, were equally impressive. As Alexei and Dace walked back, reminiscing, to the dormitory building where they were being housed, a violent storm raged on around them. They walked unencumbered, feeling a protective force shielding them from danger. The storm became a newsworthy event in Moscow with damage scattered all over the city. Dace and Alexei walked through the unfolding devastation as it was happening, yet they arrived at the dormitory unscathed. Perhaps the safe walk home was a good omen for Alexei in the second round. He wanted to show his countrymen the magic he still possessed. His performance was splendid. As he played, several jurors took mental note of the energy of the crowd. It was apparent: Russia's lost son had come home to win.

When the jurors met in seclusion to select the finalists, the tension of the remaining competitors was heavy. Alexei, on the other hand, armed with his inflated confidence, media attention, and backing of the crowd, felt at ease. The jury foreman strolled to the stage with the announcement. He shared his comments and congratulations before sharing the list of finalists. As each name was called, the crowd grew more and more concerned. Three names, two names left, then the final finalist. A stunned look crossed Alexei's face. The crowd buzzed in disbelief over the obvious shock they felt. Alexei's name was absent from the list. The chatter amongst the audience spread quickly, drowning out the remaining comments from the jury foreman. The flock of international press jumped on this notable development. Immediately, the competition was reported as fraudulent and unfair by hordes of journalists and other media outlets. The newspapers called for the jurors' heads, as four of the eight finalists were students of influential juror and conservatory professor Sergei Dorensky. Professor Dorensky is a true legend at the conservatory and a juror at the Cliburn competition in which Alexei had won first place. Interestingly enough, he currently taught Denis Matsuev and Vadim Rudenko, who went on to win first and second prize respectively at the Cliburn. What later was described as an epic jury scandal found many Russians suggesting that Tchaikovsky's name on the competition should be replaced with Dorensky's.

Another of the Russian jury members was Lev Naumov, Alexei's former yet beloved professor at the conservatory. He was very close friends with Tamara Popovich and loved Alexei dearly, but sadly didn't have the courage to stand up against what he later admitted had been an unfair jury. He was quoted later as saying, "Alexei was thrown over! It was not by chance he lost!" This suggested that there was a rigged panel of jurors. Alexei received as many low marks as he did high marks from the jury, which per rules canceled a number of scores, leaving Alexei with a slightly above average score. This only seemed to fuel the scandal conspiracy. Alexei failed to make the finals in what became the biggest news of the entire competition.

The talented Freddy Kempf's third place finish also contributed to the scandal, since once Alexei had been given his shocking early exit, the crowd was convinced Kempf deserved the gold. At the awards ceremony, as the highly coveted awards were announced, Alexei, against competition protocol, refused to attend. His audience favorite award never found its way to him and sits to this day in an unknown conservatory closet. This loss was personally devastating to him. Alexei sank further into his own personal torment. A depression enveloped him as another much-needed validation fell short. His hiatus from performing in Moscow continued, as his next performance wasn't until two years later.

The 1998 Tchaikovsky International Piano Competition was attended by two of Alexei's former Cliburn handlers, Alann Sampson and Richard Rodzinski, who were there for more than just the enjoyment of a world-class competition. The two Cliburn execs were hosted by Russian Yakov Kasman, who lived not far from the conservatory where he currently taught for the equivalent of twenty-five dollars a month. Kasman had placed well at many renowned pianist competitions, including the 1992 Artur Rubenstein Competition. Kasman had also taken the silver medal at the 1997 Tenth Van Cliburn Competition, which had garnered for him a wealth of popularity. He lived though not as a celebrated Russian pianist, but in near poverty. The economy in Russia remained bleak even for someone as successful as Kasman.

As Rodzinski and Sampson arrived at Kasman's tiny Moscow apartment, their fears became realized. Sampson had been warned by Kasman prior to the visit to wear no jewelry, speak no English, cover your blonde hair, and remain as inconspicuous as possible. They arrived at a run-down dilapidated apartment complex. Kasman and his wife had a young daughter and were protected by a large steel front door leaving no doubt that entry was by permission only. The apartment consisted of a tiny kitchen connected to a small living room filled only with hundreds of classical music CD's and a worn easy chair. Connected to the living room was a small solitary bedroom, containing a single bed. This tiny bed also served as the seat for his piano, which filled the remainder of the room. Kasman's wonderful hospitality to Sampson and Rodzinski couldn't outweigh the squalor that this sensational piano talent lived in. Drinks were served in mason jars representing the couple's finest glassware. Kasman then played a new Handel piece he had been working on for the upcoming Tchaikovsky Competition in which he was entered. Before commencing his recital for the guests, Kasman asked the pair to use their imagination for the "G" note, as his piano lacked the key. The entire scene horrified the visiting duo as this man, well respected throughout the world, lived in such terrible conditions. As the music ended, Kasman's mood turned serious. He took them into the living room and carefully explained. At the conclusion of the Tchaikovsky Competition, Kasman, along with his wife and child, would be heading to the United States for a concert engagement in the state of Alabama. Then Kasman informed Sampson and Rodzinski that he would not be returning to Russia. He needed their help in defecting to the United States. An unknown man awaited the young couple in Alabama with aid and a job. The two, now complicit, were asked to take the very few of Kasman's prized possessions back with them to ensure their survival. Rodzinski was given an armful of sheet music to haul back with him to the United States along with an assortment of mason jars that the Kasman's couldn't bear to part with. The visit came to an end as Kasman drove Rodzinski and Sampson to the conservatory for that evening's portion of the Tchaikovsky Competition. The lack of a floorboard in Kasman's car distracted the Americans from swirling thoughts of the impending defection and potential trouble. Kasman had little interest in the competition, as his prize awaited him in America.

The time following the Tchaikovsky Competition was bitter for Alexei. His concert schedule limped on, but Alexei became increasingly more difficult to work with. His depression made being in his company intolerable. He refused to travel anywhere without Dace, even when she asked to stay home. He began cancelling engagements if Dace could not be with him. Dace was often made to go with him. Those who knew him best found him extraordinarily pale, and his hands trembled. He had the appearance of man in the need of much sleep.[1]

At home, Dace found him clingy and unable to be alone. On short trips to the store, Alexei insisted on accompanying her. Alexei began to lose trust in everyone and even questioned Dace's devotion to him. She, of course, never wavered for a second. He became afraid of losing her. The couple traveled to Greece, Japan, Latvia, and a few other European locales for sporadic performances, but nothing aided Alexei with his depression. He felt misunderstood by the world around him. Alexei's response to promoters' directions was outright rebellion, which further unraveled what were once the makings of a magnificent career. One of the few bright points came from a Korean piano student who wrote to Alexei telling him that he had dreamed of taking lessons from him. Alexei received these types of requests on occasion, but this time he decided to engage the young student. The young man visited the Sultanov house in Fort Worth three times, for two days at a time. When the time came for the Korean to pay Alexei, he refused to take his money.

Alexei, in 1999, embarked on a three-week eight-city Japanese tour, which mostly consisted of recitals but did include performances with the Osaka Century Orchestra and the Tokyo Philharmonic. It was during a press interview with the *Japan Times* that he learned his celebrity had continually grown in Japan. Back in 1996, a Japanese television romantic drama series entitled *Long Vacation* had used Alexei for one of its episodes, unbeknownst to him. The eleven-episode series outlined the ups and downs of relationships amidst the deep ongoing Japanese economic recession. The highly rated show found its male heartthrob lead, Takuya Kimura, playing the part of Hidetoshi Sena, who had aspirations to become a professional pianist. In one of the later episodes, Sena attends a recital concert at Suntory Hall in which the pianist was the fictional Sutalsnov, a clear homage to Alexei. The popularity of the show amongst the younger viewers gave Alexei an influx of new young female fans. Sena at the series conclusion makes it to Boston and joins the Symphony Orchestra. Alexei, when asked about his thoughts on the cameo, suggested sheepishly that now he could play whatever music he liked.

Yusuke Murakami, the founder of the Alexei Sultanov Fan Club in Japan, approached Alexei after this recent Tokyo performance and shared that he had stumbled onto several wonderful and rare Vladimir Horowitz transcriptions, which he then gave to Alexei. Alexei was very thankful to receive these treasures from his hero. For Alexei's next four concerts, he played as encores these Horowitz transcriptions of Mendelssohn's *Wedding March*, Bizet's *Carmen*, and Saint-Saëns's *Danse Macabre*, each lasting five or six minutes.[2]

Two years after his crushing defeat at the Tchaikovsky, Alexei finally returned to Moscow when he received an offer he wanted: to play at the Gnessin Music College Hall. The college was founded by the three Gnessin sisters, all conservatory graduates in 1895, and remains the most elite music school in Moscow, second only to the conservatory. On Alexei's return, he performed Chopin's Piano Sonata No.3 as well as Liszt's Piano Sonata No. 2. Chopin and Liszt reportedly had a lifelong rivalry, which led them to competitively compose works so difficult that ordinary professionals wouldn't dare attempt them. The recital was attended by all lucky enough to get tickets. The applause was so genuine and moving that Alexei gave three encore performances. Alexei stayed for a few extra days to teach a master's class to the college. For many of the young up-and-coming musical students, Alexei was their hero.

Then Alexei received a call requesting him to play a recital at the Star Festival in Liepaja, Latvia, a coastal town three hours from Riga. The festival didn't have enough money to afford an artist such as Alexei, so he accepted the five hundred dollars-plus airfare and lodging, just for the opportunity to go home with Dace. As the concert promoters announced the concert schedule to the public, Alexei's name caused a run on the tickets. When Alexei arrived alongside Dace for the event, he learned that the event had sold out within days of its announcement. The promoter was so happy with the event that he proposed Alexei play a second performance. He quickly accepted the opportunity and word again quickly spread.

Before he made it to Riga a week later, the event was oversold. When Alexei took the stage, he was in front of a packed theatre as well as a stage full of extra people. Alexei was surrounded by the very people who loved him. Alexei found solace here for the first time in a while.

The dawn of 2001 found Dace beginning a new job working for Dr. Kramer, which irked Alexei. She felt the desire to be more productive in her life, aside from just following Alexei around and planning his travels. Dace found comfort working for the same man who helped Alexei many years prior. Dr. Ed Kramer had found the spot of gray matter on Alexei's brain scan when the no one else could. Initially, Dace received a phone call from Dr. Kramer, inquiring if she would like to come in twice a week to work, as Dr. Kramer badly needed help. Dace convinced Alexei of her strong desire to help people. She learned on the fly the business of intervertebral disc decompression therapy (IDD). She learned more and more aspects of Dr. Kramer's business, as the demands of the office required her to wear many hats. Dace made quick friends with staffer Judy Enriquez, and the two became the primary managers of the office. Dr. Kramer started Dace at ten dollars an hour. The extra money was helpful to the Sultanovs as the performance income waned, but the role Dace had helping Dr. Kramer's patients gave her life real purpose.

Dr. Kramer's patients now became her patients. She loved them and cared for them as if they were her own. The patients in turn fell in love with Dace, her cello, her caring bubbly personality, and her thick

Russian accent. When time allowed, she played her cello at the office, stealing away the stresses of the patients. There was an old marine who went by Sargent Cornell that saw Dr. Kramer for his severe Parkinson's along with his chronic back treatments. Dace was treating his lower back and grew to love this Vietnam Vet's militaristic demeanor. He arrived with memorabilia to show off and stories to share. This old Marine loved his visits to Dr. Kramer's office, mainly to see Dace and hear her cello. Sargent Cornell had endured kidney dialysis treatment for many years. One week, he made a decision to refuse dialysis, making the ultimate decision to let himself die. He endured violent itching spasms attributed to his dire need for dialysis. Dace was swamped with work one day when Sargent Cornell came to see Dr. Kramer. Dr. Kramer had an idea to help soothe the ailing man and fetched Dace away from her duties and into his patient room. Dace gladly agreed to play her cello for him. Dr. Kramer wanted to try an experiment which involved the power and effects of music, Dace's music. The plan paid off almost instantly, as Sargent Cornell stopped itching and instead began smiling. This dying man, hardened from his unforgettable wartime experiences, sat motionless listening to Dace and her cello. A tear ran down his cheek. When Dace's cello finally stopped, Sargent Cornell had a calmness about him. He seemed at peace. The next day at work, Sargent Cornell's wife telephoned Dr. Kramer's office to share the news that he had passed away during the night. The news came as a shock, but all who were present for the cello recital knew he died at peace.

Dace's two-day-a-week part-time job quickly became full-time and blossomed into a twelve-year career. Years later, when Dr. Kramer closed the practice for retirement, she was earning seventeen dollars an hour. This hourly paycheck would have made her a woman of privilege back home in Riga. Dace felt empowered by her earnings. She had the occasional opportunities to play her cello publicly and privately, earning her two hundred dollars per appearance. She had regular cello bookings with the Fort Worth Chamber Music Society, which often played at the Kimball Art Museum. Dace's bookings were all the result of word-of-mouth publicity. Alexei, on the other hand, generally refused concerts that paid him less than three thousand dollars, even as his bookings remained sparce. His luck improved, however, when Yusaka Osavi, a big Japanese pop star, contacted Alexei directly about a project. Osavi, along with a Japanese recording company, traveled to Fort Worth in order for Alexei to transcribe and rearrange his pop music for piano. Alexei listened to Osavi's songs eight or nine times in a row, then sat down and played them on the piano in their entirety. Osavi sat watching in bewilderment while Alexei turned his hit into what he considered a masterpiece. The job was hardly challenging, but it was fun and took Alexei less than three hours at a Dallas recording studio. Alexei enjoyed this work and was paid forty thousand dollars as thanks.[1]

39
Bump in the Night

Alexei and Dace's time together at home in Fort Worth remained sacred to them. No one passed judgement or controlled Alexei there. As Alexei's music retreated further from the performing halls, he pushed farther away from his great talent. When at home, he filled his time with anything not having to do with music. The couple still loved to cook together and often performed beautifully in the kitchen. Alexei showed sporadic signs of his old self as his thirst for fun always kept the kitchen entertainment on overload. His childish manner, brought on by a longing for a childhood he never had, helped conceal a lifelong deep-rooted secret. Since early in his life, Alexei had struggled with bulimia, most likely a result of his stress-filled youth. After a meal, Alexei often excused himself to the restroom to secretly purge the food from his chronically sensitive stomach. Dace was aware but never realized its severity. A recent diagnosis of lactose intolerance aggravated the condition.

On February 21, 2001, Dace prepared French onion soup for the couple's dinner. They planned to watch a movie after dinner. The French onion soup was one of the couple's favorites, even with the cheese component that Alexei now knew was a bad idea. Temptation gave in for him and he consumed the entire bowl of soup, cheese and all. The symptoms he expected sent Alexei to the restroom to vomit. This time was no different from the hundreds of other times he retched into the toilet. This purging experience often left him lightheaded, and he required a few moments to regain his composure. This time, he threw up mightily until he grew dizzy and lost his balance. In an instant, Alexei collapsed and hit the left side of his head upon the corner of the porcelain sink next to the toilet. Mere seconds later, Alexei collected himself on the floor and discovered the small, raised knot on his forehead. The pain was not severe enough to alarm him greatly. He slowly rose to his feet and looked in the mirror, finding no blood coming from the bump. A few minutes later, he left the restroom feeling strong enough to return to Dace. She immediately saw his head and grew concerned. Alexei assured her that he was okay, and the matter quickly faded. The incident seemed to be over and done with. Alexei applied ice to the bump periodically during the movie to relieve some of the swelling. The couple finished the movie and retired to bed. When Alexei woke the next morning, he felt weak and slightly dazed but brushed it off as minor symptoms from bumping his head.

Over the next couple of days, his condition progressively worsened. His strength was fleeting, and his left arm began to not cooperate with his brain. Five days after bumping his head, Alexei awoke early and found he could not use his left arm at all. Dace finally disobeyed Alexei's wishes and telephoned Dr. Kramer, who knew Alexei's medical history best. Dr. Kramer told them to head to his office. Dr. Kramer did an assessment and quickly surmised that Alexei's condition was serious and ordered him immediately to the Emergency Room at the Osteopathic Medical Center. The treating physician ordered a CT scan of Alexei's brain, revealing a large pooling of blood inside Alexei's skull. The blood was putting tremendous pressure on his brain, resulting in loss of skin color, coordination, and movement in his left arm. This subdural hematoma required surgery to remove the blood and subsequent pressure, so Alexei was prepped almost immediately. Nurses shaved off Alexei's long hair on the right side of his head to prepare the skull for the surgeons to cut a bone flap where the remnants of the knot still lay. Alexei was given the drug Mannitol, which helps relax the brain for such an invasive procedure. The surgeons utilized a three-pin Mayfield skull clamp to hold the head steady. Then, burr holes were cut, which in turn allowed a special cranial saw called a craniotome to cut a two-inch by two-inch square out of Alexei's skull, exposing the dura or membrane that encases the brain. The dura was carefully opened to allow the doctors to drain the excess blood. The procedure took nearly five gruelling hours but the surgeons felt satisfied with the outcome. The dura was delicately closed and the hole in his skull was closed with the original piece of skull. He was sent to recovery, where a few hours later Alexei was revived from his sleep by the anesthetist to determine the success of the operation. As Alexei's body shrugged off the effects of the anesthesia, he climbed back to consciousness. It became immediately clear that Alexei had improved, as he was able to communicate with Dr. Kramer. As Alexei regained further consciousness, he immediately complained to the nurses that something wasn't right. The nurses attributed this to his post-surgical state. The overall prognosis was good, and a full recovery was likely and probable. Alexei could not have known that the surgeons mysteriously omitted a drainage tube from the procedure.

Alexei was sent to the ICU for recovery. Several hours later, as nurses were checking on him, they noticed that the skin around his face was blue, and he was completely unresponsive to their attempts to wake him. The blue tint suggested to nurses that Alexei was possibly bleeding internally. Dr. Kramer was immediately notified at home, where he had just arrived minutes earlier from the same hospital. He wearily jumped back in the car and sped back to the hospital. Alexei was rushed back to the X-Ray room for another CT scan, revealing more and increased bleeding from the same area, squeezing his brain over to the right, rendering him blue and unconscious. The new bleeding cut off oxygen and glucose to vital areas of his brain as blood vessels were crushed or severed completely by the tremendous pressure being put on them. The surgeons raced Alexei back to emergency surgery, as his life now hung in the balance. Damage to his brain though was now expected. The neurosurgeons on call acted quickly and had him on the operating table before Dr. Kramer arrived as counsel. The skull flaps were re-opened, releasing much of the deadly pressure. The surgeon's quick response saved Alexei's extraordinary brain, but not before he suffered five successive strokes. These strokes annihilated the thalamus region of his brain, which gave him his ability to function normally and destroyed his cognitive ability to create music. The full diagnosis wouldn't be known for some time, as Alexei remained in a coma, even as doctors peristently tried to revive him.

Panic set in for Dace as her Alosha lay unconscious in the ICU. Her questions would have no answers until Alexei woke up. Her worst fears grew as she tightly squeezed the hand of her unresponsive husband. For the next five weeks, Alexei lay in ICU amidst a room of machines all connected to him. He lay under the constant vigilance of the nurses. Dace left the ICU only when hospital rules forced her out during the nights. She brought her portable stereo from home to his recovery room and played his recordings constantly so that he might hopefully find some comfort during his coma. Her optimism never waned in spite of the doctor's warnings. Dace felt strongly that her daily actions brought positive benefits to her sleeping husband. She did not accept the doctor's warnings at face value. Alexei was not like other people. He was a fighter. He had the strength to overcome this, and she was there to help him. The five weeks crawled by until finally doctors decided it was time to wake him. Nurses carefully monitored his slow return back to consciousness. Dace felt he would be okay even after Dr. Kramer repeatedly warned her that Alexei would not be the same man she had known. As Alexei broke free of the coma, he gently squeezed the hand that held his. This momentarily boosted Dace's confidence, but she increasingly came to realize that Alexei was indeed not the same.

The nurses administered a series of tests once he was fully awake so that his condition could be evaluated. His responses to their tests quickly shed light on the extent of the damage. When they asked Alexei to move his left arm, they discovered he couldn't. Even his fingers of his left hand were unresponsive. It was quickly established that Alexei couldn't move the entire left side of his body. The situation quickly grew darker. Alexei was not able to respond verbally to the doctor or nurse's commands. Something happened during the brain swell which stole away his ability to speak. The doctors and staff met to investigate and reached the conclusion that the effects of anesthesia had triggered in Alexei a massive debilitating stroke that rendered him mute and partially paralyzed. His life was now in limbo, and his prognosis was deemed uncertain. Alexei Sultanov was alive, but he would never again play the piano. Both sides of his thalamus, which control the brain's ability to process the body's complex messages, suffered irreparable damage. The tissues of his midbrain were starved of oxygen long enough to leave Alexei with permanent and total blindness in his left eye. Alexei's pons, which facilitates the brain's ability to send messages to rest of body, was severely starved, thus destroying critical motor function for him. The suddenness of it all had Dr. Kramer reeling. He compared the images of Alexei's brain scans to a meteorological study of a swirling storm. Dr. Kramer was the first person to know the truth. His professionalism prevailed, but emotionally he was crushed. Alexei Sultanov would never fully recover from this. He was able to comprehend what was happening and what was being said but could not react physically nor verbally. The genius of Alexei Sultanov was no more.

40
Papulnik

Faizul anxiously boarded a plane in Moscow. Dace had telephoned the Sultanovs in Moscow to share the news that Alexei was waking up from his five-week coma. Faizul had busily gathered all the money the family could muster to buy his ticket to Fort Worth. There was not money enough for a ticket for Natalia, nor would the Russian government have allowed it, so she remained behind. As Faizul arrived on the scene, he was overcome with emotions set aside for broken-hearted fathers. Tears poured down Alexei's face when his *Papulnik* walked into his hospital room. Faizul's deep sorrow and massive confusion over what to do next left him feeling numb and helpless. Dace, though, lifted herself out of despair to spearhead the next steps. A plan was constructed with Dr. Kramer for Alexei's rehabilitation and recovery. Alexei was given ample time to process what had transpired and what was in store for him.

On March 22, Alexei was moved by ambulance twenty-nine miles away to the Baylor Institute for Rehabilitation in Dallas, where his real struggle began. The Baylor Institute utilized a special funding source in order to assist with the intensive therapy Alexei now required. Due to the Sultanov's not having insurance and now little income, the Alexei Sultanov Benefit Fund was set up at local Landmark Bank to help bridge the financial gap for the suddenly struggling family. The news of Alexei's arrival had the hospital staff anxious to begin work on the prodigy. The rehabilitation staff was ready when the ambulance pulled in. They started him gently at first but always pushed him to try what they were asking of him. Priority number one was to instill in him a desire to want to improve. The work was long and slow but kept Alexei's body constantly moving. As the days of rehab grew, Alexei's paralysis slowly lessened. The staff picked up quickly on this and thus pushed him harder. Progress was measured but noticeably steady. Faizul slept in the corner of the hospital room on a cot, so he was near Alexei around the clock. Each morning, *Papulnik* dragged his precious son from his bed to begin his rehab. His day began early with efforts aimed at teaching Alexei how to walk again. Faizul often sang to Alexei some Russian children's songs or musical scales. Dace wasn't ever far away and stepped in when she could.

Alexei began to show signs of improvement. During therapy sessions, he used his crippled left arm in a very gentle game of arm wrestling. When he was placed on his feet, he managed on his own for short periods of time. A therapist even coaxed a rare laugh out of Alexei. Faizul and Dace never missed a single moment of his rehab. She sat by his side, talked to him, and played his favorite music to comfort him. The efforts asked of Alexei were grueling and painful, but very slowly small improvements took shape. The days consisted of speech therapy, physical therapy, occupational therapy, and hydrotherapy, which was his favorite because he loved to be in the pool. Then one morning his mouth made a tiny sound that caused those in the room to uniformly cheer. When prodded, his efforts to talk were humongous, but out came a barely audible whisper. Dace arrived everyday full of positivity for the tasks ahead. She typically brought with her get well cards, which arrived at the house daily along with hundreds of emails offering support for his fans' ailing star. Natalia Sultanov, still unable to make the trip, routinely wrote her son letters with large hand printed letters of the Russian alphabet on them. Each letter began with short encouraging words for Alexei. Dace would tape these to the wall in Alexei's room.

"A is for Alexei. Endlessly lovable son, we are praying for your recovery. D is for Dace, the angel savior, for Alexei," she wrote.

In a few short weeks, Alexei's voice had returned enough for simple conversation. He expressed tremendous remorse, increasingly apologizing to Dace, Faizul, and nearly every visiting guest for what he believed he was putting them through. Every response was similar. Do not worry, please relax, and get well soon. Alexei's mobility also slowly returned, and he discovered over time that with his stronger right hand, he could tinker on the portable electric piano Dace had brought. His daily improvements became more apparent as Alexei molded the highly technical rapid movements of Chopin into a much simpler one-handed inspirational concert. He attempted to draw from his repertoire as much as his right hand would allow. At night, when Alexei was alone with Faizul in the corner, he wondered out loud if this is all was just a dream. The sad reality was almost too much for him to bear. His can-do attitude during the day was replaced with bouts of extreme sorrow at night. His life now felt out of his control.

Then, several weeks later, during a routine checkup, the doctor noticed Alexei had developed an abnormality on his left Achilles tendon, which promised to impair any future ability to walk. An orthopedic surgeon was consulted who deemed surgery the best option to correct the issue. The procedure was of the routine variety with a high probability of success. Alexei was prepped and administered a general anesthesia to put him to sleep for the procedure. The operation on his foot was indeed successful and Alexei was sent to the recovery room. Alexei awoke from his induced slumber and nurses quickly discovered that most of his progress since the massive strokes had been wiped away. Alexei was left nearly helpless. It was abundantly clear that anesthesia could no longer be utilized as it caused a violent reaction inside Alexei's brain. Alexei lost his ability to speak once again. The mobility he gained was gone. Without Dace there to drag him along, Alexei would have given up. Doctors collectively felt that any semblance of normalcy for Alexei was no longer a possibility. Tamara Popovich, who had flown to New York for a work engagement, pulled some strings and flew in to see Alexei. She had not seen him in some time and found the scene of her most special prodigy lying motionless completely heartbreaking. The rigid and stone-faced piano teacher was reduced to bouts of sobbing.

41

Beverly

Beverly Archibald went to the curb to retrieve her morning paper just like any other day, but this morning something caught her attention. A front-page story outlined a disabling stroke suffered by local world renowned pianist, Alexei Sultanov. The same man who was married to one of her favorite former students. The stroke left him paralyzed on the left side of his body, ending what was an illustrious piano career before he had even reached creative maturity. Beverly felt so compelled to reach out to the couple after reading the tragic morning newspaper story that she contacted Mary Rogers, who had written the article. She asked to be connected to Dace so that she could be of service. When Beverly telephoned the Sultanov's room at Baylor rehab, Faizul answred in hius limited, broken English. She carefully navigated through and left word for Dace that she called. Dace called her back that day from the hospital and invited her to visit them. Beverly arrived with daffodils on her first visit, which was Dace's favorite flower. Beverly quickly became reengaged with Dace and became a close confidant to her. Dace felt at ease talking to her and began asking Beverly for much-needed help. Beverly never sugarcoated anything. Dace saw this and appreciated her candor. When Faizul or the Abeles came to visit Alexei, Beverly would inevitably become their chauffeurs around Fort Worth. Regardless of location, the store, the hospital, the rehab pool, to run household errands, or even later on to have margaritas—there was Beverly. The magic of Beverly was how she took such care of Faizul, Janis, and Benita without the ability to communicate in the same language. Neither spoke the others dialect but they found a way to communicate. Most impressively, Faizul's birthday fell during one of his later visits, and Beverly was tasked one day with keeping Faizul busy so that that Dace and friends could prepare a surprise party for him. To get the house empty, Beverly took Faizul to her house and showed him how to use the vacuum without the crutch of verbal communication. She then left to go help set up his forthcoming surprise. Faizul became understandably furious after four hours had passed, as the floors had been vacuumed repeatedly and he'd had no word from anyone. He had no way to leave nor anyone to help him understand what he was actually doing there. He was a prisoner in a relatively unknown woman's house on his birthday. When Beverly finally returned, Faizul exhibited the most awkward and confusing temper tantrum that Beverly had ever seen. He remained angry up until he met his surprise, half an hour later back at the Sultanov home.

Beverly's friendship began to pay off in other ways as well. When Alexei had his strokes, he lost many abilities, including the ability to earn. Hospital and medical care of this nature tend to carry with them a hefty price tag. Alexei's was especially steep. The bills started slowly, and Dace used the money that Alexei had accumulated from his concerts to keep the creditors at bay. As time progressed, anyone affiliated with the Sultanovs began to realize that the Alexei of old would never be back. The bills finally caught up to them. The phone began ringing more and more often at random times of the day as collectors sought immediate payment for various bills. The phone calls mounted and became such an annoyance that Dace moved her house phone into a closet where it often sat unanswered. Susan and Jon Wilcox always were at the ready with their checkbooks to keep the unrelenting creditors off their backs. The Sultanovs' support group consisted of a large collection of friends—those from years past and those new—just wanting to help. Enough people joined the cause and were flush enough to offer the couple some financial assistance. Beverly, several times, paid the Sultanov's property taxes when Dace could not get there with the little she had. Neighbors and friends regularly mowed her lawn, collected her mail, brought her fresh clothes, and handled other household chores. None of these friends ever needed thanks.

Dace and Beverly's friendship steadily blossomed. Beverly referred lovingly to Dace as a bottle of champagne. When Beverly was put into a nursing home years later due to her waning health, Dace was there at her side. Beverly privately told Dace that she was through and ready to die, but in a heart-to-heart discussion with Dace, Beverly changed her mind. Dace began visiting her weekly, bringing freshly made treats and plenty of conversation. These short bits of time away offered her much needed conversation. In February 2002, a Russian Societal Club with the unique name of the Russian Committee of the Records of Planet awarded Alexei a diploma for the Outstanding Pianist of the end of the twentieth century and the beginning of the twenty-first century. Alexei found no delight in this.

When Alexei was released from the Baylor Institute, his therapists and expert motivators stayed behind. Dace became his life support. Alexei could not eat, bathe, move, or use the restroom without her. His restarted recovery worked much slower than previously. Doctors and therapists had stabilized Alexei enough that the slow nature of his rehabilitation could be carried out from home. He was enrolled in the outpatient services, as well, to continue his rehab. The weight of Alexei's care fell directly on Dace's shoulders. She attacked each and every hurdle with maximum confidence. Alexei's survival now depended solely on her, and she decidedly would not let him down. His ability to communicate his needs to her was no longer verbal. Dace's questions going forward needed to be ones that Alexei could answer with a one-finger, yes or two-finger, no. Dace only asked Alexei simple questions now, thus removing all real dialogue. The absence of Alexei's voice in her life was a shock to Dace. She desperately wanted to talk to him. The intolerable sense of loss she felt though was well masked in her passion to fully rehabilitate him. Dace knew the doctors were wrong, and her Alexei would prove them all wrong. Faizul, who had been there since Alexei's rise from the five-week coma, finally left to go home after nearly six months by his son's side. A grand and heartfelt going-away party was held. Dace's life now showed its true face after Faizul left. At that time the Russian government forbid two family members from leaving the country at the same time, so Natalia was not allowed to travel to America with her husband. Natalia seemed to be uninterested in traveling to Texas, however. Natalia continued her loving and consistent correspondence with her crippled son, but for personal reasons never made the trip to Texas. Perhaps she could not bear

Alexei's mother Natalia Sultanov. *Dace Collection.*

to see her remarkable son suffering so tremendously.

A somber calm permeated the Sultanovs' once-active home. Their own music now became a distant memory. The Yamaha grand piano sat quietly in its spot gathering a heavy coat of dust. Alexei's outpatient rehabilitation assignment took place at the Southwest Medical Center, where Dace drove him twenty-nine miles to Dallas two or three times a week for nearly six months. Patty Winchester entered their lives and quickly became a trusted friend. She was tasked with getting Alexei walking again, which doctors now felt was impossible. Patty loaded Alexei into a large machine dubbed the "walking machine." Its purpose was to move Alexei's legs in a walking motion while supporting his body weight. The machine created a sense of hope for Dace as it gave her glimpses of the Alexei she knew. The efforts required of Alexei were always substantial and caused him a great deal of physical pain. The monotony of each day's slow and unhurried progress forced Dace to manufacture events to continually encourage Alexei. She would not allow him to sink into further despair.

Christmas time, which normally was a great source of joy for Alexei, now held no importance. Dace arranged for the once spontaneous couple to participate in Fort Worth's Jingle Bell Run even though Alexei was confined to a wheelchair. Dace pushed Alexei's wheelchair through the streets of the course. In the annual Festival of Lights, they were asked to ride in the parade upon a large trailer, and Alexei's wheelchair was covered in Christmas lights for the occasion. Dace knew her husband didn't want this, but perhaps the cheering public would resonate somehow with him. Dace kept the couple's Christmas traditions intact and decorated the house in extraordinary fashion after Alexei's downfall. She would not let the things he loved fall away.

Dace and Alexei's financial troubles continued to mount as Alexei's rehab continued. Dace sought to ease the debt burden by finding a few odd jobs. She catered lunches to a few doctor's offices she had connections to. Medical bills arrived almost daily from current and past hospitals and doctors, which exceeded well north of one hundred thousand dollars. She often tried calling the hospital to make a deal that she could afford. She was successful in getting some relief, but it was never enough. As no true solution presented itself, friends suggested filing for bankruptcy to escape the crushing weight of their bills. Dace worried that they would lose their house. Friends, new and old, came out of the woodwork to offer help. Several organized benefit concerts to help them. One such concert was created with the participation of a multitude of local musicians who knew the Sultanovs. The large music event raised over thirty thousand dollars. An idea was suggested which gained traction amongst her circle to put Alexei in a nursing home as Dace was drowning in responsibilities. She quickly cut off anyone who suggested separating the two. As the pressures continued to grow, Dace needed respite and sought the advice of a lawyer. In 2002, the Sultanovs' filed for Chapter 11 bankruptcy to free themselves from their insurmountable debt.

42
2003

On March 1, 2003, Alexei developed meningitis or an infection of the spinal fluid and began having seizures due to his 104-degree fever. The doctor at Plaza Medical Center reasoned that during the surgery to install a Baclofen Pump the previous summer, Alexei likely contracted the meningitis. The pump did not seem to be helping him like his caretakers anticipated. He suffered from continuous high-grade fevers caused by the ongoing infection of his spinal fluid. The Baclofen pump consisted of a circular metallic pump implanted under the skin along with a catheter which delivered medicine directly into Alexei's spinal fluid. Baclofen is a medicine used as a muscle spasticity relaxant for people suffering from multiple sclerosis, spinal cord injuries, and other neurological diseases. Alexei's new pump kept him continually sedated and wobbly in appearance, which wasn't the desired result. The meningitis grew worse and sent Alexei into shock. The problem seemed to be the pump itself. Dr. Claussen, who had installed the Baclofen pump, refused to remove it because of the difficulty involved in installing it, even as Alexei lay there dying. He informed Dace that he would no longer treat Alexei, if that was the path they wanted to follow.

Dr. Kate, an infectious disease specialist at Plaza Medical Center, assumed command of the situation and quickly jumped into a screaming match with Dr. Claussen over the issue. Alexei needed the pump out quickly. Dr. Kate luckily prevailed, and Dr. Classen walked. The fluid in the spine had become dangerously infected and thus Dr. Kate decided that in order to save Alexei, she needed to order the surgical removal all of foreign objects from his body—in particular the Baclofen Pump. This surgery was severe enough that Alexei spent the next five weeks in the neurological ICU at the Plaza Medical Center. Even given the risks to Alexei and his adverse reactions to anesthesia, doctors deemed the risk was worth taking. Dace kept a vigilant watch over Alexei for the duration of his stay, often sleeping on the floor of the waiting room when her body could stay awake no longer. Faizul fortunately had been in Fort Worth visiting when all this went down, so he was able to be near and assist Dace with his ailing son. Alexei was given a new shunt, which allowed fluids to move around the body through this new small hole. In lieu of the Baclofen Pump, doctors felt oral medications would have to suffice.

Alexei was finally allowed to move out of ICU and into a private room where his newest recovery began, and Dace finally had a couch to sleep on. On April 8, Alexei was transferred back to HealthSouth for further advanced rehabilitation more suited to Alexei's everchanging needs. These continuous setbacks and restarts did take their toll on Alexei's psyche. His recovery seemed to be railroaded by something new at every turn. Eventually, he showed enough stability and again was released and sent home. Inside he was restless and alert, but with no means of action. He was trapped in his broken body without control of his faculties, his time, or his health, which slid him further into depression.

At home his piano sat idly by. His daily activities took him near enough to his piano to constantly remind him of his loss. With no foreseeable solutions to help Alexei's severe condition, a HealthSouth therapist suggested a woman named Donna Witten. Donna worked at a clinic, Partners in Therapy, close to their southwest Fort Worth home and was a known pain whisperer. She was no ordinary therapist though. She had a special gift. Donna held a Master of Science degree in physical therapy, where she specialized in orthopedic and neurological therapy. Donna's unique approach to her craft stemmed from a promise she made to God early in her career. If He were gracious enough to get her through physical therapy school unscathed, then she would focus her life to help those who needed her, no matter what the reason.

Dace arrived at Donna's clinic pushing Alexei's wheelchair. Donna remembered Alexei's name from the widely read 2001 *Star Telegram* newspaper article. Donna knew this patient had been a special talent on the piano, but now needed her help. Alexei arrived with few motor skills, little communicative abilities, and a complete absence of hope. His most current issue involved severe pain from one of his ribs that had popped out of place due to the frail nature of his body. Donna relied heavily on Dace to communicate what she wanted Alexei to do during the therapy sessions. Donna went to work immediately on Alexei's painful rib and the additional muscle cramping that he was experiencing. She implemented a very strict policy of effort and trust. Donna's careful and meticulous treatments of Alexei ultimately worked the painful rib back to its regular position, relieving most of Alexei's pain. Once the rib was corrected, Donna began a steady routine of stretches and manual therapies designed to decrease his abnormal muscle tone inflicted by his strokes. The plan was to rebuild Alexei from the ground up and give him back some of his lost mobility. Alexei discovered he enjoyed working with the Swiss ball. Alexei was placed both face down and face up on the giant inflated plastic therapy ball. Donna even visited the Sultanovs' house once to assist with the visiting Benita's ailing back, endearing herself to Dace's mother.

Her intensive therapy on Alexei began showing slight results after the first two weeks. A spark of optimism seemed to follow. Donna took such an interest in helping Alexei that once the Sultanovs' visits to this clinic became unaffordable, Donna offered to come by their house twice a week to work on Alexei. When Donna first arrived at the Sultanov house, she was greeted by an enthusiastic Dace along with a therapy mat and table and railings on the walls, evidence of Dace's drive to rehabilitate Alexei. The sessions lasted one to two hours with a focus on improving his transitions from wheelchair to mat, bed, toilet, and back. Donna continued seeing Alexei for the next two years and the results, albeit slow, began to materialize. She never again charged them for her services.

43

Rebirth

Alexei's progress continued slowly as more and more people joined the cause. Alexei celebrated his thirty-fourth birthday in August with aspirational pneumonia, however, which sent him to the hospital for two days. He received many birthday visitors to his room at the hospital and then again at a second party at home with a thirty-four-candle bonfire atop his cake. Dace began to tell people openly that they were witnessing a true miracle with Alexei. His mobilization therapies and his beloved rides on the therapy horses were showing continual benefit. His specialized therapies from Donna Witten and her administered exercises had corrected his ongoing adjustment issues which continually caused him tremendous amounts of pain. Hope loomed large for Dace. She approached each day with renewed vigor as Alexei's needs took precedence over her own. Dace rarely had time to herself, as her work consumed the other half of her life. Dace's birthday was approaching, but it mattered little to her. Two years had passed since those five strokes ravaged Alexei's mind and body in the hospital. The stroke robbed him of more than just his genius. It stole his motivation and subsequent ability to create. Alexei lacked any desire to play the piano again. He refused to cooperate with Dace's continuous pleas to try, so much so that she finally ceased all efforts to push him back to the piano and thwarted any attempts by others to motivate him to play. Dace discovered that the mere sound of music stirred up a firestorm of emotions in his crippled brain that added to his suffering. So Dace strategically kept music away from Alexei, so as not to upset him.

Then something happened. On the pleasant night of October 12, 2003, the Sultanov house was quietly celebrating Dace's thirty-fifth birthday with several friends, including their new therapist stalwart, Donna Witten. Donna's selfless passion for Alexei's therapy had endeared her to Dace. But her birthday gift to Dace this evening was much more personal. When friends and family begged Alexei to try and play the piano again, Dace always intervened, and when she couldn't, Alexei closed his eyes and ignored all requests. Dace was always the first line of defense for her husband. Donna was used to this type of challenge, though. After all, she took on a most desperate and helpless Alexei.

On the night of Dace's birthday, Donna broke protocol and announced to Alexei in front of the room that she wanted him to play for Dace. Dace's expression revealed her shock. Dace immediately tried to steer her away from this request, but Donna held firm. She expected this, and without hesitation blew right past Dace's defenses. Donna went the extra measure and wheeled Alexei's shrunken frame right up to his ebony Yamaha grand piano. Dace was mortified. The room now hushed as bewilderment set in. Alexei, she knew, could not fight back but was crumbling inside. Donna, not wasting time, reached for Alexei's weak but usable right hand and placed it firmly onto the keyboard. Dace performed beautifully in her continued attempts to subvert Donna's actions. "Oh, my goodness, it's late," when in fact it was not. She knew her husband could not be swayed back into playing. Donna's voice now amplified, "Alexei, I would like you to play, 'Happy Birthday' for your wife," in a tone that suggested nothing but business. Donna had sensed that Alexei might suffer from a form of Locked-in Syndrome (LIS), which posits that mentally he was completely aware and able but had lost most of his brain's motor responses. She felt Alexei had it in him to play again but just needed the proper motivation and therapy. "Alexei, play for your wife!" Alexei remained motionless.

Everyone in the room stood still, not knowing how to behave. Donna chirped again, "Alexei, Let's go!" When suddenly, his hand moved ever so slightly, and Alexei gingerly placed the fingers of his right hand on the correct keys required of this simple tune. Then his fingers independently moved. What came out was anything but melodic and was hardly audible due to weakness in his right hand. The output was unremarkable, but the attempt was impressive. The crowd looked on in astonishment. Donna then kneeled beside his wheelchair putting her face within inches of Alexei's, leaving no doubt of what she said next. Staring him sternly in the face, she told him, "I want you to play the piano again. You are a fighter, and you can do this! If you want to come back, you can do this! And when you take the stage again, I will either be your page turner, or I will be sitting in the center of the front row. And I will be there to applaud."

Dace remembers those words perfectly and how she stopped dead in her tracks. Her experience told her that this kind of pressure would either cause Alexei to openly weep and/or send him deeper into his depression. Either result felt like a punch to the gut for her to see him suffer further. Donna, on the other hand, knew what she was doing. Her face-to-face encounter with Alexei filled her with the determination to proceed. She saw it in his eyes. "I saw that it was still there," she said. "I knew the music still lived inside him." Donna wasn't finished giving though. Seizing the momentum on Dace's birthday and granting the best gift of the evening, Donna told Alexei, "I want you to learn, 'O Holy Night' and play it for me at Christmas." This monumental challenge gave Alexei two months' time. The seed had been planted, and Donna had opened back up Alexei's will to try. Donna's attitude and positivity seemed to perfectly match Dace; except she managed just what Dace couldn't muster. She refused to bow down to Alexei's abstinence and allow his depression to ruin what was left of him. Donna became Alexei's secret weapon on his road back to music. Alexei's answer to Donna's challenge surprised Dace completely. He answered affirmatively with just one finger. Donna later told Dace that, "When I'm working with him, I want his music playing in the background." Dace's experience got the best of her. "We can't do that." "It makes him very sad, and it makes him cry when he hears himself play like he used to," she told Donna privately. Donna met her halfway, "Fine, play his favorite music." "Just play anything."

From that moment on, when Donna came to work with Alexei twice a week, there was always jazz, pop, rock, symphonies, or operas playing in the house. Dace played the likes of Earth Wind and Fire, Stevie Wonder, Dona Summer, and Al Jarreau to spice it up. Donna began each therapy session by placing Alexei's paralyzed body on a large, inflated ball where she stretched his tensed limbs. She made him stand on his legs unused in over two years to force their damaged synapses to fire and hopefully walk, one day. Donna pried open the fingers of Alexei's permanently clenched left fist, working to give it usefulness, however small it might be. Alexei's lack of incentive to believe in recovery found its turning point in this music. Since Dace's rudimentary birthday piano recital, Alexei now responded in optimistic fashion. He suddenly and noticeably pushed himself as hard as his frail body let him. Stroke patients, from Donna's experience, typically respond with trepidation and caution when attempting new therapies for fear of getting hurt. Alexei was no such patient. Donna now had to restrain him from attempts that were currently too progressive. Alexei quickly regained his drive to accomplish the tasks set upon him. Donna admitted that "Alexei was still an incredible risk-taker, still an adrenaline junkie. That's why I could turn him upside down on that ball and he wouldn't bat an eye."

Each therapy session was unique and especially compelling to any who bore witness. Donna had reached into Alexei's soul and hit the restart. The music being piped in resonated through Alexei, creating an electric-like surge of effort beyond what logic could explain. He stretched, reached, endured, pushed harder than he ever imagined his broken body could possibly handle. Although Alexei could only manage but a few single muffled words, his efforts at the rehab hospital and then at home with Donna gave him noticeable progress which fueled in him a desire to improve. His meager attempt at playing "Happy Birthday" for his wife against his will had magically released the hold his depression held over him. Alexei became proud again and threw himself into relearning the piano. Initially, the feeble fingers on his right hand were too weak to even depress a single piano key, whereas this once mighty performer had snapped many a string with his forceful pounding on the keys. Alexei's road would not ever be easy or explainable, but somehow he had captured the desire to try. Donna began working with Alexei daily, combining physical therapies, speech therapy, and of course practicing their music together.

Friends new to this experiment often were overheard questioning if Alexei would ever find enough capacity to form a tune. So, Dace bought a small keyboard for him to practice on for short periods each day. His strength wasn't enough for him to sit upright at first, so Dace sat immediately next to him on his left to keep him from falling over. She used her shoulder and arm to prop him up just enough where he could place his right hand on the keys. His neurologist Dr. Kramer described the notes he played as some form of gibberish, as they held no recognizable musical quality. A few weeks into it, though, Dace began to hear what she knew to be notes from, "O Holy Night," which Alexei had somehow rediscovered. Alexei's vision was so impaired that he wasn't able to make out the notes on a page several inches away, so he was limited to only his memory.

There was biting cold in the air that evening, but no one minded nor remembered it. It was December 23, 2003, and the Sultanovs' annual Christmas party was underway. It was a small gathering of fifteen of their friends along with Faizul and Benita, who had both flown in for the holidays. The invitation brought them here, but the pretense that Alexei would be playing a song made this party a must-see. Donna arrived and anxiously waited for the moment. The party was joyous, but the nervousness amongst the crowd was palpable. The collection of friends enjoyed Dace's home-cooked Latvian appetizers, along with plenty of cocktails. And then came the moment everyone had been waiting for. Faizul telephoned Natalia at home in Moscow, so that she could potentially hear what everyone silently prayed would actually happen. With all eyes and ears intently tuned in toward the grand Yamaha piano, the room fell silent. Dace wheeled Alexei to the keyboard. She lifted him from his chair and positioned him on the piano bench, then sat herself to his left in what would become her signature placement alongside Alexei. Without delay, Alexei's right arm reached out to the keys, as did both of Dace's, who would be accompanying. The emotionally charged room closed in. Alexei's fingers softly depressed the E key as Dace added the C Major arpeggios. Jaws dropped and eyes welled up. The inseparable couple began slowly but the unmistakable notes filled the room with "O Holy Night."

The living room became awash in joy. The song lasted merely a minute, but its impact was deep. As they concluded their short rendition of this very simple Christmas melody, Natalia, Alexei's mother from over five thousand miles away in a place unimaginable to most in the room, asked Faizul to place the phone to her son's ear. Alexei heard nothing for a short period, as Natalia needed time to compose herself. Covered with tears, she said, "Alosha," using his nickname, "This is just the beginning." "I love

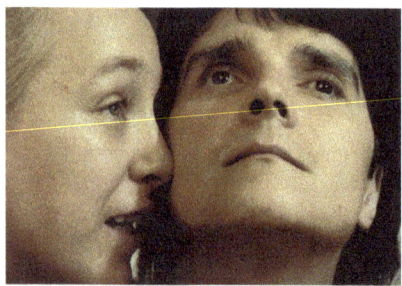

Dace whispers encouragement to Alexei. *Dace Collection.*

Alexei practicing his comeback with Beverly and Dace. *Dace Collection.*

you just like God, with no limits." The concerned room witnessed tears stream on Alexei's face, but he was not alone. Every eye in the room was being wiped. They had after all witnessed what, to them, was indeed a Christmas miracle. The miracle continued as Alexei performed several more one-handed renditions of Christmas favorites he had been practicing, accompanied now with the large in-house choir.

Howard Reich's *Chicago Tribune* interview years later described this moment. Alexei no longer was rehearsing under threats from his parents or teachers, nor to win prizes for fame and lucre. Perhaps for the first time in his life, Alexei was playing the piano purely to make music.[1]

The retooled Alexei now exhibited a strong desire to play again and even anticipated waking up and being placed in front of the keyboard. Dace was always there, right beside him, supporting him in every conceivable manner. After that Christmas night miracle, Alexei worked as hard on his piano as the strength in his body allowed. This signaled a huge step in any rehabilitation project, the desire to improve. Alexei's severe disability became more of a challenge in his head now. He realized some semblance of happiness when he was with the piano. Dace jumped into finding opportunities to further Alexei's rehabilitation. She pulled all the strings she knew to pull and started to arrange for him to play small recitals at churches, nursing homes, offices, and at senior centers. The opportunity to share this remarkable story made him an easy booking.

Each opportunity, no matter how small or insignificant, was monumental in Alexei's eyes. Dace discovered one day from Alexei's reaction to a small crowd's applause that he was acutely aware of how his playing affected those listening. People's reactions, often emotional, strengthened Alexei's resolve. As his concert calendar began to fill, his setup routine streamlined. Dace wrestled Alexei from the car and placed him in his wheelchair. She wheeled him inside the locale and positioned him front and center. Then she hauled in his large portable Yamaha piano along with its necessary accoutrements from the car and arranged the keyboard before him. Dace was required to handle all the heavy lifting, in its truest sense. Once the stage was set and Alexei was ready, she breathed deeply, lifted Alexei from his wheelchair, and then slid him onto the piano bench. She quickly sidled up next to him, left side of course, as his trusted lean-to. There she clasped his useless left hand with her right and gently squeezed. She offered up a giant smile to those in the audience, indicating they were ready.

At every performance, Alexei's story was shared with the crowd by an authorized person. This was immediately followed with their performance. Regardless of venue or crowd, emotions played heavily upon their audiences. Alexei never refused a performance request. One year to the day after the Christmas Eve miracle, the couple returned to Plaza Medical Center, where Alexei spent so much time in Critical Care Unit (CCU) for the more serious patients. They played Christmas carols for all the patients and their families. One family so moved by the performance commented, "What a wonderful Christmas present miracle for all who were there." In January, they played during a church service at Westside Unitarian Universalist Church, again to a most appreciative audience. Then, in February, they were invited to Tarrant County College, where they performed for an audience of students and faculty. Both of these performances garnered them standing ovations. The following month, they played at Fort Worth's Harris Hospital at a support group for stroke victims.

Everywhere they performed, their music and their message touched the hearts of all who heard them. Playing publicly again brought a message of hope, both for Alexei and for those suffering who heard him. Their constant message and mantra were simple but fitting. It followed them everywhere they played.

44

Never Give Up

Now that Alexei had found a new outlook on the piano, he began to willingly accept more and more of Dace's musical requests. He understood that his music was no longer the main draw, but playing in front of a crowd, however small, felt remarkably similar to moments on the grander stage. People wanted to see and hear the story of his life. The annual Christmas Concert, always held at the Sultanov home, became a highlighted tradition for so many. Many friends and family packed the couples southeast Fort Worth home to witness Alexei playing the melody with his right hand while Dace played the accompaniment. The concert repertoire comprised many of the Christmas favorites and a grand sing-along always erupted in the house. The gift of the 2004 event came when Dace, after much coaxing, finally ended her self-imposed cello ban. Dace had put away her cello and her performing talent so that her full efforts were behind Alexei. Her drive was strong to help her ailing husband, but her soul was left starving for nourishment without her musical outlet. Dace had vowed that she would not play her cello again until Alexei accompanied her. She, until that night, politely refused, as Alexei didn't seem ready. The friendly pleas, coupled with the magic of the Christmas Eve moment, finally bore fruit.

Dace gave in to the power of the moment and retrieved Mr. Cello from the closet. What transpired was not lost on anyone. Alexei could not manage to sit on the piano bench without Dace, so she put him into his wheelchair to play so that he could remain upright, and she could play her cello alongside him. Alexei initiated his most recently practiced piece. Dace joined in nearly

Alexei working with Dace. *Dace Collection*.

effortlessly after a solitary deep breath and silent prayer. The couple played a simple version of Franz Schubert's 1825 *Ellen's Third Song*, also known by its more popular name, *Ave Maria*, leaving the entire room drying their eyes as they clung to every note. Most there were overcome with emotion. Tears began to stream down Dace's face as she also recognized the significance of this moment. This special night touched Alexei as well, as his eyes showed signs of moisture. This evening opened a door of opportunity for the couple. The evening prompted the two to practice together, something they rarely did when Alexei was touring the planet. As days became months, Alexei showed steady improvement with control of the fingers on his right hand as well as his coordination with Dace's cello. When Alexei's father, Faizul, turned sixty in May of that year, Dace and Alexei performed several practiced selections for the occasion. Dace played Mr. Cello with Alexei by her side playing his beloved Yamaha grand, which Dace had rightfully named the magic piano.

45
The Grind

The daily grind at the Sultanov house was anything but simple. Alexei required round-the-clock care, which Dace steered entirely. Alexei woke up promptly at seven each morning with Dace sitting him up. The initial effort was to get to the bathroom, but Dace preferred that Alexei attempt the journey using what little faculties he could manage. Since his left side had no function, she acted as his aid. Alexei could almost balance on his right leg, but moving required her assistance. After all the setbacks, Alexei showed remarkable progress with his right hand. He was eventually able to brush his teeth. Dace utilized a doctor-prescribed arm frame that stretched out his left arm in hopes of regaining some use. In the shower was a special shower chair where he sat while Dace washed him. Once dry and dressed, Dace combed and braided his long hair. Often, he ate breakfast in the bedroom for simplicity's sake. Dace had begun to give him small chores to help prepare meals. Almost daily, Dace drove him to the local Benbrook Lake, near the YMCA. Dace lifted him from the car to the water's edge at Baca Beach, so that he could exercise his damaged body in the refreshing water. Alexei loved being in the water, and she knew it.

Alexei especially loved for Dace to bring a large jar of cherries and they would sit on the shore eating cherries and throwing the pits into the water. The couple often wondered if a cherry tree would one day sprout up on the shores of Lake Benbrook. When the weather wasn't cooperating, they used the YMCA pool to rehab. They performed therapies on their own accord. Dace noticed Alexei's legs moved much easier in water, and she pushed every day for further efforts. Every day after lunchtime, Alexei took a nap for a couple of hours. Dace caught up with everyday household chores. After his nap, Dace would coax some piano playing out of him.

Alexei's repertoire improved, as did his appearances. One special appearance on a June evening in 2004 found them at Dr. Kramer's office amidst his multitude of patients, all clamoring to see this inspirational man play. The acoustics and setup were far from adequate, but considering the circumstances, it was perfect. Dr. Kramer introduced Alexei to his waiting room as one the world's greatest pianists who was beginning his comeback tour. Dace led the countdown into Tchaikovsky's Opus 39, also known as *Sweet Dreams*, which was a series of short pieces composed for children. An electronic rhythm track that assisted Alexei with the beat and tempo, Dace's accompaniment also helped Alexei when his reflexes failed him. Alexei was always given the most important and noticeable parts, the melody. All eyes were on Alexei's fingers, and he rarely missed a note. His hours of practice gave him enough confidence to meet Dace's accompaniment and win the crowd over. Alexei and Dace played Dr. Kramer's waiting room as if it were Carnegie Hall and the applause felt as much. Alexei's work at home armed him with a growing confidence. He unveiled Schubert's Impromptu Op. 90, D.899, No.4 in A flat, in his greatly modified arrangement. He even found courage enough to tap out a few notes from Mozart's Piano Concerto No. 21, which elicited an unusual in-performance applause. They closed the performance with *O Sole Mio*, which lifted the tempo and the crowd. People began shouting out requests, impossible until another time, after Alexei had time to practice. But Alexei undoubtedly behaved as a changed man, and his musical comeback was in motion.

Alexei's strength continued to improve, and the results encouraged Dace to push him harder. The world would see her Alexei return to glory. There would always be large parts of him that never functioned as they once had, but with anyone struggling to overcome the effects of a massive stroke such as his, realizing one's own progress creates the most powerful motivator. Alexei continually pushed himself, and now he looked at his biggest feat yet: Rachmaninov's Piano Concerto No. 3.[1] This piece gives most pianists pause due to its complexity. This composition is not for the faint of heart, let alone a man with one good hand. This piece was hardly possible without two highly functioning hands. It had been one of Alexei's favorites when he was on top of the world. Now it became his Mount Everest. He desperately needed to reach its summit to feel further validation. His lonely five fingers played his new creation as his mind planned his fingers' next move. He isolated the critical notes of the piece, hoping to keep the core of the song intact.

Alexei discovered that he still possessed his gift of perfect pitch. Listening to a new song, he quickly found its key and chords. His brain seemed to have retained its gift, but getting his hand to react was the trick. Dace played for him a recording of "My Funny Valentine," sung by the Queen of Jazz Ella Fitzgerald, and Alexei tapped out the notes before the song ended. This new song came with a bonus. Ella Fitzgerald's unmistakable "horn-like" sound brought slow and heavy tears from Alexei. When Dace witnessed this, it only reconfirmed that music still mattered to him. Its magical spell still held onto Alexei's soul.

The unorthodox concert schedule kept Alexei engaged in his craft now. The questions that repeatedly came out from those that heard him were always the same. How can a person that can neither walk, talk, see clearly, nor move one side of his body manage such incredibly intricate pieces of music? The answer may lie beyond what medicine could ever explain but rather somewhere in the magic of music and its effects on the brain.

Dr. Mark Tramo, director of the Institute for Music and Brain Science at Harvard University, was hired by the *Chicago Tribune* in 2003 to study and evaluate Alexei Sultanov's CT scans and MRIs. The *Tribune* was seeking possible answers to the same questions. The findings were of most interest to columnist Howard Reich, who was documenting Alexei's journey through recovery for his introspective series on Alexei. Tramo told Reich, "Regardless of how devastated he may look from the outside, on the inside he's actually very much preserved." Tramo explained that Alexei's strokes killed his ability to handle incoming information from the rest of his body. "The hand to the hot stove test would have failed completely." Simple things like waving to a friend or shooing a fly were lost. Tramo observed, "Yet his cerebral cortex—the outer shell of nerve cells that researchers believe helps to manage how we understand our world—seemed untouched by the strokes of 2001. His musical abilities, emotional life, abstract reasoning, and those structures of the brain that govern intellectual and aesthetic emotional life were actually spared. His memory for music was preserved." Tramo seemed to suggest that a human can be robbed of any number of bodily functions by a stroke, but by sheer determination and will power, some of these lost things can be reclaimed. Alexei was slowly getting back some of what he lost.

After his resurgence, Alexei was able to attempt jazz on the piano without fear of scolding from Popovich. She actually visited Alexei and heard some of his jazz and finally opened up to the idea. Alexei utilized the varying tempos and rhythms produced by the electronic keyboard and tapped out melodies alongside jazz songs from favorites like Ella Fitzgerald and Duke Ellington. Empowered by his ability to inspire people, Alexei felt a desire to help as many as he could.

Beverly Archibald remained the steadfast friend that Dace desperately needed. Beverly, because of her sphere of influence, unceremoniously became the couple's unofficial booking agent.

46

Beautiful Mind

As scientific research continues to unlock new mysteries about the human experience, we are increasingly discovering how much further we must go to understand the complexities of our brains. Neuroscientists regularly make new discoveriesabout the effects of music on the brain. Music opens up parts of the brain to learning by association. Alexei's brain, while deeply damaged, still had a functioning frontal lobe, which reasons, plans, and helps him concentrate while playing, although now in a much smaller capacity. The auditory cortex of his brain, which helps process sound and subsequently pitch, tone, and melody, was still firing on all cylinders albeit stronger on his right side. One might watch Alexei play and wonder how he was able to recall the notes before they were played when seemingly everything about him was irreversibly changed. The answer depends on whom you ask. Doctors and researchers have for years argued over what part of the brain governs music. The right side versus left side debate is just that, a debate.

The greatest minds in cognitive study have long wrestled over this topic, but those involved with Alexei collectively saw the healing powers being unlocked inside his brain and realized the impossible task of ever explaining this. The whys and hows of Alexei's slow climb out of invalidism lacked an easy explanation. Alexei's brain was essentially repairing itself through processes that a collection of doctors would have a hard time agreeing upon. The vastness of Alexei's cranial musical library was not damaged but rather was being opened back up. He still knew how to play as he once did in Kioi Hall in Japan, but his crippled body wasn't able to keep up with his brain. This was changing, though. With each passing day, Dace could sense the forces at work in Alexei. She still believed Alexei would recover fully from this, even when no one else did.

47

Come on, Aileen

Aileen Hummel sat quietly delighted in her ticketed seat at the Fort Worth Convention Center, where she carefully listened to the six Cliburn finalists perform. She had witnessed nearly every round, and now she joined the crowd with her enthusiasm for the finals. A classical music lover since she was young, this was her happy place. Her attention perked up as she read the program, which outlined the next two performances, and she couldn't wait. Elisso Bolkvadze was scheduled to play Mozart's Piano Concerto no. 21 in C Major along with the Fort Worth Chamber Orchestra. She loved this piece. Elisso's second performance was of Saint Saens's Piano Concerto no. 2 with the Fort Worth Symphony Orchestra. It was received with thunderous applause, including her own. As Aileen now watched the final round unfold, she was rewarded with one of her other favorites, Beethoven's *Appassionata* by a young Soviet prodigy who was all the rage amongst the patrons. This young Soviet had been her favorite since she first heard him play back in the preliminary round. Aileen found herself spellbound by Alexei's command of the music and unique, powerful method of play. She decided that she wanted Alexei to win. He wasn't like the others, and she loved that. When Dudley Moore announced what she and so many in attendance desired, she felt personally rewarded.

Aileen had recently become a registered member of the exclusive music fraternity Sigma Alpha Iota. SAI, as it's commonly called, is an international fraternity of musicians charged with educating its members and the public by providing the necessary resources. The philanthropic arm of SAI seeks to empower community outreach programs, collegiate musical associations, and individuals with their grant money. Music was Aileen's life, and the SAI's mission was dear to her heart.

The name Alexei Sultanov hadn't really registered with Aileen for over a decade since the 1989 Cliburn Competition, although she heard his recordings on the radio from time to time. She knew him only by what she heard. The always-modest Aileen gave her heart and soul to music but in a much different way than Alexei did. Aileen's gift was healing people with music. Aileen's skill set was music therapy, and her path would one day lead her straight to Alexei's door.

Aileen studied music education at La Sierra University in Riverside, California. Her parents moved her here from the Philippines in the late sixties at the age of fourteen. Education was important in her house, although music played a bigger role. At La Sierra University, Aileen discovered that music had more benefits than sheer enjoyment. After graduation, she was hired as a choir director in Spokane, Washington, where after three years she recognized that music therapy was her calling. Her application to Texas Women's University in Denton, Texas, was accepted, and so she began her advanced studies. She worked also as a teacher's assistant while she studied. In no time she had earned her Master of Arts in music therapy. Her time was carefully spent learning, but when Jim arrived in her life, a romance blossomed quickly. Jim was working on his PhD in epidemiology, the study of disease patterns, at TWU. Aileen moved to Fort Worth with Jim after they married. After she graduated, she began her full-time career as a music therapist at the James L. West Alzheimer Center on Summit Avenue in Fort Worth.

 Music therapy is defined as a creative arts therapy process utilizing music to improve patient's physical and mental health by means of physical, emotional, mental, social, aesthetic, and spiritual methods. Music is a powerful tool for healing, and is incorporated in many forms of therapy.

Aileen focused on people suffering from dementia and those in hospice or terminally ill. Her goal was to ease the suffering of those facing the end of their lives and, with luck, to prolong their time. Music therapy helps patients exercise their brains, and there is documented proof that it slows the progression of their dementia. Terminal patients

Louise Canafax, (left) in her backstage mother duties.

often quickly regress once they enter into a nursing home. These patients forget important details of their own lives, such as children's names and even their own names, but they amazingly enough recall, with great emotion, songs they have heard. The brain retains the lyrics and melodies of songs so easily and the recall triggers are easily tapped. Patients, she found, remembered names of people, places, and things when put into the context of a song. Her patients used a song to help them remember certain things that otherwise were stolen from their memories.

Music-based exercises also engage patients to socialize with other people when these patients typically tend to seal off the outside world. Aileen developed songs and melodies enabling her patients to recall memories more easily. Certain songs trigger certain memories in any of us. Ultimately, her patients would die, but Aileen's work attempted to give them a more dignified exit from this life.

Aileen had picked up the morning paper on May 13, 2001, to read about the ongoing Eleventh Van Cliburn International Piano Competition, when a story by columnist Mary Rogers snared her eye. The same story that brought Beverly into the fold captured Aileen as well. She became immediately consumed with the story regarding his stroke and subsequent rehabilitation. She knew that she wanted to meet and offer him some of her music therapy. She vividly recalled being mesmerized watching him play at the Eighth Cliburn Competition so many years prior. But how does one contact a celebrity during such a tremendous life changing event? Her desire to help never waned, but the months turned to years before the opportunity finally opened up. Aileen had spread her idea amongst her friends, who unprovoked donated several hundred dollars to the cause. In the spring of 2005 Aileen connected with a woman named Louise Canafax through her musical fraternity, Sigma Alpha Iota. Louise, she learned, had regularly worked with the Van Cliburn competition. Louise held the title of backstage mother to the contestants of the Cliburn Competition for many years. This thankless role consisted of ensuring the competitors had everything ready for their performance. From clothing issues to food and drink, advice, consolation, and encouragement, Louise was the behind-the-scenes be-all and end-all engineer for all who graced the Cliburn stage. She was the last face they saw before entering the stage and the first face they saw upon exiting. She got to know most of the competitors intimately as they proceeded through the rounds. She became a trusted emissary to those who needed a friendly face so far from their homes.

Louise had developed a personal friendship with the Sultanovs after the competition. After Alexei's accident, Louise continued her support of the increasingly desperate couple. Her primary occupation, though, was teaching music at the local college prep school, Trinity Valley, where she worked with children of all ages. Aileen contacted Louise and told her of the money she wished to donate to the Sultanovs. Louise saw potential in bringing Aileen and Alexei together, so she asked Aileen to accompany her to their home once Alexei was released from the rehabilitation hospital. Aileen recalls the first meeting as one of amazement upon witnessing the tremendous energy that Dace exuded, even as she faced the couple's difficult situation. Dace even prepared chocolate covered strawberries for her new guest, as well as a fruit salad adorned with little umbrellas. Aileen fell in love with Dace's positive energy. Dace introduced Aileen to Alexei, who sat motionless in the living room. Aileen got right to the point and explained to them the benefits of music therapy and how Alexei might benefit from it. Alexei, unable to speak, showed little emotion or reaction to the idea. Dace took up the slack and after a few questions told Aileen that Alexei would love the opportunity. Aileen knew instantly that this was a special woman. Dace believed Aileen had something of value to offer Alexei, so soft plans were made to coordinate the two. Dace also took a liking to Aileen as well.

48

What So Proudly We Hailed

The prospect of becoming a US citizen had been growing in the couple's minds since early in their marriage. They both had obtained green cards though their immigration lawyer in Dallas, but political or diplomatic issues always seemed to be a threat to their permanent safety. Dace, during a visit back home to see her family, visited the US embassy in Moscow to apply for US citizenship. The plan was set in motion for her but with no guarantees. When Alexei suffered his series of strokes, the prospect of his citizenship was put on the back burner, as his care required maximum effort. At the turn of the century the idea resurfaced, and the couple, with their attorney, filed the correct forms in Dallas. Months turned into years with no word back. Their financial position didn't allow them to push very hard. Their legal counsel ran into one roadblock after another trying to determine the hold-up. Dace's calls to the Immigration and Naturalization Service (INS) office were never returned. The couple's frustrations mounted, and they nearly lost hope that citizenship would ever happen for them. Dace, inspired by her husband's progress, pressed a friend for help. Through this friend, she was able to make an appointment to see US House Representative from the State of Texas, Kay Granger, to request help. Rep. Granger found out quickly that the INS had mysteriously lost the Sultanov's paperwork, and the internal log jam kept assistance at bay. Rep. Granger, using her pull, got the Sultanovs an immigration interview for eligibility scheduled in Dallas, a wonderful step forward. Because of Alexei's inability to speak, a special interview was setup with the INS agent. Alexei was allowed to answer the agent's questions with a one-finger yes or a two-finger no. The unorthodox interview went off without a hitch. The Sultanovs had long known the correct answers to the required naturalization test. They left the interview feeling supremely confident in their performance. The INS agent cut Alexei a little slack, given his condition. Then it was time to wait again, and wait they did. Word finally arrived in the mail. The Sultanovs were to be sworn in as American citizens on May 9th, 2004.

Faizul boarded the plane at Sheremetevo International Airport in Moscow for the sixteen-hour flight. Some time passed since his last visit. He had been coming to Fort Worth twice a year to visit and stayed several months each time. He packed lightly as he always did and carried with him a new video recorder. This visit was more special and positive than the previous. He was scheduled to celebrate Thanksgiving of 2004 with them, but there was something even bigger happening on this visit. The monumental day arrived, along with Faizul and a small gathering of the Sultanovs' friends. The Sultanovs had passed their two-part naturalization test proving their understanding of American history, civics, and the English language. Alexei, it turned out, had aced his simplified version. A huge crowd of more than one thousand strangers joined together for the Oath of Allegiance Ceremony in the packed main ballroom at the Fort Worth Convention Center. The Sultanovs turned over their green cards to the appropriate authorities upon entering. The ceremony was mandatory for new citizens to complete the process. US citizenship guaranteed several rights not granted by their green cards. The Sultanovs could not be deported to Russia for any reason. They could travel abroad without a visa, whenever and wherever they liked, without fear of being detained. They now had access to federal benefits, including the right to vote, as any citizen might have. Lastly, they could apply for a green card for their families, if desired, and any children would live as US citizens.

The media was on hand as was US Magistrate Judge Charles Bleil, who presided over the grand event. He had been approached weeks

Alexei fulfilling his dream to become a U.S. citizen.
Dace Collection.

ago with a unique idea and hurriedly approved it. Most everyone in attendance was completing his or her own special ceremony to become a United States citizen and thus had no idea as to the plan in place. The swearing-in ceremony took place as the diverse array of people from across the world stood with raised right hands. As Judge Bleil's words were carefully repeated, heavy emotions were on display everywhere you looked. Dace, on cue, pushed Alexei's wheelchair through the crowd right up in front of Judge Bleil. Dace beamed with pride and Alexei showed reaction enough that Dace knew he was proud. Then, Judge Bleil addressed the premeditated portion he had so hastily approved for the Sultanovs: "Ladies and gentlemen, it is my distinct pleasure to introduce a very special new citizen. Alexei Sultanov, winner of the 1989 Van Cliburn International Piano Competition, a world class concert pianist, has come here today after losing the ability to perform, from a devastating series of strokes, which left him partially paralyzed." Judge Bleil made several more comments regarding his struggle and subsequent rehabilitation, then introduced America's newest miracle citizen and wife. Dace switched on his portable electric piano and took a seat in a chair on Alexei's left. Alexei's strong right hand lifted to the keyboard and joined Dace's two hands playing the chords and the rhythm for "America the Beautiful." The sentiment was pure and realized by all in attendance. Alexei's wheelchair supported a wooden pole rising from the back, which in turn supported a sizable American flag hanging slack without the wind to blow it. Alexei wore a bright red shirt and Dace, a dress fashioned out of an American flag. The lights from the news cameras didn't faze the couple. This was their moment, and indeed they savored it. The crowd now grasping the situation struggled to get a visual on the two. The lights from the media circus forced the crowd to further realize something special was happening, and they were somehow involved. Faizul was perched up front recording this for Natalia back home. He beamed with pride, as did Donna Witten, who sat front row as promised. Dace felt prepared for this moment but stood little chance against the overwhelming emotions, and a steady stream of tears ran down her face as she played.

The significance of this event was little known to the crowd. It was fifteen years ago in nearly the same exact space that the nineteen-year boy wonder had captured the hearts of the music world winning gold at the 1989 Van Cliburn competition. Once the song concluded, Alexei heard the familiar sound that concluded each of his performances. This was the most memorable applause of his life. Now it rewarded his soul for his painstaking journey. The applause was long and loud. Everyone stood now, fully engaged in the power of the moment. Alexei even raised his right hand and slowly waved to the crowd in a show of appreciation. Alexei, unable to vocalize his thoughts, soaked it all in. This was his day, and the media ran with it. Alexei and Dace received their Certificates of Naturalization, their undeniable proof of citizenship. Their dreams had come true.

Finally, they were Americans!

49
James L. West

In the months that followed his triumphant performance at his swearing in, Alexei didn't rest. He pushed on in the hospital and nursing home circuit. His purpose was now clear: to inspire others and, in doing so, to heal himself. The two worked interchangeably for Alexei. Alexei's set list expanded with popular classical compositions and several folk songs from Texas. "Deep in the Heart of Texas" always got the biggest crowd reaction. One day Aileen stopped by the Sultanov house to visit. She couldn't help but notice the Christmas lights that still were strung about the house long after the holiday season. Aileen came asking Dace if she and Alexei would be interested in visiting the James L. West Alzheimer Center to play for the residents. Dace immediately accepted, and a deal was stuck.

On June 13, 2005, Dace positioned Alexei and accompanying gear in front of the residents of James L. West. Alexei felt better this day as he brought along his newest conquest, Adagio Opus 70, from Shuman, in his new modified format. The crowd gathered as news of his arrival reached the residents and their respective families. As Dace began sharing their story, nearly every resident emerged from their rooms, as did the center's on-duty employees. The energy of the room quickly warmed as eyes twinkled and lips curved upward. Alexei's right hand, accompanied by Dace's cello, proceeded to inspire the many terminal and suffering people at the James L. West Center. Aileen could not have known the effect this had on her. She was humbled by Dace's efforts to get Alexei out of the car and into the building, all the while carrying his keyboard with her other arm. She made the physical effort look easy when quite the contrary was obviously true. Aileen couldn't believe the emotional responses from nearly all the patients who witnessed the performance. The gentle, deep sound emanating from her cello found resonance everywhere Aileen looked. The music was opening emotional doors to her patients long thought to be shuttered. The room was transformed from one of chronic suffering into one of soul-soothing tenderness.

The performance left many of the residents openly emotional. Many of them expressed emotions they hadn't exhibited in some time. The power of their story made Alexei and Dace an unstoppable inspirational force. Dace, though, was now the center of attention, and the positive energy she displayed affected everyone. Women and men alike marveled at her herculean efforts. As the performance concluded, Dace found herself hugging each resident as she packed up to go. Several of the residents shared that her music had triggered memories of long ago, and they wanted to share their tearful appreciation.

50
Overslept

Benita Abele arrived at the Dallas Fort Worth International airport exhausted yet anxious to see her daughter and recovering son-in-law. The sixty-degree weather back home in Riga, Latvia, was replaced by a seasonally warm start to the Texas summer. Dace and Alexei met her at the airport gate with an arrangement of flowers. Benita embraced both deeply. These annual trips never seemed enough. Benita was overjoyed to see her precious Dace again. That night, June 28, 2005, Alexei, in his wheelchair, cooked steaks on the small electric grill in the kitchen as he now had strength enough to flip the T-bones. Alexei had a hard, fast rule—meat must marinate for a full twenty-four hours before cooking. This activity and involvement made him feel useful and good. It was an old Latvian tradition to share a meal with newly arrived guests. Dace and Benita made lots of plans for the week, including taking Alexei swimming at the local YMCA the next morning. All the next day's activities were planned around being home that next evening to see the series conclusion of Alexei's favorite TV show, *The Real Gilligan's Island*. Benita was enjoying her time with the couple. The steaks on that first evening came out perfectly as did the rest of the welcoming meal. After dinner, they even had time for a movie, which Dace had to translate entirely for her. The ladies were more interested in their conversation anyway. Mom and daughter stayed up for hours after Alexei went to bed at ten o'clock, chatting in Latvian. The night went long for them, and the morning came quick.

The breakfast for the three led to the swim. The daytime together was not only meaningful for Alexei but showed Benita that Alexei was making tangible progress. The day went as planned, and Alexei's anticipation of his evening's program gave him added energy. As the couple settled in that evening for *The Real Gilligan's Island*, there was a sense of comfort after a day well spent. This offshoot reality television show saw contestants participate in challenges based on the 1960s television show, *Gilligan's Island*. Professional bombshells Nicole Eggert, Rachel Hunter, Erika Eleniak, and Angie Everhart filled the "Ginger" role over the show's two seasons. Alexei's enjoyment of the show gave Dace comfort. Afterwards, Alexei was put to bed as he showed his expected signs of tiredness. Alexei, Dace, and Benita were due to get up early for Alexei's next outdoor swim therapy session before the day got too hot. The ladies, though, had so much more to catch up on before bed.

As Alexei drifted off to sleep, the ladies brought each other up to date in the living room. Hours later, after Dace had come to bed, Alexei's paralyzed body twitched, which signaled to Dace to reposition him. He required repositioning every couple of hours as he slept, which she had done faithfully since his series of strokes. At midnight, Alexei's tiny movements signaled Dace that he needed a restroom trip, which instantly woke her. Dace had become an incredibly light sleeper since Alexei needed her so often during the night. The slightest movement by Alexei never failed to awaken Dace. Her sleep was disturbed again around four thirty a.m., which snapped Dace awake. Alexei need only to be repositioned this time. She gently moved him enough to make him comfortable, and they both quickly dozed back off. She knew that seven o'clock alarm was coming quickly.

She awoke to the sound of Benita outside watering the plants, which she so often loved to do at their home. Her eyes jerked open, and she turned to look at the alarm clock. The red digitized numbers read nine! She had overslept, and she never oversleeps. She rolled over to Alexei. "Alosha, wake up, we have to get to the lake!" Dace sat up, energized by her tardiness. Dace repeated again, this time more emphatically. Alexei remained still. There was no response, so she forcibly nudged his shoulder but still nothing. Dace, always so in tune with Alexei's idiosyncrasies, realized seconds later that he wasn't breathing. Panic took over instantly. "Mama! Mama!" Dace screamed for her mother, who dropped

Alexei Sultanov professional headshot. *Dace Collection*.

the garden hose and came running. She burst into the room only to see Dace sitting atop Alexei pumping her palms into his chest with a phone cradled to her ear. This was an image one doesn't soon forget. Dace pleaded to the 911 operator to call an ambulance. "My husband is not breathing! He is blue! I woke up, and he is not breathing," she frantically explained to the woman on the other end. After sharing her address, Dace was instructed to place Alexei on the hard floor and administer CPR. Dace lifted his upper body. Benita, now in sheer panic as well, grabbed his legs and they lowered him to the floor. When she attempted mouth-to-mouth resuscitation, Dace's first breath met much resistance, as did her second. Alexei's lungs did not want to accept air. She put her head on his chest and listened for a heartbeat. She got nothing. The neighborhood was jolted awake minutes later as the firetruck burst onto the scene followed shortly after by the ambulance. A host of uniformed people ran inside with equipment in tow. Neighbors had come outside and watched from their yards. The paramedics replaced Dace with a more proficient method of CPR. The room was loud and chaotic as strangers now shouted at Alexei to breathe while they administered compressions to his chest. No pulse. No movement. Dace and Benita crouched beside them calling out to him, helpless. Nothing!

At nine thirty-four in the morning on June 30, 2005, Alexei's eyes were carefully closed. He looked peaceful as he was pronounced dead. The paramedics pulled a thin blue sheet over Alexei's body still resting on the floor. Dace and Benita knelt nearby, frozen in the moment, motionless and speechless. Dr. Ed Kramer arrived at the house around eleven thirty to assess the body. His examination confirmed that Alexei passed away somewhere between four thirty and nine o'clock that morning from cardiopulmonary arrest. More simply, his heart stopped. Kramer explained the term brainstem dysautoregulation, which meant that the strokes Alexei suffered had damaged the brainstem enough to disturb the regularity of his respiration and heartbeat. Dr. Kramer knew that the actual reason might never be known, but Alexei had been a walking time bomb. His long private battle with bulimia may also have contributed to his strokes and subsequent death. Dr. Kramer was certain of one thing. Alexei slipped away quietly during his sleep. There did not seem to be any symptoms of a struggle to pass. Dace, who was still in the throes of shock, listened blankly as Dr. Kramer carefully explained what was to happen, and that he did not feel an autopsy was necessary. Her husband's body had suffered enough. Everything seemed to be moving at lightning speed for Dace. He was just there, and now he was gone. Her *Alosha* was hers no more. Alexei had been living on borrowed time since his strokes, and as sudden and shocking as this was, it was not unexpected in the medical community.

Dace's mind soon was awash in grief. "What do I do now?" Alexei would not, could not just leave her behind. She collected herself long enough before the coroner removed Alexei's body to retrieve a pair of scissors and cut off her husband's long brownish braid. This small piece of Alexei would stay with her forever. Sadness spread as numbness through her body. Dace recalled thinking something bad was now going to happen to her. Dace stopped ruminating when she realized that she had to pick up the phone and call his parents in Moscow. Her hands trembled as she slowly dialed the number. The hardest call of her life. Faizul cheerfully answered the phone that evening in their apartment. In seconds, the phone fell from Faizul's hands and Dace heard only screaming and wailing on the other end. There was nothing left to say. Later that day, Dace informed the rest of her inner circle of the tragic news.

51
Picking up the Pieces

Faizul boarded the plane in Moscow the next day, alone. He had rapidly sold his last cello, his favorite, to pay the substantial airfare to get to Fort Worth. Natalia would not be joining him as upon receiving Dace's call, she had locked herself in a bedroom, where she remained for two weeks. Faizul landed on July 2nd. After the most horrifically long and painful flight to Fort Worth, he had little strength. He found no sleep knowing he would never again see his son. Every second seemed like an hour.

In accordance with Alexei's long-stated wishes, his body was quickly cremated. Only his ashes were waiting for Faizul. A spot was picked out for those ashes on a shelf in the Sultanovs' living room, a spot surrounded by a multitude of stuffed animals and toys that the couple had accumulated over the years. This was perhaps a symbolic gesture to the childhood he had never realized. Faizul arrived at the house disconsolate and unwilling to speak to anyone. The visitors came by the throngs and Dace's numbness continued. Benita made the effort, but she knew Dace needed to mourn. Every day, people showed up with food and more food. People kept handing her Vodka drinks to help her pain. Friends often found her cradling his ashes or the lock of hair she kept by her bedside. Faizul would later take some of his son's ashes back home to spread in Moscow and at his birthplace in Tashkent. Dace's father Janis took ashes back to their country home in Skujinas. These remains were scattered underneath the one-hundred-twenty-year-old oak tree planted by Dace's grandfather. Alexei had once found a wonderful patch of king mushrooms underneath this cherished oak.

A memorial service was planned in the days that followed. The new Modern Art Museum opened for an official public memorial. Many dignitaries showed up to offer Dace and her family their condolences, including Van Cliburn, who showed considerable emotion during his comments. The multitude of people who helped the couple attended. Over one hundred fans crammed into the auditorium. Dace, donning the same red, white, and blue ensemble that had debuted at the citizenship swearing in, heard none of it. She sat in the back, oblivious to it all, and openly wept. Janis arrived days earlier and stayed till mid-August. Benita remained in Fort Worth for another month consoling her Dace every moment of that time. She gently urged Dace to come back to Riga with her. Dace's family shared this desire. There she would have time to grieve and a quiet place in Skujinas to hide. Dace never even considered it. Aileen, who was never far away, shared a story with Dace after the memorial that touched Dace through her despair. Aileen, along with being Alexei's music therapist, also held her private pilot's license. She had promised months ago to take Alexei flying with her. Now that the opportunity no longer existed, Aileen felt terrible remorse for putting it off, as she remembered how excited he had been. She hugged her friend Dace warmly and expressed her sorrow for not coming through for Alexei on his promised plane trip. Dace, without pause, suggested to Aileen that she could still come through for him.

Donna Witten had just arrived back in town from a trip to Alaska the day before the memorial. The trip was a celebration of Donna's mother's seventy-fifth birthday. Joining the birthday trip was another of Donna's special patients, a man suffering heavily from multiple systems atrophies or MSA, along with some of his family. Alaska had been a bucket list item for all people involved. The trip was everything they dreamt it would be. When Donna arrived home that Sunday, she called Dace to share her amazing experience, completely unaware of what had transpired. When the phone was handed to Dace, Donna immediately sensed a change. When Dace didn't respond to Donna's happy tone, Donna inquired, "Dace, what's wrong?" The silence was interrupted when Dace burst into a tearful wailing. "He's gone! Alexei is gone!" she sobbed. It took a few seconds for Donna to process this news. She was thrown into shock learning about Alexei this way. Dace painfully shared

Alexei Sultanov Memorial poster. *Dace Collection.*

as much as she could through bouts of sobbing. The next day, Donna and her mother arrived late to the memorial service at the Modern Museum, where they took a seat next to their acquaintance, *Chicago Tribune* reporter Howard Reich. His comprehensive chronicling of Alexei Sultanov's recovery from a series of debilitating strokes now had reached its sad conclusion.

Back in 2004, in Bolzano, Italy, Alexei's old Soviet rival and friend Alexander Shtarkman was working on an upcoming piano competition when news that Alexei had passed reached him. The news hit him hard, until he learned it was a false rumor. Shtarkman remembered an old Soviet saying that if someone was incorrectly reported to have died, then that person would go on to live a long and healthy life. The second and actual death notice of Alexei reached Shtarkman in early July, 2005, proving that Soviet adage to be unfounded. Shtarkman was deeply saddened and recalled the tremendous unfairness of his longtime friend's life. His friend was now gone, and with him an unimaginable talent.

It was a Sunday, August 7, and Dace orchestrated a private memorial and birthday celebration for Alexei on their favorite beach in Galveston, Sunny Beach. An incredible number of friends showed up. Faizul had since returned home to Tashkent and Natalia, who would never see Dace again after Alexei's death. For the memorial, Dace traveled to the Texas coastal town with Aileen in her small single-engine Cessna 172 airplane along with fellow friend and pilot, Peter Brown. Dace never once let go of Alexei's ashes during the hour and forty-five-minute flight. Her plan was to release his ashes midair over a particularly favorite beach of Alexei's. Several days prior, Aileen borrowed another Cessna just to practice the upcoming maneuver, as hers was in the shop being serviced. She used a five-pound bag of sugar as practice to ensure there were no screw-ups during the actual ceremony.

As the practice run commenced, Aileen released the sugar from the window, simulating the dropping of the ashes, only for it to blow straight back into the cockpit, covering the interior of the loaner plane. This was cause for concern in handling Alexei's ashes. She luckily was able to vacuum the sugar out of the plane before the plane's owner found out. Aileen had the idea to build a modified tube to aid in getting the ashes out of the plane and toward the earth below. Janis, who had flown in with Benita after Alexei's passing, used his craftsmanship to construct a workable model, which he painted red. On the morning of the day typically used to celebrate Alexei's birth, Dace, Aileen's pilot friend Peter, and *Chicago Tribune* photographer Zbigniew Bzdak (Mr. Z) clambered aboard Aileen's four-seat freshly serviced Cessna 172 and readied for takeoff on runway 32 at Scholes International Airport in Galveston, Texas. Aileen stayed on the ground for this special occasion. None of the required permits from the City of Galveston, the Environmental Protection Agency, or the Coast Guard ever arrived, making the mission illegitimate. Dace had brought red roses from her garden at home and a few more she ordered at her motel in Galveston. She pulled off the rose petals and mixed them up among Alexei's ashes in order for those on the ground to better see them fall. She placed the ashes and rose petals into the red hand-painted cylinder, which was his favorite color. Those there for the memorial gathered on the beach near where the drop was to happen. In attendance were Benita and Janis Abele, who had ridden down with Donna and her mother. The language barrier was so great that hardly a word was spoken during the five-hour trip.

At a rest stop, Donna and her mother bought Janis and Benita a Coke and a Snickers bar, their universal offering of kindness. The two pairs, unable to communicate, listened to the radio to pass the awkward time. Also attending the memorial were Beverly Archibald, Howard Reich from the *Chicago Tribune*, who had completed the final paragraph of his marvelous three-part story of the life and death of Alexei, as well as Dr. Ed and Sheri Kramer and their children. The group met on a specific beach as instructed. Dr. Kramer threw open his car doors and blasted a bootleg CD of Alexei playing Mozart's *Concert Rondo in D Major* when he was just seven years old. At the music's conclusion, the group pushed forward to the waterline and in unison sang, *Happy Birthday to You*. After all, this day would have been his thirty-sixth birthday. As the song ended, the group was awash in quiet. Then, as if on cue, the little Cessna appeared noisily in the sky. The plane circled the drop point a few times, then departed as quickly as it had entered, with no dispersal of ashes. The ground-based group looked on in confusion, wondering what to do next. Fifteen minutes later, the Cessna returned much lower, at around four hundred feet of altitude. Dace, as it turned out, was having second thoughts about letting his ashes go. "I don't know if I want to do this," she sobbed to the crew. She finally succumbed, knowing that's what Alexei would have wanted. As the plane reached the desired position and the crowd stood in place, the plane's crew exhaled. Photographer Bzdak opened the cockpit window, and Dace aimed the tube of ashes at the ground.

The moment happened with a puff of smoke in a simple yet remarkable commemoration. A thunderous applause came from the beach, which couldn't be heard from the plane. As tears rolled down Dace's face, Alexei was laid to rest into the warm waters of Galveston Bay. The plane hurriedly flew back to the airport, where Dace jumped out before the propellers had ceased their rotation and ran into the terminal building. She emerged after fifteen or so minutes from the restroom visibly upset. Dace now joined those on the beach and the spirit of her Alexei. She arrived at the spot and hugged everyone there. She grabbed a bottle and poured champagne into everyone's waiting red paper cup and then walked slowly out into the ocean alone. She stood waist deep peering out at the horizon. She whispered to her Alexei an emotional goodbye and turned up her red cup. This was her final goodbye to the love of her life. Alexei was now symbolically as free as the ocean he so much loved during his formative years. Returning to shore, Dace told everyone, "Now, Alexei can play with both hands again."

October 12 no longer mattered to Dace, but still several friends decided to throw her a surprise birthday party in the hopes of bringing her some cheer. The months leading up to her birthday were especially rough for Dace. Donna, who had witnessed much suffering and death due to her line of work helping the severely disabled, had never recalled seeing someone grieve as hard as Dace did. She had shut down since Alexei's death in June. She hardly ate, bathed, cared for her appearance, handled any financial matters of the household, or reached out to family and friends. She was heard several times declaring that she would never play her cello again. She would never marry again. Never love again. She strongly believed that her death was imminent. She could not be left alone without Alexei. She knew not how or when, but she believed she was not long for this world. Her appearance was a far cry from her normally attractive and bubbly self. Those like Donna who stopped by her house to check on her had long since begun to worry about her health and future. She spent much time alone, lost in an inescapable sadness, often crying alone and sometimes to those who visited. Beverly

Photo carried around by Dace for many years after his passing. *Dace Collection.*

again took the reins to get everyone in action for the surprise party. Nearly every one of her phone calls went to someone she didn't yet know. The show of support was tremendous. Dace was picked up by Sheri Kramer on the premise that she needed her help with a few errands. Sherri managed to get lost, which struck Dace as peculiar when she asked Dace where the damn Mimi's Café was. She immediately suspected Sheri was up to something, just not what. The thought of her birthday had not registered much since the loss. They finally arrived at Mimi's Café and entered the restaurant. Dace clutched her small-framed photo of Alexei, which never left her side.

As they entered, Dace noticed a long table with many people sitting having what seemed like a good time. She reasoned someone was having a wedding celebration there. Suddenly, the same table began to sing happy birthday. It took her several seconds to put the pieces together, but then the faces finally began to register. She couldn't contain her first smile in a while as she took her place at the celebratory table and placed Alexei's picture in front of her. The smile on her face seemed to magnify with each new face she encountered. The moment was powerful and being with all her friends brought a brief happiness to Dace. For a brief time, she was happy. As the party waned and time came to return home, her deep sadness returned. She bid farewell to Sheri and closed her front door. At home, everything reminded her of Alexei. She felt all the pain and anguish seep into her, stealing her strength as she collapsed into a chair. There she sat crumpled in sadness and despair for what seemed like hours. Strange thoughts crept their way into her brain. Thoughts that often accompany significant loss. Then something happened. Somebody was there. She felt a ferocity rush through her like a gale-force wind surging through her body. Its power lifted her from the chair and pushed her. The force was unlike anything she had ever felt. Her sadness temporarily paused as her body moved without her understanding and she found her hand reaching for the closet door, the same closet where Mr. Cello sat gathering dust. Her trembling hands reached out and lifted her old friend. Tears fell from her eyes. She carried Mr. Cello to the nearby piano bench where Alexei had spent so much time. She tightly cradled the instrument and began to pull the bow slowly across its strings. A calmness spread over her. She knew right then that music was her therapy. It was an epiphany. She played emotionally, opening wide the window to her soul. She felt as if Alexei was there with her. Her pain subsided as the minutes turned to hours. She was raised from her despair with what Dace understood to be Alexei's spirit urging her onward. She recognized that she must now play for herself, for Alexei, and for others, as inspiration for anyone who needed it. Alexei had given Dace a spiritual birthday gift of inspiration in order to keep their love alive.

Dace treasured this day as the most monumentally important of her entire life. Even today, Mr. Cello bears the marks of tear-stained wood upon its battered, broken, healed, and inspirationally constructed frame. One cannot know Dace for very long without also knowing Mr. Cello and his tear-stained badges. Several days after Dace's spiritual awakening, she received a telephone call from her mother back in Riga. Janis had suffered a heart attack due to the stress he had been under at work. Janis did survive the ordeal and undertook a much easier work schedule going forward. Janis remained a volunteer with Riga's National Guard called Zemessargi or Army of the Earth, but now with a much more restricted role. After Alexei passed, the hurt for Dace piled up as the medical bills kept coming. Due to the bureaucratic formalities, the couple did not receive Medicare for the first year and half since the initial series of strokes. When it finally kicked in, they received a fifteen-hundred-dollar disability check each month. This money barely scratched the surface of the money they truly needed. Upon Alexei's death, the Medicare disability money abruptly stopped. Dace suddenly was drowning in a growing sea of debt. Out of necessity, Dace commenced working at Dr. Kramer's office three months after Alexei's passing, but it barely put a dent into the debt. But the job gave her something to take her mind off her new reality. When at home, she played her cello constantly to override her emotional paralysis. Dace frequently spoke to Alexei as if he were still there. The healing properties of her cello were developing, but they couldn't salvage her entire day. Her grief looked for any opportunity to come forth. Mr. Cello was fighting a difficult battle. The death of Alexei left an incredible hole in Dace's life. She tried mightily to fill this void with pictures and mementos of him. She constructed a massive shrine to her lost love on the largest wall of her house, directly behind the piano where he once played. The shrine contained pictures of Alexei at different stages of his life, portrait paintings from fans, mementos collected over the years, and a few of the special promotional posters they saved. One couldn't visit Dace's house without becoming enveloped by her lingering love for Alexei. The small, framed picture of Alexei that traveled everywhere with her was evidence of her unshakable devotion to him.

Dace played Mr. Cello to remember. She played Mr. Cello as her outlet for her sadness. Aileen began visiting and playing the piano with Dace. The two found some peace when they were together, lost in their music. Performance opportunities trickled in. Slowly, Dace and Aileen began to play for small crowds in retirement homes, hospitals, private homes; places that Aileen had arranged for them to play. The music bestowed powerful benefits on those audiences, but Dace often drew the greatest succor from these moments. As she became more and more comfortable playing in public again, people began to reward her time with small monetary donations. She desperately needed the money, and so her performance calendar began to slowly fill. She thrust herself into her job and her music as the only sources of relief from her heavy blanket of sorrow.

As Alexei's death neared its first anniversary, Donna came to the rescue again. Dace was now on the lookout for performing gigs—especially ones that could help her pay some of her bills. The work at Dr. Kramer's office was tough and arduous, but she still wasn't making enough to get ahead. Donna found an opportunity that was perfect for Dace. Donna learned of a deaf young man with a severe case of cerebral palsy who required regularly scheduled physical therapy to stretch and work his diminishing muscles. Knowing that Dace was quite capable, Donna gave her specific instructions on how to treat the patient. Chris Moran was immediately smitten with Dace. Initially, her cello frightened him, but quickly he grew to love Mr. Cello. Her biweekly visits after work became the highlights of his week. Dace often implemented unorthodox activities for Chris to keep him active. Several times Donna came to inspect and discovered Chris and Dace jumping up and down wildly or performing some activity Dace had invented on the spot, in lieu of more traditional therapies. Donna knew that Dace was good for Chris and that she cared for him, so she overlooked these alternative treatment methods. Chris also became one of Dace biggest cello fans. Chris, although deaf, felt the deep rich tones of her cello permeate his body, which soothed him when medicine failed. Chris's parents took him often to see Dace's performances wherever they materialized. Chris found tremendous comfort under Dace's care and always showered her with kisses upon her departure, a clear and wonderful violation of the therapist/patient relationship. Chris's parents additionally were very good financially to Dace. She continued these therapies with Chris until his family departed for Ohio years later, in 2017.

As time crept by, Dace's inspirational performances gained steam. In 2007, Aileen introduced Dace to Dr. Mugur Doroftei, the musical director of the children's orchestra at the Seventh Day Adventist school in Keene, Texas, some thirty minutes south of Fort Worth. Dr. Doroftei, born in Romania, wanted Dace to play alongside his children's orchestra. Dace, not a Seventh Day Adventist but never one to let something as simple as religion get in the way, jumped at the opportunity headfirst. Dace accompanied the children's orchestra for the next seven years until Maestro Doroftei was forced to retire.

Dace's inspirational cello concerts began to capture more and more people's attention. People began reaching out to her and Mr. Cello for increasingly broader audiences. When Donna's mother reached the notable age of eighty, there was Dace playing the birthday party and stealing the show. Each performance she gave was uniquely special. She drew heavily on her emotions each time, which always captured and inspired her audiences.

52
Mt. Fuji 2009

Alexei, even after death, remained popular throughout the world and especially in Japan. Alexei's Official Fan Club in Tokyo boasted thousands of hardcore devotees and was continually led by its founder, Yusuke Murakami. One especially devoted fan was a lady named Kazuko Narumi. Kazuko learned of Alexei Sultanov by sheer accident. After one especially difficult day at work she was browsing the CD collection at the Tower Records store in Tokyo and randomly selected a recording of a performance by Alexei. She took it home to investigate. The music she heard moved her so deeply that she felt compelled to search him out and stumbled onto the Alexei Sultanov Fan Club. She contacted Yusuke Murakami, whose love of Alexei's music led him to create the club. Kazuko became deeply connected to his music and so inspired that she began painting portraits of Alexei. One of these portraits hung on Dace's memorial wall at home. When Kazuko learned of Alexei's passing, she was so heartbroken that she immediately reached out to Dace, as she wanted so badly to honor him with a memorial concert in Tokyo. Dace was hardly ready to attend an event such as this, let alone play, as she was requested to do, but she didn't want to spoil Kazuko's tribute to late husband. Dace reluctantly agreed to go, but only if her new pseudo sister, Aileen, was allowed to join her. Kazuko provided Dace with a cello to play so she wouldn't have to haul Mr. Cello across the planet.

Witnessing the love the Japanese people had for Alexei surely carried some emotional weight. Upon arrival at the Tokyo Bunka Kaikan

Concert Hall, Dace was greeted as an incoming celebrity. Fans took pictures, asked for autographs, and treated her as if she were Alexei himself. After she settled in, Dace was introduced to her loaner cello, a gigantic sixty-thousand-dollar French beast that she instantly struggled with due to its larger size, heavier strings, and the short period of time afforded her to prepare the virtuoso program for the concert. The trip was scheduled to last a week, with three to four days of practice culminating in the memorial event. The practice halls were in the basement of the beautiful concert hall. Dace's seasoned hands were worn raw and bloody from rehearsing on the heavy new cello strings. Sergei Sultanov, Alexei's brother from Russia, was also invited to play in place of Alexei. Sergei was a fine pianist in his own right, but admittedly not on par with his brother. Dace and Sergei somehow found sync and rose to the occasion. They delighted the Japanese crowd with Rachmaninoff's *Vocalise, Carmen Fantasy* and Rhapsody on a Theme of Paganini. A lovely Japanese string quartet filled the remaining roster for the event. The memorial drew almost three hundred people, and the money raised was earmarked for Dace's newest brainchild. It was soon to become Dace's new life's mission, to raise enough money to design and build money to design and build a lasting tribute: The Alexei Sultanov Memorial Fountain. This fountain would awe and inspire those who visited, and would promote Alexei's most important goal: to inspire those in need. The projected cost was high and the location unsure, but Fort Worth would someday be decorated by this creation. The trip to Japan came with the stipulation that any money raised went toward the proposed memorial.

During her visit, Dace, realizing she would have a few days to burn after the concert, hatched the idea to climb Japan's highest peak, Mt. Fuji, and spread some of Alexei's remaining ashes, which she now carried with her. The 12,389-foot sacred dormant stratovolcano has been a constant source of inspiration for many artists, and remained a very popular pilgrimage spot. Kazuko did not want her to go for the obvious reasons. Dace had never climbed a mountain, nor did she have the proper gear or training for such an undertaking. These obstacles meant little to Dace. Finally, after much back and forth, Kazuko relented and gave her blessing. Kazuko, as Dace's host, joined the excursion, hoping to ensure her safety. Aileen and Sergei joined the excursion as well. The memorial concert gave the fans everything they hoped for.

The Alexei-themed performance moved the audience to tears more than once. Dace played passionately for her lost love, so much so that she hardly noticed the blood flowing from her fingertips as they moved upon the coarse strings. Once the memorial concert concluded, the next morning the new mountaineers embarked. Professional mountain guides were hired by Kazuko who led her group slowly up the mountain. Their scheduled three-day climb began at station #5, which lay near the base of the perfectly symmetrical mountain. They climbed with much effort, but the group's progress was steady, and they successfully made it to station #8 on day one, before darkness set in. They had followed a well-defined trail cut into the mountainside. The lodging for the trip consisted of crudely built plywood huts at stations along the way. The quarters were so tight that the climbing party slept side by side. The 8th station was a mere eighteen hundred treacherous vertical feet from the summit. The plan was to rise early and make the summit.

Then began the long, fast decent to the bottom. Dace brought along a small container of Alexei's ashes, which she planned to leave at the summit, her primary reason for the ascent. She knew that Alexei would enjoy a place such as this where he could watch over the world. Dace and Aileen never got comfortable enough to sleep, so they spent most of their evening watching the others sleep.

Then a typhoon hit around midnight. The heavy winds easily woke everyone, as did the trailing torrential rains. The mountain guides made the emergency call to abandon the trip and head down immediately. Their hut would not provide suitable safety from this storm, so morning couldn't wait. The typhoon revealed countless mudslides to the group. The ill-equipped group, freezing, pulled on every piece of clothing they brought along and were provided with ponchos by the guides. It wasn't long, however, before the entire group was soaked and chilled to the bone. Aileen, in her first foray into climbing, made her escape wearing tennis shoes, which is all she brought along. Each and every step she took was a contest to stay upright. She could not seem to gain any foothold on the pitch black, muddy, rain-soaked terrain. Dace, who trailed Aileen, helped her to up nearly each time she fell. Aileen helplessly made her way down the mountain. Even with the pounding of the typhoon, the descent, per the laws of gravity, was much faster than the ascent. As daylight broke, the scene around them was chaotic, but now, at least, they could see. It took them almost until evening to reach the safety of the base camp. The horrific climb was officially over. Kazuko, as exhausted as the others, suggested that they go straight to a nearby hot springs so they might warm their core temperatures. Each of them was suffering from some level of hypothermia. The joyous relief of being off the mountain was unanimous. Exhaustion overcame them all as they were shuttled to the nearby hot springs. Upon arrival, the scene was one reminiscent of the movie *Caligula*. Dozens of people running around naked amidst the ongoing storm. As surprised as they were, everyone was too sore and worn out to care. The warm spring waters reheated the group enough to stave off any danger of hypothermia. The longest day ended when they finally made it back to their hotel and collapsed in their rooms. Knowing their ordeal was over undoubtedly gave them total relief.

Before the sun had broken the horizon the next day, Tokyo was hit with a six-point-five magnitude earthquake, shaking the entire country. Dace was jarred awake thinking she was on a boat in the middle of a rolling sea. The quake caused widespread destruction throughout the city, but the loss of life was minimal. Dace, Aileen, and Sergei survived unscathed and used the remaining few days to gingerly explore the destruction and witness the aftereffects of the earthquake. The trip's mission was not all a loss. Dace managed to scatter a small bottle of Alexei's ashes as they were departing from Station #8 in the midst of the storm. There on Mt. Fuji, Alexei could watch over the people who so dearly loved him.

53
Final Curtain

On August 27, 2012, Van Cliburn's publicist announced to the world that the famed pianist had been diagnosed with advanced prostate cancer, coupled with widespread bone metastases. He was receiving round-the-clock care at his home in Fort Worth, where close friends suggested he was resting comfortably. The lack of update was no surprise as Van had always been a very private person. The rumor mill for years stoked his desire to avoid the public eye as much as possible. Aside from beloved trips to New York, where he took in the opera, and recurring visits to Russia, Van kept well to himself. That privacy ended six months later when on February 27, 2013, at the age of seventy-eight, Van Cliburn was pronounced dead.

Fort Worth mourned its lost son, one of the true pioneers of the music world, on March 3, 2013. Van stood as a longtime member of the Broadway Baptist Church in Fort Worth, where he regularly attended, and where his funeral was held. The Broadway Baptist Church had long welcomed openly gay members, much to the chagrin of the state's largest Baptist group, the Southern Baptist Convention, which it cut ties to in 2009. The Broadway Baptist Church, which embraced all those wanting to worship God, utilized every inch of available space for the funeral service. The Broadway Baptist Church sent Van home with a most fitting tribute by the Fort Worth Symphony's performance of Rachmaninoff's Symphony No.2 in E Minor, Opus 27. Paul Harvey Jr., the famed son of legendary radio storyteller Paul Harvey, read a poem entitled, *Steal*

Alexei spending time with Van. *Dace Collection.*

Not Away, written by Van Cliburn. The funeral featured tributes from President George W. Bush, Texas Governor Rick Perry, President Barack Obama, and Russian President Vladimir Putin, to name but a few.

Van's legacy spread like wildfire across Fort Worth's landscape in honorary fashion. Notably, prior to the publication of this book, The Van Cliburn Concert Hall celebrated its grand opening, immediately becoming a uniquely modern world-class music hall on the campus of Texas Christian University. Its location was no coincidence, built directly across the street from aging Ed Landreth Hall, where his competition got its beginning. The Van Cliburn Concert Hall now hosts the first two rounds of the great Van Cliburn International Piano competition. Van was entombed at the Greenwood Memorial Park Mausoleum in Fort Worth. His gorgeous, marble adorned mausoleum, lined with ornate life-size statues of the United States founding patriots, remains one of the most visited sites at the cemetery. Van is entombed next to his beloved mother, Rildia Bee. Van's life was truly remarkable and continues to be retold by countless writers, journalists, and videographers, far beyond the borders of the city he called home.

What do you say about a man like this? He stood at an imposing height, yet behaved in a gentle and caring manner. He was the epitome of elegance and refinement. His presence was felt wherever he went. He hated the attention he drew, but knew his presence was needed. He infiltrated the iron curtain when it was most impenetrable to pull off one of the great musical victories in the history of classical music. Van's victory in Moscow was all the more extraordinary given the fact that this competition was created to demonstrate to the world the cultural superiority of the Soviets during the Cold War. Van's victory came on the heels of a monumental Soviet technology victory in the form of the Sputnik launch in October 1957, which initiated the Space Age. Van's victory had helped usher in the end the Cold War and launch a period of peaceful coexistence. As the world dealt with the passing of a legend, Dace struggled with the ongoing task of repurposing her life.

The distance between them strained the relationship between Dace and Alexei's parents. Faizul remained the more open of the two since Alexei's premature death. He remains in contact with Dace and regularly inquires if she's okay. Natalia has dealt with the loss differently. She no longer wishes communication with Dace, as the pain remains too much for her. Alexei's parents still teach music and live on Begovaya Street in Moscow, as it's their solace. After Alexei's passing, they held a memorable memorial tribute concert in Moscow, which gave his Russian friends and family a chance to honor their departed friend.

54
Sitting on the Terrace

All of Dace's life has been inundated with music. Her cello, with its grief-stricken scars, is with her nearly every minute of every day. Mr. Cello is more than a cherished instrument. He is her answer to life's biggest riddle. Why am I here? Dace's life had been re-purposed after her tragedy, now placing her directly in front of those most in need of her gift. Music remains her constant and required therapy. Music brought her back to life. Now she uses its magical power to bring life to people suffering through their own personal struggles. There were almost one hundred elderly people seated in the large conference room at Trinity Terrace retirement home, which is located just west of downtown Fort Worth. Dace begins to pull her bow across Mr. Cello's resonant body. The wonderous and soul-soothing sound envelopes the attentive room. Every eye is fixed on her. Each person in the room encompasses a lifetime of stories, loves, and unforgettable moments slowly reaching their end. While Dace shares small snippets of her life's story between pieces, the teary eyes from the crowd suggest something magical in their own minds. One can't help but ponder life's great purpose in this room. Had they lived their best life? Had they done their best? Had they lived a purposeful life? How much time did they have left? Was heaven awaiting them? Would death be painful? In this moment, music became the conduit to life's most important matters. Dace wasn't alone in her struggles through life. Here, everyone had known life's difficulties, and as their own journeys neared their conclusions they found understanding and solace.

Dace with her treasured Mr. Cello. *Dace Collection.*

In the Buddhist religion, the lotus flower is associated with purity, spiritual awakening, and faithfulness.[1] The beautiful flower's emergence from its muddy pond represents a rebirth. The lotus fittingly represented to Alexei his emergence from a muddy life. He had always loved the lotus flower and its spiritual significance. Alexei witnessed the lotus growing beautifully from muddy ponds several times while performing in Japan. After the strokes and once he returned to playing, Alexei felt the lotus best embodied his philosophy. His life was irreconcilably changed by the strokes, when nearly everything precious to him taken away.

Through the midst of his suffering, his strong desire to inspire people gave his life purpose. Alexei was, after all, tapping out creative melodies on his parent's piano at age two, trying to send a message. His message now carries on with Dace. Her undying love for Alexei spills forth in all she does. One can feel both her love and her pain flowing through Mr. Cello.

Upon her death, Dace has arranged to have her body transported to UT Southwestern Medical Center in Dallas. She has outlined carefully in her will that her body be donated so that it can be utilized for medical research. There, student doctors will undoubtedly find the innerworkings of one of God's special creations. When she is done giving, she wants her body to give once more.

What they will never find is the magical energy inside her that makes her unique. Her front row seat to the magic of life can't be discovered or researched. Her stubborn ability to find only the positive side of everything is a special talent. Losing one's partner in life shakes a person down to the core. Grief can consume and forever change the personality of the affected person. Dace had every reason to give up and every reason to leave that cello in its closet. She embodies the power of love and what it means to truly live. Life is not a destination but simply a journey meant to be experienced, sadness included, otherwise how might one know what joy really is? For the last three years, on Sunday mornings, Dace has played Mr. Cello for the homeless at First United Methodist Church in downtown Fort Worth. Her music, along with church-volunteer-prepared food has become a cherished event for those lacking life's most basic needs. Dace knows most of the attendees by name as they know hers. While her music may not offer them a solution to their problems, the happiness they exude during the event is palpable. While the Alexei Sultanov Inspirational Fountain is her life's mission, she selflessly plays hope into people who need it most.

In the pandemic year of 2020, beloved local artist Jimmy Jenkins crafted a large donut-shaped metallic sculpture that contains a waterfall pouring from its center. The Alexei Sultanov Inspirational Fountain was donated and dedicated on September 8, 2023, in the Fort Worth Botanical Gardens, as Dace played Mr. Cello nearby. The monumental task of raising the million dollars for her vision had been completed with the selfless acts of a few, creating a lasting tribute honoring the legacy of Alexei. Here, Alexei Sultanov's name would live to inspire others as he had done in life. Dace carries on her mission to give back through her music and her life. On June 24, 2024, in a small private ceremony, Dace's rebirth was complete with her marriage to longtime friend, Ben, who taught Dace to love again. The couple moved to Oregon and live happily on a beautiful plot of land that the bought together, high in the hills overlooking the Pacific.

(THE END)

THE CURSE OF THE CLIBURN

STEVEN DE GROOTE is the 1977 Grand Prize winner of the Van Cliburn Piano Competition. In 1981, he was honored by a resolution from the Texas Senate for outstanding contributions to music. In 1985, as an amateur pilot, he crashed his small private plane outside of Phoenix, puncturing his lung and aorta. After barely surviving, he would recover to fly and perform again. In 1989, after returning to South Africa, he developed tuberculosis and pneumonia, a complication from AIDS, which would take him to the hospital and days later, take his life.

JOSE FEGHALI is the 1985 Grand Prize winner of the Van Cliburn Piano Competition. On December 9, 2014, Jose Feghali was found dead in his Fort Worth home from an apparent self-inflicted gunshot wound. The fifty-three-year-old avid chamber musician had performed over one thousand concerts worldwide in every conceivable venue and earned the utmost respect of his peers. He had gone on to develop software for high fidelity streaming of music lessons, which was widely used throughout the world. He was also a true champion for Fort Worth's music scene and in turn, much adored. He was an artist in residence at Texas Christian University's school of piano from 1990 until his death. He was curious, inquisitive, and brilliant when described by those who knew him best and deeply troubled in a way very few knew.

ALEXEI SULTANOV is the 1989 Grand Prize winner of the Van Cliburn Piano Competition. He died in 2005 from effects of a series of debilitating strokes, taking prematurely from the world a recognized yet misunderstood genius. Alexei would have turned fifty years old the summer of 2019. Dace celebrates his birthday with an annual Birthday Memorial Concert. The year 2019 also marks thirty years since Alexei took home the gold medal.

VADYM KHOLODENKO is the 2013 Grand Prize winner of the Van Cliburn Piano Competition. On March 17, 2016, he discovered the bodies of his two young children, age 5 and 20 months, deceased inside their Benbrook, Texas home. Police took his estranged wife Sofia into custody. Her lifetime was filled with bouts of depression that started at age eighteen in Russia, after her failure to place at a piano competition. After her marriage to Vadym ended, she was in and out of mental facilities, once after throwing herself in front of a moving vehicle and lying down in a busy street. She came to believe that the devil had taken possession her and her children, which led to her horrific crime. She was found not guilty by reason of insanity for suffocating her children with a pillow on July 16, 2018, and committed to a psychiatric hospital, where she remains.

WHERE THEY ARE NOW (2024)

BEVERLY ARCHIBALD was a fiercely independent woman and educator who taught English in Fort Worth and abroad. She taught English as a second language to many including the Sultanovs, and became a close confidant of Dace's. Beverly kept her faculties to the end, but her body slowed down. On January 14, 2021, Beverly passed away peacefully. She was a devoted friend to many.

SASHA SHTARKMAN remains friends with Denise Mullins (Chupp). He is married to his wife Maria. The couple has two sons. He has been a professor at the Peabody Institute in Baltimore since 2002, where he has earned the respect of the faculty. He visits his home in Moscow twice a year to teach masters classes.

JON AND SUSAN WILCOX would go on to host four more competitors during the subsequent years in 1993 (Mikhail Yanovitsky), 1997 (Michail Dantchenko), 2001 (Maxim Manoukov), and 2005 (Lilian Akopova). They developed a relationship with each one. All were outstanding talents but without a Cliburn gold medal to call their own. None would elicit the fervor that Alexei created. The Wilcoxes are now retired and pursue a variety of volunteer activities. Jon enjoys riding his bike, frequently (#1 Fort Worth STRAVA rider). They continue to maintain ties to the Sultanov and Abele families. The Wilcoxes regularly take trips to Russia to visit their friends there. Jon was honored, in 2021, by the popular Fort Worth bike-sharing program for the milestone achievement of riding more than ten thousand miles on the shared bikes.

JOHN GIORDANO SR., now 86, is retired and completing his anecdotal biography due out around the same time as this book. He and wife Mary Alice enjoy their days together. John remains Music Director Emeritus of the Fort Worth Symphony Orchestra. Back in the spring of 1998, Texas Christian University honored him with the John Giordano Piano Wing. They also bestowed him the title of Distinguished Fellow in Music. In 2021, his memoirs entitled *Speak Loudly and Carry a Little Stick* were published by TCU Press to high acclaim.

AILEEN HUMMEL continues to provide music therapy to a bevy of people in need. She keeps current with her pilot license and attends annually the EAA Airventure in Oshkosh, Wisconsin, which boasts being the largest gathering of pilots in the world. Aileen on occasion plays piano alongside Dace for music bookings wherever they may fall.

DONNA WITTEN is in the midst of her thirty-fourth year as a physical therapist. She cares for her aging mother and her rescue dog Tucker. An avid fan of TV's *America's Got Talent* and a former violinist, Donna works for the Christian Care Outpatient Therapy Clinic and volunteers therapy to the neediest and those who have fallen through the cracks.

DENISE MULLINS, formerly Chupp, a semi-retired community arts advocate, worked at the Cliburn from 1987–93, then formed Denise Mullins Artist Management Company, where she managed Alexei's Soviet counterpart Alexander Shtarkman and acclaimed cellist Gary Hoffman. She would become the Fine Arts Director at Fort Worth Country Day for two and half years. Denise booked over five hundred concerts during her time at the Cliburn. She enjoys her children Kirstin and Thomas, and still finds time to spend in Guana Cay, Bahamas, at her little beach house named "Nowhere." Denise has recently remarried Pat Ashcroft.

DR. TAMAS UNGAR performs and teaches frequently all over the globe. He remains the Executive Director of Piano Texas International Academy & Festival and is a member of the TCU Piano Faculty. Three of his students were invited to participate in the Eleventh Van Cliburn International Piano Competition, a remarkable achievement very few teachers can boast.

Since 1989, Tamas Ungár has been a regular guest teacher at the most important music centers in the United States, China, and the world. In 2006, he was appointed Artistic Director of the Beijing International Piano Festival and Artistic Advisor for China's legendary music educator, Zhou Guangren, and her Summer Piano Institute. Dr. Ungar's most important contribution is his tireless effort to help young artists find and reach their goals.

DANNY SALIBA has turned over reins of the Steinway business to his son Casey. Danny still handles the service and concert side of the business. He regularly visits the many colleges across the southwest promoting Steinway and, more importantly, music. His tremendous efforts have trickled down to high schools, where he lobbied and succeeded in placing a piano in every school in the Fort Worth public school system (136 in all) in order to introduce music to young students. He has turned Texas Christian University into the world's first all-Steinway school. TCU owns northward of one hundred twenty Steinways. Saliba serves as president of the Clavier Group.

NATASHA POGORELOVA, mother of Alexei, has remained a violin teacher in Moscow since her son's passing. She remains close to her other son Sergei, who lives in Moscow. They sold the apartment Alexei bought for them, upgraded to a nicer place, and live comfortably.

FAIZUL SULTANOV, Alexei's father, still checks on Dace from time to time. He finds some comfort in Dace's well-being. He still teaches the cello and conducting lessons at M.A. Balakirev, Children's School of the Arts.

JANIS ABELE, father of Dace, worked for the city of Riga in the art projects and promotional department for many years. His efforts there and in the city park named Mezaparks were utilized for tourism. He retired in 2003. He enjoys traveling with Benita to the Lofoten Islands in Norway to visit Dace's brother Maris and his family. He is active in community theatre and enjoys creating cell phone photo exhibits.

BENITA ABELE, mother of Dace, still teaches piano lessons privately in Riga. She still loves going to opera, theatre, and concerts with Janis. Dace speaks with mom and dad daily via Skype.

SERGEI SULTANOV, brother of Alexei, teaches piano at M.A. Balakirev, Children's School of the Arts in Moscow, and accompanies his parents' music students on piano. He accompanies most of the performers at the three schools he teaches in. He married Korean-born Natasha. He and his wife welcomed a baby girl named Masha to the family.

RICHARD RODZINSKI now heads the richest piano competition the world has ever seen in First China International Piano Competition, with a grand prize of $150,000 and a three-year management contract. Prior to that, Richard rebuilt the Tchaikovsky Competition after it faced potential closure. Early on, he was artistic administrator for the San Francisco and MET Operas. His career has spanned the world, and his musical influence is seen everywhere. He enjoys photography, biking, and tennis with the rare free time he enjoys. He is married to Elizabeth and together they have two children, Juliana and Alexander. Rodzinski declined to be interviewed for this book.

ALANN SAMPSON, a graduate of Arlington Heights High School in Fort Worth, then TCU and Barnard School, refers to herself as a "closet pianist" who studied Greek and reads Russian. She serves on the Fort Worth Symphony Orchestra board. Her passion is to help bring music and art to the masses. She helped found the Fort Worth Country Day School in 1963, a year after volunteering as an usher at the first Cliburn Competition. She works as a virtual assistant for Ashley Null, the world's foremost expert on Thomas Cranmer (leader of English Reformation as well as Archbishop of Canterbury) in Berlin. Null is chairman of the board of theology in Cairo, Egypt, as well as chaplain for the U.S. Olympic swim team.

TAMARA POPOVICH had a storied teaching career and was responsible for the success of many Soviet and Russian pianists, none more so than Alexei. She would pass away from natural causes in 2010 at age of eighty-four, five years after the death of her prized pupil, Alexei. Her career at the Uspensky Music School lasted fifty years. Her unique style of teaching the piano resulted in significant recognition and the education of numerous award-winning pianists, including current world bombshell sensation, Lola Astanova. Popovich had brought a small group of young students to New York in the early 1990's for a Russian-sponsored students' concert. Alexei, who was in town to see Popovich, doted on the ten-year-old Astanova and bought for her a life-sized Barbie from famed toy store FAO Swartz. Popovich always considered Alexei her most prized and unique pupil.

JAMES WILLIAMS recently retired as the head concert technician at Texas Christian University. He has handled the piano technician duties for the Dallas Symphony Orchestra, Fort Worth Symphony Orchestra, El Paso Symphony Orchestra, Van Cliburn Concert Series, Piano Texas, and rides Enduro motocross along with his wife, a piano tuner as well, and his son. This degreed petroleum technologist of fifteen years can still hold his own in a room full of wildcatters. He has been known to hunt quail across the plains of Texas. He won the 2008 and 2010 Provost's Academic Affairs Outstanding Staff Award. Nominated for the 2010 Chancellor's Staff award for Outstanding Service, he lost out for the overall award to TCU head football coach Gary Patterson who was fresh off the school's 2011 Rose Bowl Championship. Williams spends much of his retirement working at his ranch.

LEV NAUMOV, the Godfather of the Russian Piano School, was Alexei's professor during his time at the Conservatory. He had a storied career as pianist, composer, and teacher. He produced some of Russia's most famous pianists during his forty-year plus career. His role in the Tchaikovsky scandal riddled him with guilt for the remainder of his life. He passed away at the age of eighty nearly two months after Alexei did.

JOSE CARLOS COCORELLI, the silver medalist, would make his Carnegie Hall debut in 1991 but later would retire from performing to become a Buddhist monk in France. Years later, he would return but as a piano teacher in Fresnay-sur-Sarthe in France.

SIMON PEDRONI, gold medalist at the ninth Van Cliburn Piano Competition in 1993, would embark on a stellar recording and performing career that continues today. He made his conducting debut in 2015 for John Williams's Star Wars music performance in Italy. In 2024, the album *John Williams: Reimagined* was released and transcribed by Pedroni.

SASHA KORSANTIA lives in Boston with wife Neya. He is a professor of piano on the faculty of the New England Conservatory. After his 1993 Cliburn snub, Alexander Korsantia received first prize and gold medal at the Arthur Rubinstein Piano Master Competition in 1995 in Tel Aviv. In 1999, he was awarded the prestigious Medal of Honor by Georgian President Eduard Shevardnadze for his contributions to his country's arts. Georgian National TV released a full-length documentary about him in 2003. The next year, Korsantia performed at the inauguration of Georgian President Saakashvili. He performs often in his homeland of Georgia.

VAN CLIBURN left an indelible impression on the world. There was never a man more gentlemanly than Van. Over the course of his career, he earned more than $51 million, but his legacy is what made him special. His gifts to the world of music are immeasurable. His contributions to the world in terms of peace and building bridges may very well be his greatest accomplishment. Van's life had gone on in storybook fashion with accolades and performances coming in at a frantic pace until the day he decided he had had enough. The fortune Cliburn had amassed from his talents would give him an opulent life, and years later the ability to care for his beloved mother Rildia Bee at his Fort Worth mansion. In 1978, his father passed, and shortly thereafter his manager Sol Hurok, which caused Van to begin a hiatus from public life. He would still play on occasion, but only on a limited basis such as when heads of state or presidents came calling. In July 2001, Van was awarded the Presidential Medal of Freedom in 2004 by then President George W. Bush. He also was awarded the Russian Order of Friendship. These two awards are the highest civilian/Foreign Service awards in each country. The reason Van was so loved by Soviets was because he reminded them of who they were. He represented America and the gift of freedom. He best described playing the piano as picking an incredibly perfect rose from your garden and with the utmost care, delivering it to your audience.

APPENDIX A

Alexei Sultanov's main repertoire:

Bach	Preludes and Fugues from Well Tempered Clavier
Bach	Invencions
Bach	Concertos for Piano and Orchestra
Haydn	Sonatas *E flat major, Hob XVI ob98*
Haydn	Concerto for Piano and Orchestra in D major
Scarlatti	Sonatas
Clementi	Sonata in F-sharp minor
Mozart	Sonatas *in C major and in F major, A major*
Mozart	Concertos
Beethoven	Sonatas, Rondo
Beethoven	Concertos (#1, #3)
Schubert	Impromptus *Schubert Sonata in B flat Maj*
Schumann	Arabesque
Schumann	Youth Album
Chopin	Sonata in B minor #3
Chopin	Ballades, Scherzos, Waltzes, Polonaises, *Ballade #1 and #4 4 Scherzos*
Chopin	Mazurkas, Preludies, Etudes, Nocturnes, Impromptus
Chopin	Works for Piano and Orchestra
Chopin	Concerto No.2 in F minor
Chopin-Liszt	Songs
Liszt	Mephisto Waltz, Transcendante Etudes *F major* *Sousa-Horowitz Stars and Stripes forever*
Liszt	Hungarian Rhapsodies, Paganini Studies *Liszt-Horowitz - Hungarian Rhaps #2 #15*
Liszt	Sonata in B minor
Tchaikovsky	The seasons, Dumka, The Children's Album
Tchaikovsky	Concerto No.1
Rachmaninoff	Etude Tableaux, Polka *Preludes Rachmaninoff Preludes*
Rachmaninoff	Sonata No.2
Rachmaninoff	Concertos (#2, #3)
Mendelssohn	Songs without Words *Mendelssohn- Horowitz Wedding March*
Skriabin	Etudes, Sonatas *#5*
Schostakovich	Concertos
Prokofiev	Sonatas (#3, #6, #7) *Saint-Saens Liszt Horowitz Danse Macabre*
Prokofiev	Concertos (#2, #3)
Gershvin	Rhapsody in Blue
Poulenc	Concertos *Bizet-Horowitz Carmen Variations*

Chamber Music:

Mozart	Violin Sonatas
Beethoven	Sonatas for cello and piano
Beethoven	Sonatas for violin and piano
Beethoven	Trios
Schubert	Sonata "Arpeggione"
Schubert	Trio
Brahms	Sonatas for cello and piano
Brahms	Sonata for violin and piano
Prokofiev	Sonata for cello and piano
Franck	Sonata for violin and piano
Dvorak	Piano Quintet
Rachmaninoff	Sonata for cello and piano

20th Century music of the following countries:
Belgium- Devreese Mascarade
Japan- Transcriptions of the Ballades by Yutaka Ozaki
Uzbekistan- Jalil Toccata for piano
Mansurov- Impromtu for 2 pianos and orchestra
Salihov- Toccata for 2 pianos and orchestra
Greece   Kyriakis- Ballades
Georgia   Balanchevadze- Concerto for piano and orchestra
USA   W.Schumann- Chester Variations

Also is involved in Jazz and Pop music repertoire

Favorite Solo Repertoire

APPENDIX B

Alexei Sultanov's concerts, orchestra tours, recordings etc.

1989.

June 6	Winning the Van Cliburn International Piano Competition
	documentary film of Peter Rosen "Here to Make Music" by RCA Victor
	life recording of the competition by Teldec
	"Today Show" on NBC television
June 13	Kennedy Center Washington D.C.
June 17	Johnny Carson Show on NBC television in Los Angeles
June 21	Ambassador Auditorium in Pasadena California
June 22	Schleswig Holstein Music Festival with *Yehudi Menuhin* conducting Festival Orchestra
July 12	Northwood Orchestra concert in Michigan *Don Jaeger* conducting
July 18	Interlochen Festival Orchestra in Michigan *Kenneth Schermerhorn* conducting
July 22	Detroit recital, Michigan
July 23	Pittsburg Symphony Orchestra in Great Wood Festival, *Stanislaw Skrowaczewski* cond
July 26	David Letterman Show on CBS television in New York
July 27	Meeting with Vladimir Horowitz in New York, 14 East 94th Street at 21:00
July 27	Amsterdam recital at the Royal Concertgebouw Halle, Holland
August 7	La Roque D'Antheron Festival in France
August 10	Lucerne recital, Switzerland
August 30	London recital in Wigmore Hall, England
Sept. 5	recording in London with London Symphony Orchestra and *Maxim Shostakovich*
Sept.9-11	Warsaw recital, Poland
Sept. 14	concert with Tampere Philharmonic Orchestra *Leonid Grin* conducting, Finland
Sept. 19	Berlin Festival, Germany
Oct. 3	Fort Worth recital USA
Oct. 6	St.Paul recital, Minnesota USA
Oct. 8	Portland recital, Oregon USA
Oct. 13	concert with Springfield Symphony Orch. *Raymond Harvey* cond. Massachusetts
Oct. 19	concert with Detroit Symphony Orch. *Raymond Harvey* cond. Michigan
Oct. 24	Russian Festival in San Diego, California
Oct. 29	concert with Fresno Symphony Orchestra California, *Lawrence Southerland* cond.
Nov. 30	concert with San Antonio Symphony *Gerhardt Zimmermann* cond. Texas, USA
Dec. 11	recital in Bonn, Germany
Dec. 13	Festival Pro in Banhof Rolandseck, Germany
Dec. 14	recital in Herkulessaal Munchen, Germany
Dec. 17	recital in Hannover, Germany

1990.

Jan. 10	recital in Munich, Germany
Jan. 28	recital in Carmel, California USA
Jan. 30	recital in Seattle, Washington state USA
Feb. 2	recital in Kahilu Theatre, Kamuela, Hawaii
Feb. 4	recital in Kauai, Hawaii
Feb. 6	recital in Brigham, Oahu Hawaii
Feb. 7	recital in Mililani, Oahu Hawaii
Feb. 8	recital in Honolulu, Oahu Hawaii
Feb. 14	concert with New Orleans Symphony Orchestra *Raymond Harvey* conducting
Feb. 23	recital in Denton, Texas USA
Feb. 25	recital in Krannert Center Urbana, Illinois USA
March 5	recital in Bonn, Germany
March 11	recital in Rotterdam, Holland

1990. cont.

March 15	recital in Barcelona, Spain
March 22	concert with Royal Philharmony Orchestra in London's Festival Hall England
April 19	concert with Rochester Symphony Orchestra *Gilbert Varga* conducting USA
April 20	recital in Genesco, NY USA
April 22	recital in Buffalo, NY USA
April 30	recital in Amherst, Massachusetts USA
May 3	recital in Carnegie Hall New York, USA
May 5	concert with Fort Worth Symphony Orchestra *John Giordano* conducting USA
May 12	recital in Louvre Paris, France
May 17	recital in Zurich, Switzerland
May 20	recital in Milan's Music Conservatory, Italy
May 22	recital in La Fenice Venice, Italy
June 10	Naantali Festival, Finland
June 30	recital in Los Angeles, California USA
July 2	Yamaha disckclavier recording in Los Angeles California USA
July 8	concert with Detroit Symphony Orchestra *Zidenek Macal* conducting
July 10	concert with Atlanta Symphony Orchestra *George Hanson* conducting USA
July 14	concert with Philadelphia Symphony Orchestra *Jose Lopez-Cobos* conducting USA
July 18	concert with Northwood Orchestra *Don Jaeger* conducting, USA
July 22	concert with Milwaukee Symphony Orchestra *Neal Gittelman* conducting
August 2	concert with Moscow State Orchestra in Munich *Pavel Kogan* conducting Germany
August 3	Helsinki Festival, Finland
August 15	Joroinen Festival, Finland
August 25	concert with Royal Concertgebouw Orchestra Amsterdam, *Klaus Peter Flor* conducting
August 30	Stresa Festival Theatre of the Conferences, Italy
Sept. 17	Ludwigsburg Festival, Germany
	Berlin, Germany
Oct. 5-7	concert with Sacramento Symphony Orchestra *Carter Nice* conducting California
Oct. 10	concert with Boulder Symphony Orchestra *Oswald Lehner* conducting USA
Oct. 12	recital in Fairfield, Connecticut USA
Oct. 14	recital in Monroe, Louisiana USA
Oct. 21	recital in Kahilu Theatre, Hawaii
Oct. 29	concert with Maui Symphony Orchestra *Jerry Martin* conducting Hawaii
Nov. 7	Yamaha disckclavier recording Los Angeles, California USA
Nov. 8	concert with Northern Symphony Orchestra *Hugh Wolffe* cond. Newcastle England
Nov. 9	recital in Middlesbrough, England
Nov.10-17	recital in Carlisle, England
Nov. 18	Teldec CD recording in Berlin, Germany
Nov. 21	recital in Lugano, Switzerland
Nov. 26	recital in Hamburg, Germany
Dec. 5	recital in Lisbon, Portugal
Dec. 9	recital in Cardiff, Wales
Dec. 11	recital in Heelen, Holland
	recital in Utrecht, Holland

1991.

Jan. 7, 9	City of Birmingham Orchestra *Pavo Berglund* conducting, England
Jan. 24	concert with Turku Philharmonic Orchestra *Mr. Atzmon* conducting, Finland
Jan. 27	recital in Jarvenpaa, Finland
Jan. 30	concert with Helsinki Philharmony Orchestra *Juk a-Pekka Saraste* conducting

1991 cont.

Feb. 9-12	recital in Taipei, Taiwan
Feb. 15	Tokyo Symphony Orchestra Suntory Hall, Japan
Feb. 17	Nagoya Philharmony Orchestra *Naoshiro Totsuka* conducting, Japan
Feb. 19	recital in Symphony Hall of Osaka, Japan
Feb. 20	recital in Fukuoka, Japan
Feb. 22	recital in Hiroshima, Japan
Feb. 25	recital in Suntory Hall Tokyo, Japan
March 1	recital in Seoul, Korea
March 3	recital in Hong Kong
March 7	recital in Clearwater, Florida
March 9	recital in West Palm Beach, Florida
March 12	recital in New Haven, Connecticut
March 14	recital in Houston, Texas
March 15	Ravinia Festival, Illinois
March 20	concerts with New Orleans Symphony Orchestra *Maxim Shostakovich* conducting
March 28	concerts with Dallas Symphony Orchestra *Eduardo Maza* conducting
April 2	recital in Koger Arts Center Columbia, South Carolina
April 4	recital in Greenville, South Carolina
April 6	recital in Charlottesville, Virginia
April 8	recital in Bridgewater, Virginia
April 12-13	concerts with Austin Symphony Orchestra *Sung Kwak* conducting, Texas
April 14	concert with Austin Symphony Orchestra in Temple Texas
April 26	recital in Fresno, California
April 29	recital in Miami, Florida
May 3-6	concerts with Milwaukee Symphony Orchestra *Morton Gould* conducting
May 10	recital in Raleigh Durham, Massachusetts
June 3	recital in Maryland, Md.
June 22	concert with Fort Worth Symphony Orchestra *Anshel Brusilow* conducting
July 2	recital in Scottsdale, Arizona
July 16-20	concerts in Charlievox, Michigan *Don Jaeger* conducting
Aug. 10-18	Teldec CD recording in Berlin
Sept. 21	concert with Louisville Symphony Orchestra *Lawrence Leighton Smith* conducting
Sept. 28	concert with Greensboro Symphony Orchestra *Paul Anthony Mc Rae* conducting
Oct. 2	recital in Corvalls, Oregona
Oct. 4	recital in San Luis Obispo, California
Oct. 6	recital in San Mateo, California
Oct. 8	recital in Santa Rosa, California
Oct. 10	recital in Asheville, North Carolina
Oct. 11	recital in Covington, Georgia
Oct. 14	recital in Charlotte, North Carolina
Oct. 16	recital in Sandusky, Ohoio
Oct. 18	recital in Rock Island, Illinois
Oct. 21	recital in Greenville, Texas
Oct. 24	recital in El Paso, Texas
Oct. 24	concert with Boulder Symphony Orchestra *Oswald Lehnert* conducting, Colorado
Oct. 27	recital in Great Falls, Montana
Oct. 29	recital in Billings, Montana
Nov. 8-10	concert with Toulouse Symphony Orchestra, France
Nov. 20-21	concert with Lugano Symphony Orchestra *Yoav Talmi* conducting, Switzerland
Dec. 20	recital in Athens, Greece

1992.

Jan. 25	recital in Colorado Springs, Colorado
Feb. 3-11	Teldec CD recording Berlin, Germany
Feb. 14	recital in Chatelet Theatre Paris, France
Feb. 19-21	concerts with Helsinki Philharmony Orchestra *Woldemar Nelsson* conducting
Feb. 22	concert with Oulu Philharmony Orchestra *Osmo Vanska* conducting, Finland
Feb. 25	recital in Tampere, Finland
Feb. 27	concert with Kuopio Philharmonic Orchestra *Pertti Pekkanen* conducting Finland
March 7	recital in Lafayette,Louisiana
March 9	Bayreuth Festival, Germany
March 15	recital in Sarasota, Florida
March 17	recital in Columbia Missouri
March 18	recital in Charleston, West Virginia
March 20	recital in Randolph, New Jersey
March 30	recital in Englewood, Florida
April 2	recital in Collegville, Minnesota
April 4	recital in Lima Ohio
April 8	recital in Storrs, Connecticut
April 10	recital in Elmira, New York
April 13	recital in Bordentown New Jersey
April 20	recital in Rockford, Illinois
April 21	recital in Freeport, Illinois
April 23	recital in Carbondale, Illinois
April 24	recital in Jefferson City, Missouri
April 25	recital in Guthrie, Oklahoma
April 27	recital in Topeka, Kansas
April 28	recital in Atlanta,Georgia
April 30	recital in Harrisburg, Pennsylvania
May 6	recital in Scranton, Pennsylvania
May 8	concert with Mansfield Symphony Orchestra *Jeff Holland Cook* conducting
May 30	concert with Houston Symphony Orchestra *Zdenek Macal* conducting Texas
Sept. 23-26	concerts with Kalamazoo Symphony Orchestra *Yoshimi Takeda* conducting
Oct. 1-4	concerts with New Orleans Symphony Orchestra *Maxim Shostakovich* conducting
Oct. 11	concert with Napa Valley Symphony Orchestra *Asher Raboy* cond., California
Oct. 17	recital in Duncanville, Texas
Oct. 20	concert with Waco Symphony Orchestra *Stephen Heyde* conducting, Texas
Oct. 24	recital at Kennedy Center Washington DC
Nov. 6	concert with Springfield Symphony Orchestra *Raymond Harvey* cond. Massachus.
Nov. 15	concert with Palm Beach Symphony Orchestra, Florida
Nov. 21-22	concert with Binghampton Symphony Orchestra *John Covelli* conducting, NY
Nov. 24	recital in Hopkinsville, Kentucky

1993.

Jan. 6	concert with Helsinki Philharmonic Orchestra *Peter Larsen* conducting, Finland
Jan. 9-10	concerts with Fort Worth Symphony Orchestra *John Giordano* conducting
Jan. 12	recital in Chico, California
Jan. 14	recital in Ukiah, California
Jan. 17	recital in Glendale, California
Jan. 19	recital in Wilmington, North Carolina

1993, cont.

Jan.	21	recital in Macon, Georgia
Jan.	23	recital in Coral Springs, Florida
Jan.	24	recital in Orlando, Florida
Jan.	26	recital in Huntsville, Alabama
Jan.	27	recital in Palm Springs, California
Jan.	29	recital in Lancaster, Washington
Jan.	30	recital in Everett, Washington
Feb.	1	recital in Hoquiam, Washington
Feb.	3	recital in Klamath Falls, Oregon
Feb.	5	recital in Laguna Hills, California
Feb.	12	Rundfunk Sinfonie Orchester in Berlin's Shauspielhaus *Manfred Honeck conduct.*
Feb.	17-18	with Tulsa Philharmony Orchestra in Guthrie *Bernhard Rubinstein* conducting
Feb.	20	recital in Aiken, South Carolina
Feb.	25	recital in Wheeling, West Virginia
March	4	recital in Kahilu Theater Kamuela, Hawaii
March	7	recital in Lihue Kauai, Hawaii
March	9	recital in Hilo, Hawaii
March	12-13	concerts with Warsaw Philharmonic Orchestra *Andrzej Straszynski* conduct. Poland
March	15	recital in Istanbul, Turkey
March	18	concert with Noordholland Philharmony Orchestra in Harleem, *Lucas Vis* cond.
March	19	concert in Hoofddorp with Noordholland Philharmony Orch. Holland
March	22	recital in Amsterdam, Holland
March	26-27	concerts with Florida West Coast Symphony Orchestra in Sarasota *Paul Wolfe* cond.
April	2	recital in Springfield, Illinois
April	10	recital in Anchorage, Alaska
April	13	recital in Reno, Nevada
April	23	recital in San Louis Obispo, California
May	15	recital in Memphis, Tennessee
June	29	concert in Meyerson Center Dallas, Texas
July	9	recital in Concertgebouw Amsterdam, Holland
July	12	recital in Athen's Amphitheater, Greece
July	24	recital in Mikkeili Festival, Finland
Sept.	10	concert with Duluth Symphony Orchestra *Taavo Virkhaus* conducting, Minnesota
Oct.	3	concert with Mansfield Symphony Orchestra *Ottvio De Rosa* conducting, Ohio
Oct.	9-10	concerts with Greenville Symphony Orchestra *David Pollitt* conducting, SC
Oct.	18	recital in Las Vegas, Nevada
Oct.	21-22	concerts with Tuscon Symphony Orchestra *Robert Bernhard* conducting, Arizona
Nov.	7	recital in Chads Ford, Pennsylvania
Nov.	20-21	concerts with Fresno Philharmony Orchestra, *Kate Tamarkin* cond., California

1994.

Jan.	3-7	recitals in Bermuda, Great Britain
Jan.	12-15	Tivoli festival with Aarhus Symphony Orchestra *Peter Etrup Larsen* cond. Denmark
Feb.	26	recital in Mankato, Minnesota
March	3	recital in Greenwood, Mississippi
March	10	concert with Kuopio Symphony Orchestra *Guhrer Aykal* conducting, Finland
March	11	concert with Tapiola Symphony Orchestra *Tuomas Ollila* conducting, Finland
March	17	concert with Oulu Symphony Orchestra *Peter Lilje* conducting, Finland
April	16	recital in Grants Pass, Oregon
May	7	recital in Newport News, Virginia

1994, cont.

Sept.	15-16	concerts with Boulder Philharmony Orchestra, *Oswald Lehner* conducting, Co
Sept.	25	concert with Evansville Symphony Orchestra *Alfred Savia* conducting, Indiana
Sept.	29-30	concerts with Noordholland Philharmony Orchestra in Haarlem, Holland
Oct.	15	recital in Iowa City, Iowa
Oct.	21-22	concerts in Columbia with South Carolina Symphony Orchestra *Nicolas Smith* con.
Nov.	10	recital in Sacramento, California
Nov.	18-19	concerts with El Paso Symphony Orchestra *Gurer Aykal* conducting, Texas
Nov.	22	recital in West Palm Beach Kravis Center, Florida

1995.

Jan.	28	concert with Hilton Head Symphony Orchestra *John Gosling* cond., South Carolina
Jan.	14	recital in Rapid City, South Dakota
Jan.	16	recital in Zanesville, Ohio
March	31	concert for Dallas WRR classical music radio, Texas
April	26-27	concerts with Helsinki Philharmony Orchestra *Alexandre Lazarev* cond., Finland
May	6-7	concerts with Las Cruces Symphony Orchestra *Mariana Gabbi* cond., New Mexico
August	31	concert with Dallas Symphony Orchestra *Keri-Lynn Wilson* cond., Texas
Sept. 26-Oct.20		winning the 13th Chopin International Piano Competition in Warsaw, Poland documentary film of Aleksandra Padlewska "Point of View" by Polish TV life recording of the competition by Technics co.
Nov.	9	concert with Polish Radio Orchestra in Warsaw *Wojciech Rajski* cond.,Poland
Nov.	10	recital in Bydgoszcz, Poland
Nov.	11	recital in Poznan, Poland
Nov.	13	concert in Ansbach, Germany with Polish Chamber Orchestra *W. Rajiski* cond.
Nov.	14	concert in Quakenbruck, Germany with Polish Chamber Orchestra
Nov.	15	concert in Stade, Germany with Polish Chamber Orchestra
Nov.	17	concert in Emden, Germany with Polish Chamber Orchestra
Dec.	15-16	concerts with Ankara Symphony Orchestra *Guhrer Aykal* conducting, Turkey
Dec.	23	recital in La Scala Theatre Milan, Italy

1996.

Feb.	16	recital in Stuart, Florida
March	3	recital in Springfield, Illinois
March	18	recital in Sapporo, Japan
March	21	recital in Hamamatsu Act City Hall, Japan
March	28	recital in Metropolitan Arts Space Tokyo, Japan
March	30	recital in Osaka Symphony Hall, Japan
March	31	recital in Kioi Hall Tokyo, Japan
		life recording of the recital by Arts Core co.
April	2	life recording of the recital by Arts Core co.
August	30	concert with Philharmonie of the Nations in Hamburg *Justus Frantz* cond.
Sept.	27	recital in Los Alamos, New Mexico
Oct.	8	recital in Warsaw, Poland
		life recording of the recital by International Chopin Foundation
Oct.	12	concert with Poznan Philharmony Orchestra *Grzegorz Nowak* cond., Poland
Oct.	18-19	concerts with Istanbul Symphony Orchestra, Turkey
Oct.	22	recital in Katowitze, Poland
Nov.	10	chamber music concert in Fort Worth, Texas
Nov.	28	concert in Essen, Germany with Philharmony of the Nations *Justus Frantz* cond.

NOTES

Chapter 1
1. Papulnik is a Latvian pet name for Papa

Chapter 2
1. Reich, Howard, "The Life and Rebirth of a Musical Mastermind, Stricken Genius," *Chicago Tribune*, 2005

Chapter 3
1. Smithfield, Brad, "Riga, the city with the largest collection of Art Nouveau buildings in the world," May 11, 2017, *The Vintage News*
2. Belge, Boris. "From Peace to Freedom: How Classical Music Became Political in the Soviet Union, 1964–1982," *Ab Imperio*. 2013 (2): 279–297, 2013
3. Architectuul, Salaspils: "A Soviet Memorial To Nazi Victims In Latvia," Feb. 17, 2023, www.architectuul.com
4. Interview with Dace Sultanov, 2018
5. These games made historical headlines when African American sprinters Tommie Smith and John Carlos took a stand for civil rights in America by raising their black-gloved fists and wearing black socks in lieu of shoes.

Chapter 4
1. Interview with Dace Sultanov, 2018

Chapter 5
1. *New York Times*, April 28, 1986, "Horowitz Again Hears Cheers for Leningrad," April 28, 1986
2. During the Battle of Moscow in 1941-42, Tchaikovsky's house was repurposed by the invading Germans as a soldier's barracks and a garage for motorcycles.
3. *Horowitz In Moscow*, the recorded album, known appropriately as the music recital of the century, would win a Grammy for Best Classical Album in 1988. The video recording released much later went on to become one of the greatest bestsellers in the world of classical music.
4. Interview with Dace Sultanov, 2018

Chapter 6
1. *Time* magazine, "The Texan Who Conquered Russia," May 19, 1958
2. Interview with Abele Family, 2018

Chapter 7
1. Kiger, Patrick J. National Geographic Docuseries, *Genius*, "Albert Einstein Theory of Infidelity," 2017

Chapter 8
1. Interview with Dace Sultanov, 2018

Chapter 10
1. After Tchaikovsky completed this composition in 1875, he unveiled it to his teacher, the famed Anton Rubenstein, who pronounced it "unplayable, fragmented, vulgar, and to be thrown away."
2. The jury box was filled with the likes of Soviet legends Sviatoslav Richter, jury president Emil Gilels, and Soviet composer greats Dmitri Kabalevsky and Sir Arthur Bliss, with the chairman of the competition being Dmitri Shostakovich.
3. Emil Gilels remains in the Mount Olympus group of great pianists. He was the first Soviet musician to win a major piano competition outside the USSR (Queen Elizabeth Competition in Brussels) in 1938. His well-known violinist sister Elizabeth married Leonid Kogan, another well-known Soviet violinist, who was a reported spy for the KGB. Gilels suffered mightily from diabetes later in his life. He chaired the nervous 1958 Tchaikovsky jury alongside his archrival Sviatoslav Richter.
4. Isacoff, Stuart. *When the World Stopped to Listen*, 2017
5. Reich, Howard. *Van Cliburn*, 2008

Chapter 11
1. The three competitors from the People's Republic of China, as it was later learned, had very poor conditions in which to practice. Often not even a piano was available to practice, and so to practice the young pianists utilized windows or boards, which had the black and white keys painted on them.

Chapter 12
1. Interview with Jon and Susan Wilcox, 2018.

Chapter 13
1. Henry's monumental accomplishments in life are deeply rooted in tragedy. As an eight-year-old in 1805, he fled alongside his mother and two sisters from the invading French to the mountains near his hometown of Wolfshagen, Germany. The harsh winter would orphan him when his mother and two sisters perished in the extreme cold. When his father and three older brothers, originally thought to have been killed, returned from the war, they took Henry and joined the forestry service. Years later, a bolt of lightning would strike the shelter where the Steinwegs took shelter, killing his father and brothers, and orphaning the fifteen-year Henry for the second time. Henry, alone and penniless, through sheer

determination and will overcame seemingly insurmountable odds to create the world renowned Steinway & Sons.
2. The original New York-made Steinway & Sons piano was given the number 483 because before Henry Steinway immigrated to the US, he built 482 pianos at his home in Germany. This inaugural New York Steinway was sold to the wealthy New York Griswold family for $500 and now sits on display at the Metropolitan Museum of Art in New York City.
3. *Cosmopolitan Magazine* in 1985 listed Paley as one of America's ten most eligible bachelors. This list would in fact inspire David Lettermen's creation of his Top Ten Lists.
4. The piano from John Steinway's Manhattan apartment, which Cliburn, amongst many other famed pianists, has played, now resides in Saliba's living room.
5. The prerequisites to becoming a Steinway artist are owning a Steinway, having an active concert career, and having New York-based music management. Steinway, which doesn't pay its artists, has roughly one thousand six hundred on its roster, with eight hundred being Americans.
6. Ratcliffe, Ronald. *Steinway*, 1989
7. Interview with the Wilcoxes and Dace Sultanov, 2019

Chapter 14
1. Interview with Denise Mullins, 2019 and Horowitz, Joseph. *The Ivory Trade*, 1990

Chapter 15
1. Interview with John Giordano Sr., 2019

Chapter 16
1. Gay, Wayne Lee and Rogers, Mary. *Star Telegram* articles, 1989

Chapter 17
1. The *Chester* composition is based on tunes from colonial era composer William Billings. Billings's original composition was written during the American Revolution and was adopted by the Continental Army as its marching song. Country music legend Merle Haggard, in 1983, during a concert at Billy Bobs, bought shots of Canadian Club Whiskey for the entire audience of 5,095, earning his place in the Guinness Book of World Records for the largest round ever and a bar tab of $12,737.50.

Chapter 20
1. Interview with Dace Sultanov, 2019

Chapter 21
1. Interview Denise Mullins, 2019
2. Mohr, Franz. *My Life with the Great Pianists*, Baker Publishing Group, 1996

Chapter 23
1. Interview with Wilcoxes and Dace Sultanov

Chapter 24
1. The school boasts Fort Worth alumnus and US representatives Kay Granger and Marc Veasey. The Texas Wesleyan table tennis program, one of the nation's best, boasts 65 national titles since 2002
2. Interview with Beverly Archibald, 2019

Chapter 25
1. Composed in 1834 but published posthumously in 1855, "Fantaisie Impromptu" remains one of Chopin's most popular and performed works. After Chopin's death in 1849, it remained unpublished until 1855 because of his instructions to never publish his unpublished works.

Chapter 29
1. Peters's remarkable career spanned thirty-five years singing at the MET, where she was awarded the National Medal of Arts in 1998. She had received similar fame from her television career, which included sixty-five appearances on the Ed Sullivan Show.

2. Emil Gilels, often considered one of the greatest pianists of all time, famously entertained Allied Soviet troops in 1944 with open-air recitals on the front line to boost troop morale. Gilels was approached by legendary exiled Soviet composer, Sergei Rachmaninoff, after Rachmaninoff heard his performances on the radio. Rachmaninoff was so moved by Gilels's genius and perfect pitch he anointed him his pianist successor and forwarded him the diploma and medal he himself had received from Artur Rubenstein.

Chapter 30
1. *Life* Magazine, "Santa Barbara Oil Spill," June 13, 1969
2. In an example of the magical aura of Vladimir Horowitz, Alicia de Larrocha, the 4'9" legendary Spanish pianist and composer gives a most poignant example. Long considered one the greatest piano virtuosos of the 20th century, she made her debut at age five and went on to a storied career eliciting four Grammy wins out of fourteen nominations coupled with four honorary university degrees. Larrocha, oft considered the female Horowitz because of her style of play, had just completed a recital when she learned that Horowitz had been in the audience and wished to meet her. The meeting reportedly found the world-famous Larrocha falling to her knees in front of him, overcome with emotion. She would describe the moment as one of the greatest of her life.
3. Interview with James Williams, 2019

Chapter 31
1. Interview with Tamas Ungar, 2019
2. Interview with Dace Sultanov and Murakami Yusuke, 2019

Chapter 35

1. This classic composition is one of the most well-known of all piano concertos. Tchaikovsky revised it three times after harsh criticism, and two prominent pianists of the time refused to premier it before on-tour German Hans von Bulow, to whom the piece is dedicated, played the final version on October 25, 1875, in Boston, Massachusetts. This piece became the theme for Orson Welles's famed radio series, *The Mercury Theatre on the Air.*

Chapter 36

1. Susan, notably, founded Fort Worth-based Streams and Valleys, a non-profit advocate for Fort Worth's segment of its main waterway, the Trinity River and its trails. She also was the first chairman of Fort Worth's wildly popular springtime festival, Mayfest.

Chapter 38

1. Personal Interviews with Alann Sampson, Dace Sultanov, additionally, Lee, Gary, "Tchaikovsky Finalists," *Washington Post,* June 27, 1986
2. Interview with Murakami Yusuke, 2019
3. Dace Sultanov, 2019

Chapter 43

1. Reich, Howard. "Stricken Genius," *Chicago Tribune*, 2005

Chapter 45

1. This legendary and challenging composition premiered in New York City in 1908 with Rachmaninoff accompanied by the New York Symphony.

Chapter 47

1. Two world-class ensembles finally merged in 1928, creating the legendary New York Philharmonic, as we know it.
2. I would meet Louise Canafax years earlier when I was a six-year-old in my kindergarden music room at Trinity Valley School. Louise taught music there for thirty-one years. It was at her funeral in 2017 that I learned about her role at the Van Cliburn and her connection to the Sultanovs. I remember Mrs. Canafax having tremendous patience and care for those of us who found it extremely difficult to carry the simplest of tunes.

Chapter 54

1. "Joyful Aspiration," *The Divine Lotus*, Feb. 2, 2016

BIBLIOGRAPHY

Books

Horowitz, Joseph. *The Ivory Trade: Music and the Business of Music at the Van Cliburn International Piano Competition*. Summit Books, 1990.

Isacoff, Stuart. *When the World Stopped to Listen: Van Cliburn's Cold War Triumph and Its Aftermath*. Knopf, 2017.

Mohr, Franz and Edith Schaeffer. *My Life with the Great Pianists*. Baker Books, 1992.

Ratcliffe, Ronald V. *Steinway*. Chronicle Books, 1989

Reich, Howard. *Van Cliburn: The Remarkable Life of the Famed Pianist*. Thompson Nelson Publishers, 1993.

Schonberg, Harold C. *The Lives of the Great Composers*. W. W. Norton & Company, 1987.

Newspapers

The *Chicago Tribune*
The *Fort Worth Star-Telegram*
The *Japan Times*
The *New York Times*
The *Spectator* (UK)
The *Sun Sentinel* (South Florida)
The *Washington Post*

Podcasts and Videos

Fishko, Sara. "Cliburn Takes Moscow," Fishko Files podcast, April 5, 2018.

Niles, Ben. "Note by Note," *The Making of Steinway* LI037, DVD, September, 2005.

Rosen, Peter, dir. *The Eighth Van Cliburn International Piano Competition: Here to Make Music*. 1989. The Van Cliburn Foundation.

ABOUT THE AUTHOR

J. W. Wilson is a husband, father, author, business owner, former athlete, adventurist, type 1 diabetic, and child at heart. He is the author of *Portraits of a Soldier*, his first book, also published by TCU Press. He lives in Fort Worth, Texas, with his wife, Andrea, and their two children, Ryder and Reese.

www.ingramcontent.com/pod-product-compliance
Lightning Source LLC
Chambersburg PA
CBHW040314170426
43195CB00021B/2965